STARS
OVER
SHIRALEE

Also by Sheryl McCorry

Diamonds and Dust

STARS
OVER
SHIRALEE

SHERYL McCORRY

with JANET BLAGG

MACMILLAN

Pan Macmillan Australia

Some of the people in this book have had their names changed to protect their identities.

WARNING

It is customary in some Aboriginal communities not to mention the names of or reproduce images of the recently deceased. Care and discretion should be exercised in using this book within Arnhem Land, central Australia and the Kimberley.

First published 2009 in Macmillan by Pan Macmillan Australia Pty Limited
1 Market Street, Sydney

National Library of Australia
Cataloguing-in-Publication data:

McCorry, Sheryl, 1949–

Stars over Shiralee / Sheryl McCorry.

9781405039604 (pbk.)

McCorry, Sheryl, 1949–
Ranch managers—Western Australia—Kimberley—Biography.
Ranches—Western Australia—Kimberley—Management.
Breast—Cancer—Patients—Western Australia—Kimberley—Biography.

636.01092

Typeset in 11.5 Janson Text by Midland Typesetters, Australia
Printed in Australia by McPherson's Printing Group

Papers used by Pan Macmillan Australia Pty Ltd are natural, recyclable products made from wood grown in sustainable forests. The manufacturing processes conform to the environmental regulations of the country of origin.

For Leisha and Robby

The best and most beautiful things in the world cannot be seen or even touched. They must be felt with the heart.

— Helen Keller

Contents

PROLOGUE

Autumn 1999

Squawking mobs of black cockatoos circle the ghost gums by the shed before settling themselves in the branches, their agitated screeching loud and piercing. I'm standing alone in the brown paddock, staring up at them blankly. A lazy breeze swirls around me — it ruffles the autumn leaves at my feet, but chills me to the bone. I feel cold and lonely. Some kind of change must be on the way!

I have lived in the southern country of Western Australia since 1996 — long enough to realise the elements are preparing me for winter — but my mind has a deeper pattern etched in it. I shut my eyes and see the reds and ochres of my beloved Kimberley, many thousands of kilometres away to the north, the rugged country strewn with sprawling cattle stations, many of them covering more than a million acres. I see brolgas dance on the claypan flat by the old stockyards, where the palette is blended with the many shades of pindan dust that drift above a stockyard full of cattle.

Napier and Kimberley Downs, Louisa and Bohemia, Oobagooma, Blina, Ellendale, Mount Hart and Silent Grove,

Fairfield and Kilto — all stations I once managed or owned with my husband Bob McCorry and the help of a loyal Aboriginal stock camp. I was their *yumun* — 'boss missus', they called me — before we sold up and moved the family to the southern country. But there is no going back. McCorry always drilled that into me: we can never go back.

But McCorry is dead now. Dead, I have to keep reminding myself. He will never again turn up at the homestead with guidance or advice, or to reassure me that I am still travelling in the right direction with my plans for the land, as he did all those years our lives were entwined. The deep feeling of security, of knowing McCorry was there for the children and for me, is gone. He is gone. I can't get used to it; the fact of his death keeps tripping me up, even though we'd been divorced three years when he died.

I had been married to this tough old cattleman for twenty-two years. A deep-thinking man of few words, he suffered serious depression for most of those years, and for many of them I felt I had suffered with him too. These were tough years of hard work in primitive conditions and fierce heat while we were trying to resurrect a couple of dilapidated Kimberley cattle stations for the Australian Land and Cattle Company, which was always in a state of financial struggle, and at the same time trying to keep the Burke Labor government from resuming the properties.

In the seventies we had found cases of TB amongst our cattle, but it was the mid-eighties before the government got serious about it. They threatened to take over the properties if the TB wasn't eliminated. Australian Land and Cattle managed to retain Kimberley Downs and Napier Downs, and with me as manager we went on to complete one of the largest, and most successful, TB eradication programs in the history of the west Kimberley.

Through all these challenges, which included bringing up a young and extended family in the outback, I'd long steeled myself not to take my eye from the faint glow at the end of the tunnel. There were deep personal tragedies for McCorry and I, which left us mentally and emotionally broken, but I always kept myself moving forward. For good or for bad, that was the only way I knew, and overall, when I look back, they were wonderful years.

Since I was a little girl, my dream had been to live on a cattle station in the Kimberley: whether I owned it, worked it or managed it didn't matter. After years of mustering and managing other people's properties, McCorry and I bought first Kilto station in 1986, then Fairfield in 1993. I stayed on at Kimberley and Napier Downs stations, managing them, while McCorry moved between Kilto and Fairfield and took whatever contract mustering work he could get. Our lives became more and more separate, and it seemed there were ways in which McCorry resented my independent initiative. Even so, the long history between us helped us stick together through difficult situations. But by the end of 1994 I was exhausted by the constant dramas of our life together. McCorry suffered severe physical pain from various injuries sustained over the years, and for as long as I could remember he had been prone to depression and had no energy for working through things with me. In 1995 I gave up the effort myself. We were divorced and I signed the papers to sell Fairfield so we could all move on.

For the first time in my life I felt really lost. I was forty-six and I'd been with McCorry half my life. All my adult life.

Although we were no longer married, the deep bond between us was never truly broken and we shared a lot over the next three years. In 1996 we each bought properties in the south-west that were practically within cooee of each other. And we never stopped looking out for one another. I could always count on McCorry for considered, cool-headed advice.

After my divorce, I became involved with a younger man for a while. It felt wonderful to be desired, but still, it was probably not one of my better calls, and it was over before long. But now, with McCorry gone, there was another man knocking at my door. He seemed eminently suitable, and in fact he wanted me to marry him. But I had only known him for a few months; we scarcely knew each other. What was I to say?

I wished I could ask McCorry. I'd faced a lot of difficult things in my life, but losing him was not something I was prepared for. No wonder, as I stood in that chill autumn breeze in 1999, I felt cold and lonely. Some kind of change was certainly on its way.

I need to go back and start at the time of his death, though, because that is where this story begins.

CHAPTER 1

The End of an Era

On 3 October 1998 I was watching the nurses at St John of God in the Perth suburb of Subiaco push McCorry's bed down the quiet hospital corridor. It was a chilling sight with all the tubes, bottles and bags connected to it. They put the bed in the observation room directly opposite the nurses's station, so I should have realised his time with us was coming to an end. He had cancer of the pancreas and liver — diagnosed only a week earlier — and his skin was the colour of cold campfire ashes. Only two days later, on 5 October, our daughter Leisha's twenty-first birthday, McCorry passed away.

Leisha and Robby were there as the tough old bushy left our world, leaving me with the three words I had waited twenty long years to hear: 'I love you.' Words he had battled to express to the children or to me.

I sat by his bedside watching the light that filtered through the trees outside dancing across his body. For the sake of the children I tried to pull myself together, but I trembled with the very real fear of being alone, of no longer having the old man to back me. I wasn't ready for him to die.

'Not now McCorry!' is what I wanted to scream. 'I'm not ready yet.' And neither was he. He was always so full of strategies and schemes and who knows what else. He still had plenty of plans to make. I felt like screaming and pummelling his chest.

Only days before McCorry had had the strength to refuse a bedpan. He had said to me years ago that he would die before he would ever consent to such an indignity. And since that old cattleman could get me to do just about anything, somehow, with a spider web of tangled tubes, bags and bottles, I managed to walk him to the lavatory and sit him on the throne.

He was falling forwards, and I was kneeling in front of the pedestal trying to keep him balanced, when I felt myself start to black out. A wave of heat and nausea came over me and I woke up in a chair beside McCorry's bedside to see a nurse in deep concentration taking his pulse and studying her watch. He was a deep grey colour and very still. I jolted awake and screamed, 'Wake up, wake up Bob!' Moments later a bit of colour seeped back into his frail body and his eyes slowly opened. They were vacant, there was no consciousness there, but he was still with me. I breathed again, grateful and relieved that my old cattleman was still with me.

After that, his pain only worsened, and I realised I should not have called him back to me. I had panicked, when I should have let him go. I was only thinking of myself.

Now the room was quiet; the machines and life-support equipment had been turned off. Thirteen-year-old Robby sat by his father's side, looking as if he was trying to take in some impossible fact. There were no tears for him at this point, but soon Leisha's heart-racking sobs and cries of 'Daddy, Daddy,' echoed around the hospital. Before long she had the nurses and other staff in tears. McCorry was liked by all who had attended him for that quiet, fierce dignity of his. I sat silently holding his callused old hand, travelling in my mind back to Oobagooma station, the place where it had all really started for us, so long ago now. Back there we had nothing more than a swag and a couple of working dogs each, but we were happy. The wind of the Kimberley blew around us and kept our marriage fresh for a long time. We could see each other against a wide blue sky; back then the thunder heads were way in the distance.

After McCorry's death my mother and father moved down from Northampton to stay with me and the children for a while on the Shiralee. I was grateful for their gentle and stoic comfort and support. Mother reminded me of the things McCorry would have expected of me. They were of the same era. 'Get it together, girl, you're tougher than that,' he had drilled into me often enough when the going got rough. It was true. I knew deep inside me it was time to saddle up and get on with our lives.

The Shiralee was crying out for attention: there was fertiliser to be spread and fences that needed fixing. When I bought the farm it was run down, the old wooden cattle yards a potential death trap — not that this had bothered me, it was part of the appeal. Something I could get my teeth into and make my own.

After leaving the Kimberley I had travelled through the southernmost part of Western Australia in search of a farm to call home. I felt a deep connection to this part of the world, and made Albany my base as I visited properties.

One Sunday afternoon early in 1996 I was driving in the Narrikup area, a few kilometres south of Mount Barker. I had been visiting McCorry at his place, Sleepy Hollow. He'd only been there six months; in fact, he'd followed me into the area, even though he had found his place first.

I followed For Sale signs up a little gravel road, around a bend to a slight rise, to spot a final For Sale sign placed in front of a dilapidated gateway. It was obvious the white ants had had a field day with the wooden post-and-rail entrance to the farm. Rails were broken and posts nonexistent among the kikuyu-covered shambles.

Suddenly it was as if a light bulb was turned on in my head, I saw past the falling-down front entrance, past the front paddocks that had been 'flogged to the boards' by sheep, past the neglected and broken-down fences, and on to the deep purples of the Porongurup Range beyond, the majestic backdrop to this quiet farm.

Warmth flowed through my body. I had found a home for myself and the children. There was no doubt in me. The ranges beyond reminded me of the Napier and King Leopold ranges in the west Kimberley. They had been a constant source of beauty during my life up there.

Sitting in my Landcruiser I gazed about the property and wondered if the orange-tiled house at the end of the long tree-lined driveway would be livable. It didn't matter. If it wasn't, I would live in the corrugated-iron shed partly hidden among the gum trees while I built a house. I just had to have this place, no matter what.

Thirty days later it was mine. From the beginning, in my mind, I called it the Shiralee, a name I have loved since I first heard it. The name Shiralee means 'swag', which appealed to me. But it also has another meaning — 'toil' — which also felt appropriate. I had lived in many homesteads over the years. Now I was going to put down my swag and stay.

Within six weeks the homestead was gutted, painted, carpeted and I had new curtains and blinds hung. I cut roses and lavender from the overgrown garden and filled crystal vases for the house. I watched the little wrens find the confidence to patronise my new bird feeders.

And my dreams spread through the paddocks and beyond. I was ambitious. From planning to rebuild fences and gateways, I decided I needed a new cattle yard — the panels and posts were buggered from years of wear and tear and had never been replaced. I wanted to seed the entire farm for better pasture suitable for good quality Angus cattle to graze upon. My dreams didn't stop there. I would purchase the farms around the Shiralee, making it large enough to support a decent number of cattle. I really wanted this to be a viable enterprise for me and my family.

Two years on, it was definitely a work in progress and, as on all farms, there was always plenty to do. Now I planned to purchase some weaner steers from the Albany and Mount Barker saleyards. A weaner is a young beast no longer suckling from its mother, and a steer is a young castrated bull — all young bulls are castrated, except for those saved for breeding.

I had decided to change from breeding calves to fattening steers for market after several near disasters where I ended up having to physically pull calves from the cows. In the meantime, I was in transition and had paddocks full of cows due to calve any day. These big fat Angus cows bore no resemblance to the rangy shorthorns I was used to dealing with in the north. One day I discovered a heavy heifer with her tail raised and the birth sack protruding. The young mum was showing signs of distress and I knew I had to pull the damned calf out somehow.

This was a new experience for me, something I'd never had to do in the Kimberley, where the cows calved without difficulty. I needed to yard her up if I was going to be able to help her, but I could find only horse panels saved from the girls' rodeo days. These I placed in the narrow passageway in the old sheep yard by the shed. I gently moved the heifer up into my temporary cattle race, jamming an old wooden fence post in front of her and another behind to keep her steady.

Now I had to work out how to get the calf out. Luckily, I had recently invested in a set of shiny new calf-pulling chains, so I went and fetched these. The calf's front legs had broken the birth sack and were now protruding, and I wrapped the chains around the hooves. However, it was a big calf and I couldn't find the necessary strength to pull the bugger out — and my Angus mother wasn't helping me at all. I thought, *For god's sake, help me out here, this isn't a private hospital!* I was starting to feel a bit desperate. It crossed my mind to call the vet from Mount Barker but I hesitated as I imagined my profit going out the window in vet fees.

I ventured into my shed again to see if anything inspired me in there, and returned with the old fence strainers. I figured if they could pull up a fence they could pull a calf out of a cow. I can't tell you how pleased I was that the heifer didn't kick up sheer hell and try to bolt at the sight of them. I certainly would have! I wrapped the strainers around the calf's protruding hooves and looked towards the heavens for help, thinking, *Here goes.* Then I gently jacked the calf out of the heifer without any further problems. It was a beautiful big male calf. I threw him over a yard rail to pummel the mucus out and watched him take his first breath.

I spent the rest of the calving season pulling calves. The trusty fence strainers were a blessing, and I always used them when I didn't have Robby around to help me.

*

After McCorry's funeral, the first big project was to build the new cattle yard. I decided on Witnells panels: I'd used them in the Kimberley and found them exceptionally tough and easy to work with. In no time I drew up a new yard plan and faxed it through to Perth. Witnells promptly built the panels and trucked them down to the Shiralee. Kristy, Robby and I dug the post holes and mixed cement in the wheelbarrow with a hoe. The panels were cemented into the ground and we soon had a strong, safe working yard to be proud of.

Leisha was living in the city at this time but would come home for a visit every fortnight. Kristy (who is the daughter of my cousin Mary but has been a part of my family since she was four) was nineteen and living at home with me on the farm. She had a job exercising thoroughbred horses for a trainer in Redmond, which was on the way to Albany.

Robby was at home with me too. On school days he rode his farm bike out to the main road to get the school bus into Mount Barker. Robby loved being on the farm and was a great help to me with the cattle. He spent his weekends trapping rabbits which seemed to thrive between our back paddock and a nature reserve.

I could understand his passion for trapping. My father had taught me and my younger brother Bruce how to trap dingoes when they were coming into our camp on the bauxite plateau in Arnhem Land — we worried they would attack our little silky terrier Scruffy, who was already favouring a hind leg from a dingo nip. Bruce and I decided to set our trap on the path that ran by the rubbish dump. I disguised the loop of the snare on the track with light branches while Bruce set the remaining wire up in the overhanging tree. 'We can't miss,' I said to Bruce, 'we'll get a dingo for sure.' We headed back for the camp and home and never gave our dingo trap another thought.

The following afternoon I heard my father calling out to my mother with some urgency. Dad was at the rubbish dump tangled in the noose — he'd very nearly hanged himself in our dingo trap! *Bloody hell*, I thought, and ran to get Bruce. We waited around the camp long enough to see that Dad was okay, then disappeared to the billabong to give him time to cool off. Later that evening I overheard Dad telling Mum he couldn't believe how well the trap was set up. He had taught us well! I decided I'd better ask Robby not to set his rabbit traps where he might just catch his mum.

Everyone needs a home, a place where they feel safe and at ease, and the Shiralee was our home, from the undulating green paddocks to the old farmhouse with its white pillars and old-world charm. When the lounge-room fire was burning, the warmth spread throughout the house, to the furthest of the four bedrooms. I had filled the house with a mixture of Italianate and antique furniture and hung the walls with oil paintings of Kimberley stockmen and indigenous elders. Antique vases were crowded next to framed photographs of the children on horseback. The house was packed with warmth and memories, and the children were surrounded by things they were long familiar with.

Spring was in the air and the southern country never looked more beautiful. Rolling green hills were dotted with shiny contented cattle, while reserves of native bush were bursting with glorious colour. The air was alive with bird calls, all music to my ears, but my favourite was the little blue wren that came tap-tap-tapping on my bedroom windowsill each morning to join me for my breakfast pannikin of tea. I loved the Shiralee, and increasingly I felt I could grow to settle into this country.

Keeping cattle in the gentle south-west was a very different proposition from my beloved Kimberley, and in many respects much tamer. But not always! Owning cows comes with the need of a good bull, and at the end of my first year Jan and Gray Williamson, cattle farmers in the Narrikup area, lent me a Simmental bull that was on his way to the meatworks. I was grateful for the favour, but also worried as I watched this tonne of pumped-up muscle eye my paddock fences with serious displeasure. Bulls will go through just about any fence when they want to, and this boy was not going to stick around, I thought. But he changed his mind when a couple of my smart-looking Angus girls walked by like tarts, waving their tails high in the air. Muscles immediately let out a bellow of excitement and dutifully followed to start work servicing my cows.

But the real excitement began when it was time to return him to the truck to continue on his fatal journey to the meatworks. He must have known. My Landcruiser became the bull buggy as I steadily lapped him around the paddock to show who was the boss of this outfit. Muscles didn't give up; he fought every inch of the way through the paddocks, right into the yard, charging our every move in an effort to nail at least one of us up against the rail. He was ploughing the ground in anger and sending dust flying high into the sky while blowing snot everywhere, and I had to leap for the safety of the top rail more than once. And I had thought this only happened in the Kimberley — though instead of one aggro bull going down the road, there would have been a hundred or so. Yes, I still missed the excitement of the north.

Eventually we managed to load the bull onto the truck. His black mood wasn't changing in a hurry though. He was throwing himself against the cattle crate as I stood and watched the truck disappear into the distance, rocking violently. I felt sorry for Muscles as I knew his fate.

The following season my bull problem solved itself in a different way. One beautiful misty morning I took myself and my pannikin of tea to the clover paddock to check on my cows, only to be met with a surprising and wonderful vision. Out from behind a clump of natural bush moved a superb-looking Angus bull, accompanied by several of my girls. As I sat and watched him at work, I wondered who could be the owner of this magnificent creature — he wasn't branded. And no, I had not dropped the back fence to help him over. McCorry might have done something as cheeky as that, but it wasn't my style. Then several weeks later, after I'd made a lot of phone calls trying in vain to locate the beast's rightful owner, he jumped the fence and vanished, never to visit again. But the job was done, and the offspring were as good-looking as their father.

That was my last calving season; it was at this point that I decided to sell my cows and heifers and simply deal with steers. Buy them, fatten them, sell them! This I enjoyed. To collaborate with other cattle men and women, to stand around and talk cattle weight and prices, gave me great satisfaction.

The southern cattle industry was all new to me, and talking to the locals was the best way to discover what breeds were most suitable for paddock fattening. My choice was well-bred Angus steers, because I like a good clean line of cattle, but many other breeds would have been just as good.

I found there was a lot more to making a profit in the cattle industry in the south compared to the Kimberley. Huge overheads to start with, firstly with land value — you pay a heck of a lot more dollars per acre — then fertiliser, fencing, haymaking and farm machinery. On top of all that we need to spend a lot on chemicals to control parasites in cattle and insects in pastures. If I'm lucky I'll get a halfway reasonable rainy season, the grass will grow, and the red mites and lucerne flea will leave me enough to make hay and fatten my steers. But after all that, market prices may leave me wondering if the whole deal is worth the effort.

Back when I still had my Angus girls, I envied them in one respect. They might have given me trouble calving, but their sex life was straightforward. If only my own was as uncomplicated! I am a woman, with a normal woman's desires, yet my marriage to McCorry was no ordinary affair. The twenty years between us was not so noticeable at the beginning of our life together when I was twenty-four and he was forty-four, but I would be lying if I said it wasn't obvious to me some years later when we were making love out in the bright light of day on a worn old saddle blanket under a bauhinia tree. I was lying peacefully by McCorry's side, looking at him while he sat up to roll a cigarette, when for the first time I registered just how much older he was than me. His skin was burned nearly black and wrinkly from the harsh Kimberley sun; his hands were hard and callused, and his dark hair was turning grey. For all that, his body was still hard and lean: he never carried an ounce of fat on him. Seeing our age difference so suddenly like this shocked me, but it didn't change the deep love I had for my old cattle man.

Robby, our youngest, was conceived outdoors like that. This time our saddle blanket was spread in the spinifex country on Louisa Downs and we were serenaded by the call of black cockatoos who were probably wondering what the hell was going on. And that was the last time we ever made love.

Robby was born on 28 November 1984 in Derby Hospital and McCorry and I were over the moon. Our boy felt like a gift from above after losing our firstborn, Kelly, in a terrible accident on Louisa Downs three years earlier.

The circumstances could not have been more heartbreaking. McCorry was driving the bull buggy slowly through the homestead paddock gateway when five-year-old Kelly slipped unseen from the bullbar and broke his neck. He died in my arms while we waited for the flying doctor. It was the darkest day of our lives, and maybe even more so for Bob than for me, as he blamed himself for the accident. How could he not? I understood that, I would have blamed myself if I'd been driving the bull buggy. I understood, and I never blamed him, but he tortured himself with it.

Robby's birth was a great gift, but even that was not enough to pull McCorry out of the dark hole of depression. He also suffered back pain and some painful problem with his pancreas, and the cocktail of medication he washed down with an abundance of alcohol served to widen the distance between us. He was scarcely able to make love to me any more: the 'old fella' just wouldn't work, he said. For a long time I didn't know whether McCorry had simply lost interest in me, but whatever the reason, from the time Robby was conceived to our separation eleven years later, I was celibate.

So when an old friend from the Kimberley showed up at the Shiralee, there was part of me that was ready to respond to a bit of old-fashioned attention and romancing. There was another part of me that had no intention of getting involved with a man — my energy was focused on the children, and on getting the Shiralee into good shape.

Heath was a truck driver. Tanned, fit and lean, with a distinctive handlebar moustache. And he was only thirty-four — ten years younger than me — a big difference from McCorry. I had known his family a long time — Heath and his father had repaired station vehicles and power generators for McCorry and me for many years. And when I left the station in 1995 and took Robby to Derby, I saw Heath quite often.

He began as a much-needed friend — I felt vulnerable in Derby; I was way out of my comfort zone, being in town. It was good to be away from McCorry in his darkness, yet still it was a darkness I was familiar with. Heath gave me a friendly shoulder to cry on, and later a strong arm around me.

There was an undeniable spark between us; I had first felt it back on Kimberley Downs. I was changing all the station's windmills to solar and Heath had come out to give me a quote on a solar pumping system to pump water from a bore into a dam. The dam was quite isolated, surrounded by claypan flats with the occasional ant hill and bauhinia tree white with cockatoos. While Heath measured the depth of the bore, I walked around the rim of the dam. Overhead a lone eagle circled. I turned once to see how he was doing, and found his gaze fixed on me. I felt an instant surge of desire and was immediately caught between feelings of aroused sexiness and utter fear, for I had not been with a man for more than ten years. That was all that passed between us then; we did not touch each other or remark upon the feelings that had been ignited.

In Derby, though, it wasn't long before we slipped into an affair. The hunger in me was more than ready for release and I was no longer the station manager. There was nothing to stop us from taking the physical comfort in each other that we were both seeking. Heath was an intensely sexual man and it gave me an enormous boost to feel desired after so long. In just a short time I could feel the pent-up emotions of years dissolving. I had not realised how much I had longed for this physical connection.

For the few months that Robby and I stayed in the unit in Derby, Heath was a frequent visitor. When I left to go south, that was the end of things between us. It was quite amicable. Neither of us had seen it as a long-term affair.

And so when Heath dropped into the Shiralee as an old friend, it seemed like a good idea to take up where we'd left off. He was doing a local run, and it was only a small detour to call in on me. I felt secure in him being around the children; he was friendly with them, and Robby knew him from Derby. I never thought I'd be with him for the long haul. We didn't think we were in love. I was very conscious of our age difference and he was too. He was happy spending time with me on my farm, and helped out now and then with the cattle work and building new gates and fences, but he wasn't so keen on us going out together in public. He didn't like being seen holding my hand. My pride didn't like it, but as time went on and I saw more of him, I realised I needed to fill that big gap in my life that had opened up after I left McCorry. Heath helped fill it, and I looked forward to the days he dropped in.

We were very different. He was an intense sort of man, very passionate, yet he also stood back a bit and was hard to get to know. I don't think he understood me; why, for instance, I would make myself a pannikin of tea and go and sit alone on a bale of hay in the paddock and watch the cattle feeding. I needed the open spaces and this was my way of finding some peace.

I also needed time out from him. It was very strange for me, having a lover who was so much younger and with a strong sex drive. At times I found the sexual tension between us almost too much to handle; the air seemed electrified when we were in each other's presence. It was like living in a Mills and Boon romance novel. Because it was so unfamiliar to me, I didn't know what it meant: was this what any woman my age might feel after a long sex drought? Was I simply vulnerable?

After McCorry died Heath moved in with me on the farm. Right from the start, this spelled the end of things being easy between us. I was in a very low space then and would often wake in the middle of the night sobbing. One night when I woke in tears, Heath growled angrily, 'Get over it, just get over it.' He really thought it was as simple as that: you just got over it. I felt hurt, though I told myself he had never lost anyone he had loved so he didn't understand — that was better than thinking he just didn't care. I lay there in the dark trying to convince myself that Kelly and McCorry were in a better place somewhere, together — if only I could believe it.

The next morning when Heath had gone I made my way out to the paddock with some hay for my black Angus steers. I had only recently bought these magnificent creatures and was still capable of getting a kick out of seeing them. I warmed myself with a pannikin of tea while soaking in the beauty that surrounded me. The Porongurups in all their glory stretched out beyond the horizon of natural bush and green paddocks, looking like a sleeping princess lying on her back, her outline formed by the rise and fall of the range. I counted my blessings. Leisha, Robby and Kristy were all healthy, and I was feeling much stronger in body and soul.

My thoughts turned to Heath and I felt a sudden leap of anger. How dare he tell me to get over McCorry's death? Who did he think he was? He hadn't earned the right to speak to me like that. I wanted to send him on his way, but at the same time I knew I wasn't ready for that, not yet. In one respect we were an excellent match: he kept my reawakened sex drive more than satisfied. The desire to make love was never far from the surface when we were together. I even found myself smiling out there in the paddock as I remembered how, when the urge became too much to ignore, we once ended up balancing on the seat of the four-wheeler motorbike!

And maybe it mattered to him more than I thought that I was grieving for another man. There were times I felt he was competing with Robby for my undivided attention, and he once told me he wanted to be the most important person in my life, although I hadn't taken him seriously in this. It seemed to me it was more a matter of ego — he was no more in the relationship for the long run than I was. Once, he asked me to marry him, but I didn't believe he had thought it through — he still found it difficult being seen in public with me. I told him that I wasn't ready to think about marriage, that I still needed time to deal with McCorry's death. I felt he held that against me, as if he thought he was doing me a favour and I was refusing him out of spite.

But he was also a caring person who wanted to play a positive part in my life. He once hired a horse float and drove the Landcruiser to Broome for me to collect two of our horses that had been left up there. One was Little Blue, a champion barrel-racing horse with whom Leisha had won numerous 'All Round Champion Cowgirl' titles in the Kimberley. We had retired the little mare from the rodeo circuit, but she still had plenty of go in her.

I wanted Little Blue down on the Shiralee because I figured she would help quieten my new steers in the paddock. I was still trying to find faith in these southern cattle. I worried each time I unloaded a new mob that they would crash through every paddock and fence and continue rampaging across every farm in their path till I'd lost the bloody lot. It wasn't as if I could bring in a chopper to muster them back up — well, not without upsetting the whole district. I was still thinking with a Kimberley mindset.

I was lucky to have good neighbours like Richard O'Connor, who helped guide me and did contract seeding and haymaking for me in the early years. To prepare myself for farming on these smaller acreage farms I had studied for a Diploma of Agriculture, but I always believed that local farmers were the best teachers of all. I would listen to them and then work the Shiralee my way. I'm sure the locals were wary of this woman from up north, but they watched my farming methods with great interest over the fence.

In fact my farm was looking good. I had soil-tested the paddocks halfway through 1996 and paid a local spreading contractor to lime and fertilise them. We had plenty of feed and the steers were a picture. The only problem I had was not wanting to send the cattle to market. I hated parting with them.

There came a time when I realised I was wasting my time preparing a meal for Heath on a Friday evening. He was driving big rigs Monday to Friday between Perth and Albany, a job he was very happy with, but I had a gut feeling that he was playing around on me. Then rumours reached me that he was messing around with a younger married woman who worked in the office of his transport company.

One Friday night when he came in late I was already in bed. I sat up and asked him quite bluntly, 'Heath, are you playing around on me?'

'No,' he said straightaway, not looking at me.

I didn't believe him. I could tell there was something amiss, and he just didn't want to talk to me.

'Well, if you are, you can pack your bags and get the hell out of my life,' I said angrily.

I got out of bed and went to the kitchen to brew a pot of tea. Heath disappeared out the back door into the darkness and I was left with the hum of the cicadas. I drank my tea and returned to bed, shut the light off and fell asleep, only to wake with a start to the slamming of the back door. I heard Robby's voice, calm but insistent, and Heath's answering murmur. I was just getting up to investigate when Heath came into the bedroom. Without a word he got into bed and pulled the covers up over his head. I stood and watched him for a moment, then went out to Robby's room to see him tucking the farm's .22 rifle under his pillow.

'What's going on, Robby?' I demanded. 'Is that loaded?'

'No, Mum, I've emptied it, the bullets are in the wardrobe. Everything's cool, just go back to bed.' Nothing was making sense to me, but Robby was tired and he didn't want to talk. He wrapped his arms around me, gave me a big hug and told me to sleep tight. I went back to bed where Heath was already asleep.

Morning came and everyone was busy and I didn't mention the previous night's antics. It niggled at me, but it was a couple of days later before Robby and I talked about it, when Heath was on the road.

'What was that business with the gun, Robby?' I asked.

'Mum, I got up to go to the bathroom when Heath walked in from outside with the .22. I don't know why, or what was going to happen,' Robby said, 'but he wasn't going to walk around with that gun in our house, not around you anyway.' Robby had followed Heath into the lounge room and found him sitting with his head down and the rifle in his hands. 'He looked up at me, and his face was really sad, Mum. I just took the rifle out of his hands, he didn't even try to stop me.'

A shiver ran through me and I was suddenly covered in goosebumps. I tried to get my head around what Heath might have been doing with a gun, but my mind just ran amok with terrible thoughts and unspeakable questions. Had he intended to kill himself? Or was he going to shoot me? Maybe he was simply moving the rifle from the shed to the gun cabinet — but in the middle of the night? I thanked God for my level-headed son, but I was also very angry. Robby had enough on his plate having just lost his father, he shouldn't have to be worrying about whether he had to protect his mother from a crazy lover; it was me who should have been protecting him.

I was in a dilemma. I wanted to confront Heath, but each time I was about to bring it up, I lost my nerve. Despite his denials, I had no doubt he was playing around on me and I no longer felt safe or secure with him. I should have tossed him out — in my mind it was over between us anyway — but there was always that physical connection between us. I never spoke to Heath about the gun or the other woman, and we went on like this for a little longer.

This was not the first brush with guns in my life. Some four or five years, earlier on Kimberley Downs, I had intervened between two fighting men with a gun. It was late evening and the last colours of the sunset were spreading a beautiful tranquil sky over the homestead. Jim, my right-hand man, and I were sharing pannikins of tea when cries came from the children. 'Mum! Two stockmen are fighting with a gun out there!'

We both rose at once. There was no moon or stars, and the night sky was rapidly turning pitch black. I told the children to go inside with Jim, then ran inside and grabbed a torch, and with some trepidation moved out into the dark. I could hear muffled sounds and I called out to the stockmen, but no answers came. I stood with my torch at eye level and moved it steadily until I picked up two dark silhouettes stepping warily around one another. The beam reflected off a firearm. Enraged, I yelled, 'What the fuck is going on here?' There was no answer.

I kept walking in the dark in the direction of the two men, and their slow dance continued. Still neither of them answered me, which only exacerbated my frustration. My pulse was racing, but it was more in anger than fear of copping a bullet myself. They were moving in a wide circle and finally I was close enough and made a dash for the gun. I grabbed hold of it and refused to let it go. Eventually I managed to wrest it from the stockman's hand. I walked back towards the verandah then swung around and shone the torch on the pair.

'What did you think you were going to do with this?' I yelled, furious as all hell. 'Shoot someone? What for?' Neither man answered me, they both stood with heads bowed, kicking at the dirt in front of them. 'Is there any shit involved in this?' By that I meant drugs; if there was, they'd both be on the road at first light. I searched their faces with the torch for signs of intoxication, but could see none.

I took a deep breath. 'Have either of you anything to say?' I asked a lot more calmly. They glanced towards each other and both shook their heads. I needed the lesson to sink home. 'You've disappointed me; I've lost my trust in you both. I'm keeping the gun, I'll talk to you in the morning. Go to bed.'

I emptied out the bullets from the .308 and walked into the house with it; the gun spent several nights under my bed for safekeeping before I bought it from the stockman who owned it and had it licensed in my own name.

One night at the Shiralee, not long after the business with the gun, I was rolling over in bed when I suddenly felt a lump in my breast. It was so hard, I thought my pearl necklace had broken and a pearl was pushing into my chest. But it hadn't broken, and I realised I had a distinct marble-like lump high in my right breast. Heath was beside me, and I told him, but his only response was a sense of annoyance that I seemed to be expecting some warmth or support from him for something I was probably imagining, or at least something that was in the world of older women, not younger men.

God knows what I was expecting him to say, but his utter lack of interest nearly reduced me to tears. I needed to talk to someone about this, but I made up my mind I would not burden the children or my parents until I knew what was going on. There was no one else I felt close enough to talk to about something so personal. This left me feeling very isolated. I couldn't cry; I felt only a deep, sad emptiness. The next morning I made an appointment with the travelling breast X-ray van that was currently parked in Mount Barker.

It was my first mammogram. What an education. My breasts were squeezed flat between the plates of what looked like an old-fashioned ironing press; they were pulled, prodded and tugged at by the clinic operator to get the desired shots. I was very relieved to find that they bounced back afterwards.

A couple of weeks later I received a call from a Perth clinic telling me I had an appointment in Albany for further tests. They were concerned about my left breast, though it was my right I was worried about. But after more X-rays and ultrasounds, I was given the all-clear. I should have been jumping for joy, but I was still bothered by the hard marble-like lump, which I was told was a benign cyst. I told myself to ignore it, forget it, and with that in mind I was celebrating the good news that evening when Heath asked me if I would use the Shiralee as surety to finance him for a truck and trailers to start his own trucking business. He needed $500,000.

'You want me to mortgage the Shiralee?' I asked, unable to believe what I was hearing.

He hesitated, then answered, 'Well, yes.'

Our relationship was hanging on by a thread, he didn't even *pretend* that he cared about me, and he thought I was going to risk my farm for him! *You've got to be joking*, I thought, while studying his face for some kind of expression of love or concern. There was none. 'No Heath, it's not on,' I said, and got up and left the room.

I was incensed. I thought, *Like bloody hell I'm going to mortgage my home for you! I've done some dumb things in my time but I'm not risking my farm for a man who doesn't care a damn for me*. I should've ended it then and there; I don't know why I didn't, except that the sexual attraction was still strong. I found this amazing, that you could lose your affection for a person, yet still want to make love — constantly.

It was around this time that Terry, south-west farmer and Broome caravan park owner, came into my life. I thought it was a case of close one door, and another door opens, but it turned out to be more a matter of out of the frying pan, into the fire.

I'd met Terry earlier, when he came down from Broome in 1999 to watch one of his horses run at Ascot. I had travelled to the city to visit Leisha, arguing with Heath most of the way.

That evening we all gathered for a meal and drinks at the Ascot Inn, a popular watering hole for the local racing fraternity. Terry was there too, and when he discovered that we were from the Kimberley and had been involved with cattle stations, he introduced himself. As it turned out, Terry remembered our family from a visit to the Boyanup cattle saleyards several years earlier when McCorry, Leisha, Kristy, Robby and I had made an initial trip around the south-west looking at cattle and cattle country. Back then, I later discovered, Terry thought I was one of McCorry's daughters! Old McCorry would have choked him for that.

On meeting Terry I held out my hand for him to shake. He held on to it far longer than was necessary while bombarding me with questions about my life in the Kimberley. Tall, somewhat older than me, not bad looking, and very charming, he ignored all the rest of the company, including Heath. I did not know it at the time, but he was with a young woman, Lauren, his receptionist from Broome, and he had parked her at the far end of the room with a supply of drinks and peanuts to occupy her while he came to meet me.

I had to admit I was impressed by his charm, and mildly flattered by the attention he was showering on me, but I didn't think any more about him when I returned to the Shiralee the next day. However, one thing the meeting achieved was to make it very clear to me that my relationship with Heath was no more than a childish game and I no longer wanted any part of it. There was no sense of trust between us. I finally told him he had to leave. Except for the physical connection, I could see no future for us together.

He left, though not without some unpleasantness. He felt he had made material contribution to my life on the Shiralee and thought he could waltz off with my Italian leather lounges. No way was he taking them, I'd bought them when I'd set up house. I could as legitimately have tried to lay claim to his tool box! Yet even then, we made love until the day he moved his last possessions out. The physical attraction was impossible to ignore. And when he had gone, I did miss that. But not so much that I regretted ending it.

It was two months later when, out of the blue, I answered the door to Terry. I was surprised to see him and invited him in for a cup of tea. He said he was in the area to check on some mares he had in foal at Mungrup. Mungrup was not far from the Shiralee, and he asked me if I would come along and have a look at the horses with him. I said I would so long as I was back home in time to meet Robby's school bus. I was never happy for Robby to arrive home to an empty farmhouse.

While we were out he was constantly getting calls from his receptionist and I felt awkward sitting there, keeping my peace, as it was obvious Terry was hiding the fact that he had someone else in the car with him. When we left the stud he drove on towards Albany to visit friends, ignoring my requests to return to the farm. Looking back, it is easy to recognise that here was a clear sign of a man doing exactly what he wanted, when he wanted, and having no interest in the wishes of anyone else concerned. But back then I shrugged and told myself he was probably anxious, it was our first outing.

And could he talk up a storm!

His family had farms at the Carbunup River south of Busselton where he was to help with haymaking before returning to Broome, and at Wildwood River, not far from Dunsborough, where his parents lived. They had recently bought the caravan park in Broome, which he managed part of the year, in partnership with another brother. He had been married once before, was divorced and had three grown boys.

By the time we were on our way back to the farm, Terry was offering me the world. We had similar goals in life, he said. We could travel together and farm together; my knowledge of the Kimberley would be an advantage in his tourist trade. He was painting a wonderful future for the two of us, but as we drove through the front gate of the Shiralee I was still trying to comprehend exactly what he was saying — it sounded suspiciously like a marriage proposal. And that was a bit damn quick on a first date — if this could even be called a date. *Hell*, I thought, *one man has just left my life and now another sounds like he's planning on moving in. What am I doing?*

As Terry brought his car to a slow stop by the farmhouse, still sweet-talking me, I opened the door and literally fell out onto the lawn. Frantically gathering my dignity I got up and waved my goodbyes as he drove off with promises to keep in touch. Some part of me knew what it was doing when I abandoned his car so quickly — he had the look of a man intent on pouncing! (And on another count, too, my intuition was spot on: I later learned that when he got back to Broome he said to the women who worked at the caravan park, 'I've just met the woman I'm going to marry.')

It was five o'clock, and Robby was sitting waiting for me on the verandah.

CHAPTER 2

The Importance of a Holden Statesman

*I*t was early summer 1998 and Robby, Kristy and I were moving between Sleepy Hollow (old McCorry's farm) and the Shiralee, fixing fences and checking on the cattle.

I had negotiated a lease on the farm directly behind the Shiralee for the purpose of running my steers through to market. With more land I could carry the cattle longer so they could gain more weight before I sold them. It was a wonderful thing to watch them in the finishing paddock, a gentle breeze rippling across the luscious green feed, big black steers, heads down munching. It was a beautiful picture, but it had a bitter side too. This particular mob of cattle was contracted for live export to the Middle East, but after watching a documentary on the way cattle are slaughtered in Muslim countries — slashing a hock then cutting the beast's throat — I was no longer sure this was ethical. Of course I had a family to consider — the income put food on our table, and I wasn't sure I could afford to have such scruples. The dilemma felt too much for me: it was the sort of thing I would have discussed with McCorry, and wished I could discuss with him now.

I missed this capacity to talk things over; without it I felt more alone than I could bear. It wasn't only the exports, there was so much building up in me that I couldn't talk about — my private battle of dealing not only with old McCorry's death, but with all the old anger, hurt and pain from our years together, never mind the hassles with Heath and the fear of cancer. And always memories of Kelly. But that didn't mean I was going to take Terry's wild proposals seriously. I was feeling far too vulnerable to be bringing anyone new into my life at this point.

They say everybody hurts sometime, and I was hurting big time. But I was ploughing on with my life on the farm, telling myself constantly to keep it all together, while putting on a strong and confident face.

I wasn't the only one struggling. Leisha, too, was having a hard time coming to terms with McCorry's death. She and her father had been very close. Bob had the kids late in life, and he was devoted to them. When Kelly died, there was only Leisha — Robby wasn't born then — and he clung on to her tight. He didn't want anything to happen to her.

Leisha was trying to tough it out. Watching my daughter suffer whilst unable to express her true feelings upset me deeply. I wish she'd felt able to talk to me. Instead she hit the party scene, and it seemed she'd really lost her direction. While trying to manage the farm and be there for Robby and Kristy, I began to worry that I might lose my daughter to the dangers of the city.

One night her drink was spiked in a Perth nightclub when she was out on the town with her girlfriend Jenny. Thank goodness Leisha had heard of drink spiking, because she handled it amazingly well, but I shudder to think of what might so easily have happened. The girls had a rule never to leave their drinks unattended or with a stranger. So when the drug hit her leaving her immediately heavy and dizzy, she knew the trouble had to have come from behind the bar. Catching the bouncer and barman with sickening smirks on their faces, she battled to help Jenny, who had also been drugged, down the corridor to the bathroom, to vomit up the substance before it effectively paralysed them.

Leisha willed herself not to black out. The drug affected her speech so that the people she asked for help thought she was drunk. It was my girl's steely determination that kept her awake and got the two of them out of the nightclub. In the street, they hailed a taxi and luckily got a compassionate driver who delivered them home safely. The girls recovered, but that ordeal was something Leisha did not forget in a hurry.

'Why didn't you report it to the police?' I cried when she finally told me about it a couple of weeks later. She said she thought no one would be interested; she'd heard this sort of thing was impossible to prove.

Living in Perth, she may as well have been on another planet, the distance from the Shiralee seemed so great. One beautiful crisp morning when she was visiting the farm, we were sitting on the back verandah with Robby, having a quiet moment together. It was so peaceful there, listening to the birds, and my body slowly relaxed, letting go some of the pent-up feelings I was carrying. The early morning sun warmed me, giving me strength, and I seized on the opportunity to speak.

'Leisha, do you realise the worry your brother and I go through when you're up there drinking and partying?' She raised her eyes and looked at me to show she was listening; I was grateful for that at least. 'When I get a phone call from you miles away, upset and emotional, it tears me up. It brings terrible thoughts to mind. I often end up unable to sleep,

frightened that at any moment a police officer will come to
the door bearing bad news. Please,' I begged my girl, 'Daddy
wouldn't want this, nor would Kelly. We have to try and find
our strength again and get it together, for all our sakes.'

'I know, Mum, and I will,' said my girl.

'We need to think of good memories of Daddy. Remember
how he was when we visited him at Sleepy Hollow,' I said. No
matter how sick he was in those last months, and bent over
and slow, McCorry would always make us tea and toast us
steak sandwiches. He never let us do anything, but treated
us as his treasured princesses. He really mellowed in those
last months before he died.

'You're right, Mum, that's a good memory to hold. I can
just picture him there, having us over to tea.'

Remembering the good times with her father must have
helped Leisha deal less destructively with her grief, because
gradually she stopped living such a wild life and started to
settle back into herself.

How different my life was now from the life I had in the
Kimberley. When we managed Oobagooma there was a
woman who lived in the far corner of the property, on a small
lease called Kimbolton. She was only in her late twenties, and
ran this rough area of country with her older partner and two
boys. We held this girl in high regard for she was a battler
and, like me, loved the wild outback life she was leading. She
had a great spirit. One day when our stock camp men drove
the old station truck to a tidal creek on Kimbolton to go
fishing, they stopped a little too close to the homestead and
she came out with a .303 rifle. 'Piss off!' she told them: the
stockmen did, and from that day on, the men nicknamed her
Geronimo.

At the start of the next dry season Geronimo asked some Aboriginal stockmen to help her put a mob of cattle together. They moved down from the homestead to Cone Bay in the saltwater region where they picked up about three hundred head of cleanskins (unbranded and therefore unclaimed cattle). Then they walked the cattle back, following the Stuart River to where it joined the Robinson. Both of these rivers were tidal at this point, but there was a freshwater spring just off the Stuart on Oobagooma country, with good green buffalo grass all around it.

There has always been a rule in the mustering game which states that if your cattle are in need of a drink, you may walk them into your neighbour's country and water them there, as long as you remain close to the boundaries. Geronimo's mob of cattle were thirsty and so this is what she did. Across the outback, there were no boundary fences at that time. We all knew where the boundaries were — you lined them up along prominent points in the landscape.

Now the guy who owned Oobagooma, who we called 'city slicker Monty,' happened to be flying his light aircraft back to the Oobagooma homestead from Sydney at that time and passed directly over the area where Geronimo and her team of stockmen were watering her newly found cattle. He landed at the homestead and dropped off his girlfriend with instructions to bring us the news that the Kimbolton stock camp was mustering Oobagooma country, then flew back to Derby to bring the police out to witness this heinous crime. McCorry and I were to get ourselves out there pronto.

We jumped into the old Landrover and were out there in no time. We knew Geronimo's cattle were cleanskins from Cone Bay, as the country hadn't been mustered before, but we didn't know if any branded Oobagooma cattle might have been in the mob. If there was even one, then Geronimo could be in trouble.

What a piece of work this city slicker was! For years McCorry and I had been mustering cleanskin cattle for him, and all we ever got out of it was a very ordinary wage and McCorry's tobacco. The cattle we were drafting at the Oobagooma yard at the time were cleanskins, just like Geronimo's, and he had the cheek to turn and pull an act like this — he was doing the same bloody thing! Bouncing around in the Landrover we crossed the bugger-bugger country — an Aboriginal term for rough and rugged black soil country — where we met up with Geronimo. She was holding up the mob of cattle with her stockmen. Without fences, the stockmen 'hold up' cattle, or keep them corralled, by riding around them in a circle.

'Monty's flown to Derby to get the cops,' said old McCorry. 'If there's any Oobagooma branded cattle, you could be charged with cattle stealing.'

'There's only one old Oobagooma cow in the mob, as far as I can tell,' replied Geronimo. But before we could do anything about it, the city slicker arrived in his Cessna with a cop we didn't know. Monty took the Landrover and drove the policeman around and through the mob of bellowing cattle. When he returned and pulled the vehicle up by our side, everyone was quiet and solemn. The cop stepped out of the vehicle and said to Geronimo, 'I'm going to have to charge you for having an Oobagooma cow in your mob and for mustering Oobagooma country, and now I place a lien on these cattle.' He was playing it by the book. This meant the cattle had to stay where they were, pending further investigation. It was farcical. There was nothing there to hold a mob of feral cattle up with — no cattle yard, nothing — and all this for one old Oobagooma cow, which looked like it was on its last legs anyway!

McCorry was looking pleased with himself. He clearly had something up his sleeve. He told Geronimo and her head stockman not to say a word. Geronimo was tall and lean, a bit flat chested and with her long blonde hair twisted up under her hat and wearing a man's shirt and trousers, she could be taken for a man if you didn't know better. The cop didn't know better. He waded in, boots and all. 'Do I recognise your face mate? Off a wanted poster? You're a bloody crim aren't you!'

At this, old McCorry thought it was time to play his hand. 'Hold on,' he said. 'I think you had better shut up until you get the facts straight. For a start the person you are talking to is a woman, and a bloody good one at that. Secondly, if you put a lien on these cattle, you do realise that they will be the responsibility of the crown, which in this case is you? That means these people will ride away and you will have to watch the cattle all night until reinforcements arrive from Derby.'

'Hell,' the cop said, 'I can't do that; I have to get back to town.'

'Well,' old McCorry said, 'then you're wasting your bloody time and ours too.'

'I'll be back in the morning with the sergeant,' the policeman said, and climbed aboard the Cessna with Monty. Once the plane had disappeared, McCorry told Geronimo and her stockman to push the cattle inside the Kimbolton boundary and yard them. 'Before you do,' he said, 'put a rope around the Oobagooma cow, put the barrel of your .22 well down into her ear, pull the trigger and then remove the rope. At the first sign of piccaninny daylight, walk the cattle back to the yard at the homestead. There'll be no case to answer.'

The next day McCorry and I drove out on the pretext of taking possession of the Oobagooma cow for 'city slicker' Monty. He was our boss after all. The policeman and his sergeant arrived, full of importance and pleased to be upholding the law of the land. They looked over the mob of cattle once more. 'Where's the Oobagooma cow?' asked the sergeant. I thought, *Heck, here we go.*

'She died last night in the yard on the Stuart River,' old McCorry said.

'Or maybe you shot her,' replied the surly sergeant.

'Well,' volunteered McCorry, by this time looking even more pleased with himself than he had the day before, 'you can check the cow for a bullet hole on the way back to the plane.'

The sergeant looked uncertainly at Geronimo. 'I'm going to brand these cattle with the crown brand, the broad arrow,' he said.

'Have you got the brand with you?' asked McCorry.

'No,' said the sergeant, agitated now. 'We can make one out of some number 8 fencing wire.'

Old McCorry knew this was not legal, as you can only brand with a registered brand. He also knew that if the fiasco got to court, the sergeant's ignorance would be the downfall of the prosecution. He walked over to Geronimo and spoke to her privately. 'Let them go ahead with the branding, don't say anything, you're in the clear girl. Once they get back to Derby town and read up on the stock laws, you won't hear from them again. All you have to do is paddock the cattle for 90 days, then sell the lot.' And that was the end of that.

Over the next few months Terry rang frequently, and visited whenever he came down to work on the farm on the Carbunup River. I began to look forward to his visits. We'd drive between his family's farms, talking away about our common interest in the cattle industry — I could learn from him about farming down there. Sometimes we'd be singing along to old sixties and seventies hits on the radio; we knew the same songs, it seemed like we had a lot in common. Most importantly, the kids liked him. He could be very funny, and he constantly made me laugh. These were happy days, and for the first time since McCorry had died I felt like I really didn't have a care. Terry was fun. He was big and happy and confident and he liked to have a good time. He'd take me to the races, we'd eat in nice restaurants. He liked having me on his arm; I could see he was proud being seen out with me and, after Heath, that was a real boost to my ego. We made a good-looking pair.

Yet despite how much I enjoyed his company, I really didn't know whether he was the right man for me in the long term — and it was clear he was thinking about the long term. It wasn't long since I'd shown Heath the door, and the bitterness of that ending had left me feeling wary. I wanted to take things easy, see how we were together once the first thrill had worn off. He wanted me to visit him in Broome, the sooner the better, and that seemed like a big step for me. I was dithering, and I suddenly realised I no longer believed in my own capacity to make decisions. I was looking for some guidance, the kind you might expect from an old friend who knows you well, but there was no one like that in my life now that McCorry had passed away.

In the end, I visited a psychic in Albany. I'd heard someone talking about her, saying she was the real deal. Of course I was ambivalent about seeing a psychic — it hardly seemed the action of a woman who managed cattle stations. And yet I had seen a psychic once before, at Mundijong, south of Perth, after losing Kelly. In that terrible time I was clutching at anything that might give me some relief, and it did. Now I needed to know where I was going, I needed some solid direction in my life, and I convinced myself that no harm would come as long as I didn't take it too seriously.

After a few laps around the block I pulled up outside an upmarket-looking house perched high on the hill overlooking Albany. I was met at the door by a well-dressed middle-aged woman. A quiet calmness surrounded her as she led me to a brightly lit room. We sat on opposite sides of a table and I felt quite comfortable. There were two decks of cards in front of her; she shuffled them and asked me to select a pack. I chose the blue pack. She then dealt the cards on the table in front of me. *Hell*, I thought as soon as I saw them, *this doesn't look good*. It was the death card, the same card that had appeared in the reading after Kelly's death. The psychic said it could mean either a literal death or the death of a relationship. I knew it was both. McCorry's death, and the recent end of my relationship with Heath.

I sat in a bit of a daze, not really taking in what she was saying, until I heard the words, 'A new man is coming into your life.' This grabbed my attention. I stopped peeling the nail varnish from my fingernails and raised my eyes to look at her. *How do you know this? Are you sure?* I wondered silently.

'When?' I asked.

'Very soon,' she replied, and shuffled the cards and placed several more on the table in front of me. 'He's your type of man,' she added after a moment. 'He's strong, and he knows what he wants in life.' Then she offered a rather odd detail: 'He'll be driving a Holden Statesman.' When the reading was over I walked in deep thought out to the car. *Well*, I said to myself, *I guess I'll see what the future brings*. It had been an interesting way to pass an afternoon anyway.

On his next visit, Terry arrived in a silver Holden Statesman. I had to look twice, I couldn't believe my eyes. It was a second-hand Caprice he had taken for a test drive from a car dealership in Busselton. It was pretty hard not to look at him a bit more seriously after that. I am a practical and sceptical person, and had it not been for the detail of the Holden Statesman, I would probably not have taken a lot of notice of the psychic. But I thought about the other things she had said, that he was my type of man, strong, confident, a man of the world who knew what he wanted, and I realised these were the very things I wanted in my life right now.

I was getting my old sense of self back. I knew what I wanted. Nothing fancy, I didn't want the world. I didn't want his status or his money. I just wanted a man who loved me and wasn't afraid to tell me. And Terry had made that perfectly clear often enough. I wasn't dizzily in love, and I never felt that animal spark of sexual attraction that existed between me and Heath. But I didn't want that any more. That sort of passion might be fine when you're young, but it was no use to me now. On its own, it was no basis for a relationship. I liked Terry. I felt easy and comfortable with him, and able to be myself. I liked the way we laughed and sang together and danced. If a good tune came on the radio at the Shiralee when he was visiting, he'd whisk me away from whatever I was doing and dance me around the kitchen.

So I said yes to a trip to Broome. He was delighted and I was glad to be finished with dithering. And it would be enlightening to see him on his own turf up there. Besides, we could all do with a holiday. My four brothers — Bruce, Darryl, Eric and Michael — all had mango farms and other businesses around Broome. We didn't keep in touch very much, but we all got on well when we saw each other, and it meant Leisha and Robby had cousins in town — all my brothers had wives and children. There was also John and Ben, cousins from McCorry's side of the family, who were skippers and divers for Paspaley pearls. Robby couldn't wait to hit the surf, though Kristy decided she would remain at the Shiralee — she was still riding trackwork for the trainer at Redmond and she didn't want to leave.

We set off early from home, full of confidence and holiday high spirits. The heavy grey clouds that seemed to lie like a blanket across the sky would only make for good travelling — better for the tyres and engine too, I thought. But once we had passed Perth and taken the inland road to Meekatharra we were in for a rude shock. Rain pelted down on the thirsty earth in a fury, and what were usually parched creek beds were quickly becoming angry rivers, while the plains between the rivers soon flooded to look like great dirty foaming oceans. It was frightening. I turned on the car radio to pick up the news or a weather report while constantly searching the heavens trying to read the dark racing clouds. The elements were in a hell of a hurry — the clouds, downpours and rising rivers — and I made a decision to turn around and return to Perth. We could fly to Broome for our holiday.

No sooner were we pointed towards the south when I caught the words 'Cyclone Vance' coming from a barely audible radio and knew I had made the right decision.

Terry met us at Broome's tiny airport and drove us to his caravan park where he encouraged us to stay, even though my intentions had been to go to the Mangrove Hotel overlooking the turquoise blue bay of Broome.

I felt very awkward standing in the small kitchen-cum-lounge room that was also the office and reception for the caravan park. Terry had ushered us in but had then been immediately dragged off to attend to something. The building was a small timber structure from Lord McAlpine's days of bringing Bali to Broome. The place was a hive of sweltering activity and I felt hemmed in and uncomfortable with streams of people — staff and friends and acquaintances — coming and going. One of them stood out, it was the young woman

Lauren who, I had learned by now, had been with Terry at the Ascot Inn. She was eyeing me up and down in a way that didn't look very friendly. Was there something going on between the two of them, I had to wonder. I had made it very plain to Terry that if there was another woman in his life there could be nothing between us. He had laughed at my concern and assured me there was no one.

Robby and Leisha were outside somewhere, looking over the grounds, and I had to get out too. The noise and the claustrophobic crush were making me agitated. I was trying to juggle my suitcases through the overcrowded dining area out towards the back door when, pausing for a moment to get my breath, I had a sudden memory of McCorry at the luxurious Parmelia Hilton in Perth. I was managing Kimberley Downs at the time and we were taking a rare annual holiday. The doorman was bowing graciously to receive our dusty suitcases from the waiting cab as the children stood in awe, taking in the magnificent structure and noting staircases with a potential for entertainment.

Old McCorry, legs bowed and back bent, wrestled for ownership of the luggage. He was not well. 'They're not pinching it,' I whispered. 'Let the doorman get it delivered to the room.' The memory made me smile, but then I noticed Terry smiling at me from across the room and I lifted my cases again. I needed time away from this circus atmosphere to clear my head and think. I was apprehensive and needed space to see the real picture. At forty-nine years old I had no intention of getting caught up in a disastrous relationship. I would rather be alone, I told myself, though in fact I'd never really been on my own. I suddenly felt very vulnerable and unsure what the hell I was doing.

As if he could read my mind, Terry came over and wrapped his arm around me, pulling me close while guiding me towards a bedroom; his, as it turned out. He proudly pointed out the beautiful bedroom suite, newly bought, he said, covered in crisp new linen and on the bed a beautiful bunch of roses. It was such a lovely gesture, one of those things I really appreciated in him, and I felt my worries and confusion slide away. Then another call came from the office needing his attention, and Terry had to go. I was left standing alone, immediately apprehensive again, when I felt a presence in the room with me.

I turned around to see Lauren standing there. She was a slim girl about my height, with golden tanned skin and fine blonde hair tied back in a ponytail. She wore short tight shorts and a white halter top that left her tummy bare. She looked not unlike my own girls, in fact she was probably their age. She looked puzzled, a little wary of me.

It was rather a strange and awkward way to meet, I thought.

'What are you doing here?' she asked me bluntly, and I could have said the same thing to her. Where was my privacy? But at that point I did wonder what the bloody hell I was doing there. I was definitely on the back foot. 'I'm here on holiday,' I said lightly. 'How about you?' and I turned and walked out of the bedroom before she could respond.

That evening Terry took me to dinner at the Mangrove Hotel. He was bubbly and happy and introduced me to the many people he knew there. He seemed to know everyone, and they all seemed pleased to see him. He was so enthusiastic about having me there with him that I could almost enjoy feeling so wanted and appreciated. But the business with Lauren was niggling me, and I told him about my strange encounter with her. 'Something's going on between you, isn't it?' I said. 'Why would she come in like that otherwise?'

His eyes opened wide in surprise. 'She came into the bedroom?'

'Yes, your receptionist came into the bedroom and was standing there interrogating me as though she had every right to. What's going on?'

'Absolutely nothing is going on. But you're right, her behaviour is unacceptable. I'll give her notice. She'll be gone in three days.'

'You don't have to sack her on my behalf,' I said, wishing I hadn't said anything. But he was adamant. 'There's plenty of people who want work around here,' he said. 'Now let's get on with enjoying the evening.' He raised his glass and proposed a toast, 'To us!'

It was a night when the beam of the full moon stretched across the bay. There was nothing between us and the glorious golden 'stairway to the moon', and I sipped my champagne and let the magic work on me. It was a perfect balmy Broome evening, when the air seems to caress your skin.

Still, when I went to the ladies room a little later, I found my mind buzzing again. There were practical things to work out, and our first romantic evening in Broome hardly seemed the place to decide where the children and I were going to stay. I had left it to Terry to book us into the Mangrove. He hadn't, deciding on my behalf that we'd be better off with him. Broome was in the height of the tourist season, and finding last-minute accommodation would be a problem. What to do? I couldn't think. *Come on, Sheryl,* I said to myself, *you're not a girl of twenty. Get a grip on yourself. Terry is a decent man and he's doing his best to make you comfortable.* But I was still uneasy.

I just needed time to settle my feelings down and get to know him better. Part of the problem was not really knowing him — it was all too easy to fear the worst. It occurred to me that my affair with Heath had shaken me more deeply than I'd admitted. My confidence had taken a battering. Now I wanted to say yes to Terry, who at least seemed to know what he wanted in life, and appeared to really appreciate me, yet at the same time I feared he'd be another two-timing bastard.

It was no good. I couldn't keep up this constant tension in my mind. The night was too balmy and mellow. Back at the table I drank my champagne and flashed him my best hundred-watt smile. 'Let's dance,' I said. We danced until my feet ached, and then I went back with him to his bedroom at the caravan park where we spent our first night together.

My holiday in Broome became an extended stay, with a proposal of marriage from Terry, which, dear reader, I accepted.

In hindsight, instead of marrying Terry, I should have moved in with him. But I had promised myself that I would not just live with another man after my experience with Heath. Also, I believed that being married meant I would be loved and looked after, that my husband would be there for me, just like McCorry was. My head ached with reservations, but I was vulnerable and I denied any misgivings I had at the time.

I accepted his proposal, though I told him there was no way I could live in his quarters at the caravan park. 'I've lived most of my life on cattle stations,' I told him. 'I can't live cramped up here.' I even had to share the bathroom and the kitchen when the office staff were there during the day. The next day he took me out to show me a house he had recently purchased in town. We drove slowly past; it was large and built to suit the tropics. 'Could you live here?' he asked me.

'It has polished timber floors.' *The white ants would have a ball*, I thought to myself, but I said, 'Yes, I could certainly live here.' It would be a couple of months before we could move in, and in the meantime I would be gracious about staying in his quarters.

I accepted, even though after a month Lauren was still there. When she hadn't gone after three days I looked at Terry and said, 'You couldn't do it, could you?' He seemed relieved that I understood, and said it would be easier to make it three weeks' notice. I thought he was a big softy. When she was still there a month later I decided it was not worth fussing over. She had not repeated her bizarre behaviour and we were able to be civil to one another. It was true she and Terry had their heads together a lot, but that was the nature of their work — the reception staff always had messages to pass on to him. It was always noisy, and they couldn't go shouting at each other. I had to accept that. All his office staff were women, and he was a charming man.

My initial plan to go home to the Shiralee to prepare for my marriage — which would be in June, only a few weeks away — got put off week by week. Terry just didn't want me to leave, and secretly that pleased me. It felt good to be wanted. So I enrolled Robby in school in Broome while Leisha returned to the Shiralee. She planned on getting work locally, and in the meantime she would help Kristy keep an eye on the farm.

Terry's life was structured around spending six months of the year on the family farms in the south-west and the six months of the tourist season managing the caravan park in Broome. While he was in the south-west, his sister-in-law Jean and her son Jeff, a gentle boy about Leisha's age, stepped in to manage. I knew there would always be plenty to do, and I wholeheartedly committed myself to jumping in wherever I could be useful. He seemed to value my ideas too, and wanted my input on decisions. My life could be full of happiness with a great lifestyle. So yes, I would marry Terry. The children were happy with the idea of Mum marrying again, and we would find a way to keep Sleepy Hollow and the Shiralee going.

I loved being back in the north. A few weeks later I was sitting on Broome's Cable Beach. The temperature was in the low thirties, and a clear sky met the turquoise blue sea and perfect golden sands. I was watching Robby surf, with my dusty old Akubra pulled firmly down on my head for protection from the sun. I was listening to the crackle of the coconut palm fronds in the breeze when I caught sight of a woman I had known back in the seventies when I was on Napier Downs. Her husband managed another cattle station, and I remembered her well, because she had looked down on McCorry and me for hiring Aboriginal stockmen.

She wasn't the only one. I felt the disapproval of plenty of station managers at the time for having stock camps full of black stockmen and their families. Many properties were importing their jackaroos and ringers from Queensland and even New South Wales. But I could see no reason to make a distinction between black and white, except that the black stockmen were probably more reliable — at least they were if you treated them decently — the imported white stockmen rarely stayed for the full muster season.

The woman I had just spied on the beach was particularly memorable for an event that stuck firmly in my mind. It was Derby rodeo time, August 1977. I had arrived a little late and the air was already filled with the pungent smell of cattle dust, which swirled in a fine powdery mist around the arena. A constant bellow came from the bull pen, added to by dogs barking themselves silly, and above all this noise was the strong and clear clang of the Condamine bell as the stockmen rigged their beasts ready to ride.

I stepped out of my vehicle with a newborn Leisha in my arms and was greeted by a mob of our Aboriginal stockmen's wives and their excited children. Chattering and laughing, the children pushed their mothers aside to be the first to check on the new baby. There was a beautiful feeling of togetherness, in stark contrast to the scene on the Toyota Landcruiser tray-back vehicle parked up beside me. Lounging on deckchairs were two neighbouring managers' wives, Sheila from Yeeda, and Vinegar Tits from Myrodrah (the names have been changed to protect the innocent). Both ladies elocuted perfectly while firmly gripping tumblers of whisky at ten in the morning. As I watched Kelly run off with his Aboriginal mate, Sandy Wungundin, one of the women tottered to her feet and balanced precariously on the edge of the Landcruiser tray while sizing me up with rather bleary eyes.

'How do you put up with those blacks?' she said, her little finger at right angles to her whisky glass. 'They stink!' She screwed up her nose and added, 'They're lazy and won't work.' I stood with Leisha wriggling in my arms and looked up at Vinegar Tits. Her skin looked like burned leather, and her nostrils were flared and red. I was angry but making a scene wouldn't change the woman's attitude. At that moment Betty, an Aboriginal girl from the station, brought Kelly back to my side and relieved my tired arms of the little bundle that was Leisha. She was showing my children off to her extended family and friends. I looked at Vinegar Tits and said, 'We've never had a problem we can't sort out with the people, they're top stockmen, and we always have a full stock camp.'

Her attitude might have had something to do with her husband's messing about with Aboriginal women. Over the years I got used to having station wives look down their noses at me. But none of them ever went on to manage cattle stations in their own right as I did. And, if they only knew it, I was helping to look after the legacies left behind in our stock camp by their very own husbands. I'm not saying the Aboriginal women weren't willing participants, they may well have been, but it made my blood boil to see the anguish they went through as they tried in vain to extract some form of financial support from the white managers who were the fathers of their children. Some of these managers went on to have stations of their own, but their offspring are still living in camps on the outskirts of small Kimberley towns, many of them not even aware of the truth of their inheritance.

I sat soaking up the sunshine on Cable Beach a while longer. I watched Vinegar Tits pack up and load her vehicle and leave. She hadn't seen me. As her 4WD disappeared down the road among the coconut palms, I wondered whether her attitude towards Aboriginal people had mellowed at all.

CHAPTER 3

My Wedding is Upstaged

*W*edding invitations had been ordered and mailed out to family and friends. We were marrying on 12 June 1999 in the new luxury Radisson Beach Resort south of Busselton, Terry's old stamping ground. We would fly down from Broome just before our big day, which was the anniversary of the day I lost Kelly on Louisa Downs back in 1981. It was obviously not my ideal date, but running a business meant we didn't have a lot of choice. It had been eighteen years, I told myself. Deal with it. And nothing would stop me honouring my darling boy's tragically short life.

There was something else causing me more concern. A few weeks before my wedding day my Uncle Stan, who had worked with Terry some years back, cautioned me. 'What are you doing with him, Sheryl?' he said. 'You don't need him.' He and my aunt seemed genuinely concerned and wanted to be sure I knew what I was doing, and they weren't alone. An old friend said, 'You've only known each other a short time. Do you really think you know him well enough to commit to him as his wife?'

The answer to that was that I didn't, but nor did I appreciate the attitude of such 'well-wishers'. I'd had my own doubts, I felt satisfied that there was nothing in them, and it distressed me that people would try to stir things up in this way. People change; hell, what kind of world would it be if people *didn't* change?

I was well known in Broome as a strong woman who knew her own mind. I wasn't going to change it now on the basis of gossip. And I wasn't going to insult Terry by repeating the stories to his face. I had to make a choice, and I went with my own gut feeling. It had always served me well. There was nothing going on between him and Lauren, and he seemed genuinely committed to me. Sure, he liked the races, but so did lots of people. It didn't make him an inveterate gambler. The same went for his drinking. He drank wine every night, but I never saw him drunk.

I had ordered a Vogue-designed wedding gown to be made for me in Sydney. It wouldn't exactly come in handy for chasing the steers around the paddocks if I changed my mind about the wedding, but I wasn't going to change my mind, any more than I was going to drop my plans for the Shiralee.

A week before our wedding day, any doubts I might have had that Terry cared about me were dispelled. I was lying in bed next to him when he put his arm across me to pull me closer to him and accidentally hit me high on the right breast. Absolute shock crossed his face as he noticed the lump for the first time; it was like a hard marble sitting under the skin surface. He flew out of bed to make me a doctor's appointment for the very next day.

I felt very touched by his concern and hastened to re-assure him. 'There's no need to panic,' I told him. 'I've seen several doctors about this, it's nothing. There's no pain with it.' After Heath's cavalier attitude, it felt good to have chosen someone who loved me and wanted to help, and to make him feel better I agreed to see a doctor the next day.

I wasn't worried. I had been at this point before. In the morning I arrived at the Broome Medical Centre to see Dr Sullivan, a doctor I'd known since I was eighteen years old. If there was anything wrong with me, I was certain he would find it. Sure enough, the very next day I was on a plane for Perth, and the following day I was having mammograms, ultrasounds and needle biopsies at the Mount Hospital. By the time all the procedures were over and I was sitting waiting for the results, Terry and Robby had arrived from Broome. Terry and I were two days away from being married.

Finally I was called in to the rooms of the specialist, David Ingram. Terry came in with me. The doctor straight-away explained that I had an aggressive breast cancer. He spoke quietly and calmly, and waited a moment for me to absorb the information. I suppose I was in shock, I didn't cry. I was wondering how the hell I'd been given an all-clear when I had an advanced aggressive cancer. I damned well wanted to know why it hadn't been picked up when I'd been pointing to that hard lump every time I saw a doctor. Had anyone been listening? Or was I just another hypochondriac woman? But this was not the time for anger. Right now I needed to concentrate, to decide on the best course of action, so I shut my anger down.

Looking at the doctor for the next step in this completely alien situation, I asked, 'Can we take it — my cancer — out?' He didn't hesitate. 'Yes! Of course.'

'Okay then,' I said. 'I'll be returning to the city in three weeks, can you do it then?' I wanted to get it over with as soon as possible. Dr Ingram shook his head and explained to me slowly and clearly that my cancer must come out much sooner than that, preferably the next day.

He went on to explain the choice I had — mastectomy or lumpectomy. I asked whether he advised one more than the other and he said it really was a matter of choice. Neither was more appropriate for my cancer. I opted for the lumpectomy, with radiation treatment to follow after the wedding. I was pretty sure Terry wouldn't want a wife with one breast.

Once that was decided, my main concern was about delaying the wedding, wondering how we'd be able to contact people who'd be coming from all over the country. But Terry wouldn't hear of it. 'We don't need to cancel it, lovey,' he said. 'We'll be all right. I'll be looking after you and helping in every way I can.'

When he said that, I suddenly realised that I *wanted* to call it off — completely — not just postpone it. Here was my ticket out, for the fears I'd scarcely allowed myself to acknowledge. I looked to Dr Ingram for help, but he seemed to think it was theoretically possible to travel the day of the operation. And that was it. I didn't know what else to do. It all felt bigger than me.

Out in the waiting room I told Robby. He went terribly quiet and I had no idea what was going through his mind — beyond the obvious fact that he had just lost his father and the last thing he needed to hear was that his mother had breast cancer.

From the hotel room I called Leisha at the Shiralee, then my parents. Leisha broke down in tears. Like Robby, my mother was very quiet, but it was a confident quietness. 'You will beat this cancer, Sheryl, you are strong,' she said. My mother always had great faith in me. I put the phone down and burst into tears. If this cancer got a grip on me and I was to die, my children would be alone. They were my only concern. They had already been dealt enough bad news in their short lives.

Everything seemed too much to handle and I badly needed to talk to someone, but Terry was asleep and I wasn't going to wake him up. I couldn't stop crying; I became very cold and started to shake, and then I couldn't stop shaking. Robby piled blankets on me and sat with his arms wrapped tightly around me. When I saw the tears and fear in his worried blue eyes, I made a supreme effort and pulled myself together. Terry was still sound asleep, and I wondered if he would ever really be there for me.

But I told myself that sort of thinking was coming from weakness. I was in shock. Really, this was about me and my children. Terry was such a newcomer in my life, I had to get through this on my own. I could, and I would. I suddenly had perfect confidence of that.

Bright and early the next morning the nurses at the Mount Hospital prepared me for surgery. I was first on the theatre list to give me time to come out of the anaesthetic before Terry drove me to Busselton for our wedding the following afternoon. All gowned and warm I lay dozing on the theatre gurney waiting for the operation. At one point I looked up and saw Terry in tears before a nurse ushered him from the room. I had no more tears myself. I had made up my mind that once the cancer was removed, that would be the end of it.

A pleasant voice asked me my name, and then I was wheeled into a room full of bright lights. I wished they'd turn them off so I could sleep. I registered Dr Ingram's face hovering above me, then nothing more until, what seemed like no time later, I heard my name called again, over and over. Eventually I found the will to answer. 'It's over, Sheryl,' the nurse said. 'All done.' For a moment I wondered where the heck I was, and then I remembered: my cancer was out. Instant relief flooded over me. It was over.

In the afternoon Dr Ingram came with some preliminary results. He had found two smaller cancers that had started to travel away from the main cancer. This meant I would need to have the glands removed from under my right arm to help prevent any further spreading. I could come back in three weeks for that. This news didn't affect me at all. I could only see a cancer-free future for myself. He left and I went straight back to sleep.

Meanwhile my girlfriend Joanne, who was to be my maid of honour, had arrived from Derby. Joanne had been busy rushing in and out from my hospital bed, trying to organise the final touches for my wedding. I wasn't much help; I remember very little as I drifted in and out of the anaesthetic.

My mind was still very disorganised by late afternoon. Robby was sitting next to me, holding my hand. 'You'll be all right, Mum,' he kept repeating. I was conscious that Terry was pacing up and down and asking the staff when they were going to discharge me. I had no desire to move, I just wanted to stay put. I wished that I could have told him I didn't want to move, but I still felt hazy, and wanted only to sleep. The head nursing sister also wanted me fully recovered from the anaesthetic before discharging me, and I could hear her firmly telling Terry he would have to wait. I was glad it was out of my hands and I continued to doze.

Eventually somebody helped me to dress, and Terry led me from the hospital out to the waiting hire car. We all got in, Terry, Robby, Joanne and me. I was soon asleep and remember nothing more until waking up as we pulled in to the Radisson late that evening.

Then the rush began. Leisha and Kristy had arrived from the farm and both hugged me at the same time. 'Will you be all right, Mum?' asked Kristy, who hadn't seen me since I left for Broome. Leisha's eyes were filled with tears; she hugged me so tight I had to gently push her away for fear of opening my wound.

The bridesmaids' gowns needed slight alterations, which Joanne's mother Jan Finlay would take care of. I didn't really need to be there for that, but I was awake now, and feeling quite alert. I wanted to be in the thick of things. This was my wedding, it was girl time!

We arrived at Jan's house on the Busselton waterfront at 10 pm and it wasn't until the early hours of my wedding day that all the gowns were perfect and ready to wear. It was time for me to put my weary body to bed, but my hair needed serious attention and I thought that would be better than a shot in the arm to get back some of my strength and enthusiasm. Joanne, who was a nurse, was pushing me to rest, but I figured if I could just get my hair done, there would be little else for me to do, and I could sleep then.

Barbie, a Busselton hairdresser, came to the house and styled my hair and put a touch of gold in it for me, which certainly gave it a lift, but by the time it was finished the tiredness had finally set in and I hardly cared any more. I returned to the resort in the early morning to an empty room. I was so exhausted I collapsed on the soon-to-be matrimonial bed and fell straight into a deep sleep.

When I woke the sun was high and I was still alone. I was feeling quite rested, with only a little soreness from the surgery. I went onto the balcony where there was a stunning view across the pristine white sands to the deep blue of Geographe Bay. This wasn't a part of the south I was familiar with — I didn't know anyone in the area other than Terry's family — but it was certainly beautiful. The day was still and clear, and the sparkle off the water swam before my eyes. Yes, I thought, this was as good a place to marry as any other — though a marriage celebrant in a paddock would have done just as well for me. I'm not a party girl, not into making a big fuss. But it's not every day you marry.

I went back to bed and kept a low profile through the morning. I wanted to look my best, and figured sleep would be the best restorative. The kids were fine, they didn't need me.

Leisha and Kristy were sharing a large suite of rooms with Joanne, while Robby had two friends in his room, twins Simon and David whose family rented the second house on Sleepy Hollow. The Radisson was a great place for three young mates to have fun. But not too much fun! I phoned Leisha in her room to ask her to keep an eye on them for me. I didn't want them getting up to mischief.

I was dozing when the phone rang at three in the afternoon. The girls had already started celebrations. 'How are you, Mum? Are you ready yet?' said Leisha. *My god*, I thought, *they're jovial already*. I listened to the chatter on the other end of the line for a moment, then got up to start dressing.

I was tugging and pulling at my ivory jacket trying to conceal the plaster covering the wound on my right breast. It wasn't easy, and I was feeling a bit crazy to be doing it at all. But oh, the outfit was beautiful. The gown was tailored to perfection with a full-length brocade skirt that had a delicate inbuilt train. The jacket had a cinched-in Victorian line to it, with wide collar and long sleeves and Czechoslovakian crystal buttons.

Terry was dressed and pacing around the unit while I dabbed the finishing touches to my make-up and gave myself a final spray of Chanel. Then he walked me to the girls' suite. I turned my cheek so he could kiss me, but instead he drew back and looked at me quite seriously. 'Make sure you turn up,' he said, 'and on time,' and strode off down the corridor. I was trying to decide what to make of this behaviour when the door burst open and I was suddenly enveloped in a warm wave of love and laughter. My girls were having a party.

'What's up, Mum?' asked Leisha as Kristy handed me a glass of ice submerged in Baileys Irish Cream. I flashed them a smile. 'Nothing's up at all, my darling girls, everything's wonderful.' I took a sip of the drink. It was so smooth and delicious it went straight down and I had another.

The wedding photographer arrived and photographed us in every conceivable pose bar hanging upside down from the chandeliers. We were relaxed and happy. Then there was another knock on the door and someone was there with a gift for me. I opened the slim box to find a gold bracelet. It was from Heath. No letter or message, just a card with his name. All of a sudden all the laughter left me and my body was burning. I wondered if it was obvious to everyone in the room. Was my blood pressure going through the roof or was this second thoughts? What was he playing at? More to the point, how did he know where I was? I hadn't invited him to my wedding.

Leisha tapped my arm. 'It was me, Mum. I told him. He was asking after you. I'm sorry, I hope it's okay.' I shook my head to clear away all the questions, and to indicate to her that it was nothing, I was fine.

Someone poured me another Baileys and then it was time to head for the grand entrance. Any more to drink and I knew it would be a battle to stay in control. I am not a drinker, and not twenty-four hours earlier I had been in a post-anaesthetic haze. All the alcohol surely wasn't doing me any good, but I was feeling reckless. I finished off my glass. *Soon*, I thought, *I'll be married again*. I felt uneasy. On this, my third marriage,

I had my worst case of pre-wedding nerves. My first marriage, to a Yank when I was only nineteen, was short-lived and a total disaster. I was only five years older when I married McCorry but I had really loved him. Even when it became too difficult to hold the family together, I still loved him. I suddenly didn't know whether I loved Terry at all.

Well, there was only one way to find out. 'Come on, everyone,' I called over my shoulder while gathering up my brocade skirt to protect it from the dust. The reception staff were all waving and wishing me well. 'We're going to a wedding, where's the wedding?' I cried, trying to hurry the girls along. I had no idea what room I was to be married in or, for that matter, where the bloody hell the reception would be. I was feeling very reckless.

'Up the stairs,' the receptionist replied between gusts of laughter.

'Thank you,' I said, grateful that someone knew what was going on. 'Come on, girls,' I cried, carrying my high heels as I tried to hold metres of cascading ivory up around my waist. Joanne and the girls were in similar predicaments, tripping over themselves and giggling. What a mess we were, I thought, as we made our way carefully along the endless corridors, but at least we were an elegant mess.

As we reached our destination I let my beautiful skirt fall to the floor and slipped my heels on. I walked into a room full of smiling strangers and great bouquets of flowers. I had arrived. Glancing towards Terry, I could see an expression of relief cross his face, and I was relieved too. *I'm here at last*, I thought.

Then it hit me: as I looked around I realised I was practically a stranger at my own wedding. All Terry's family and friends were there, but very few on my side. Peter Melsom, who I'd managed cattle stations for in the Kimberley, had come down from Perth, as had my old helicopter mustering pilot, Brett Nixon. Richard O'Connor and his mother Joan and a few other good neighbours from around the Shiralee were here, but other than my children — oh, and my accountant and his wife — that was it for me really.

It was almost the middle of winter, but suddenly I was burning hot. Fine beads of perspiration gathered on my forehead, the overhead lights seemed far too bright, and I started to shake. I felt a surge of nausea rising in my throat, and then, thank god, my fifteen-year-old son moved through the crowd and took a firm grip on my hand. 'Come on, Mum, come in here,' Robby said softly, and led me gently towards the podium.

It was just as well my parents and brothers had not come. Dad was not in the best of health, which made it difficult for him to travel. But if that had been the only reason, I'm sure he and my mother would have been there. Like my brothers, they were also worried about this marriage. I was their only daughter and they only ever wanted me to find happiness — and they didn't think I was going to find that with Terry.

But I was a big girl now. Their effective boycott of my wedding didn't hurt me; I understood their feelings, but I decided I would just take pleasure in proving them wrong.

Because of my condition, the marriage celebrant was keeping the vows short. I was nervous, though, and stumbled over the words, and so did Terry, but that wasn't the end of it. Where was the ring? Ed Robertson, a long-time friend of Terry's, was best man. He had trouble locating the wedding band, and for a fleeting moment I thought, *If the ring doesn't turn up, I'm not married*. I could see Terry's stress levels rising;

Ed was in a complete dither and all of a sudden I burst out laughing. I couldn't help myself. Perspiration gleamed on Ed's brow as he frantically turned out every pocket in his hired suit until eventually, with a massive sigh of relief, he muttered, 'It's here, I've got it.' Ah, we have the ring. All solemn and proper, Terry dutifully placed the wedding band on my finger — the wrong finger. As he pulled it off to have another shot, I thought, *Holy hell, I've had better days — and weddings!*

It turned out the reception was in the same room as the service. The band started playing and the evening went off with a bang. The speeches began with Terry thanking the barmaids instead of the bridesmaids — an interesting substitution, I thought. Peter Melsom spoke on my behalf, reminding my new husband that the last time he had seen me I was wielding a pocket knife for castrating 'micky' bulls on Fairfield station. With a wicked laugh, he suggested Terry think twice about playing around.

It was a strange night, alternately wonderful and disconcerting. Terry was a good dancer, lots of fun and good company, but he would disappear outside for a smoke and a yarn with his mates, leaving me for long stretches in a room of mostly strangers. As the evening went on, however, I felt increasingly mellow and contented, until finally the moment came when we said goodbye to our guests and wandered off to our suite. We were so close to the water we could hear the steady lapping of the waves on the shore.

My first thought after taking off my shoes was to put the kettle on for a cup of tea! As I waited for it to boil I gazed over the pile of wedding gifts, still in their rich wrappings, overflowing the coffee table. Then, lifting my head to look out of the window, I saw flashes of gold over the sea as moonbeams danced across the bay. The vision was perfect and I felt deeply moved to be experiencing such a profound stillness. A quiet sigh escaped my weary body.

The kettle had boiled, and I filled the cups, thinking with a wry laugh that this wasn't your typical blushing bride! Still, it was my wedding night, and a girl has to get her priorities right. Besides, I was looking forward to the conjugal bed. But as I turned to that conjugal bed I discovered Terry had completely outdone me in the priorities stakes — he was sprawled out cold, fully dressed and snoring like a train. I tried in vain to wake him. I could hardly believe it. All my mellow contentment vanished and I suddenly felt hurt by my new husband. It had been barely thirty-six hours since I'd had a serious operation. Didn't he care?

Fighting back tears, I sat on the soft leather couch in my beautiful ivory gown feeling desperately in need of a friend; I didn't even have the energy to look through the cards. Holding my head in my hands I began to sob, loudly and not caring whether anyone heard. I lay awake most of the night tossing and turning between feeling neglected and lonely, and being mad at myself for feeling upset over something so silly.

My marriage wasn't consummated that night. The next morning I thought Terry might have apologised, but he didn't, and I said nothing about my disappointment. It was as though we were two strangers — not a promising beginning to our married life, and the day didn't get a lot better.

We were having morning tea at Terry's family farm on Wildwood Road. On our way we had a close shave with another vehicle — both Terry and the other driver were travelling too fast and neither wanted to share the black-top with the other. At the Wildwood farm, Terry's mother, Molly, came out to meet us. She greeted me very warmly, and led me inside with an arm around my waist. Inside, everyone was far older than I, but I did connect with some of the old ladies.

Terry's Aunty Elsie said to him, 'You look after this girl; she's the best thing that's happened to you.' I thought that was funny — I was fifty years old!

On our return we walked back into the Radisson to a bizarre scene: a man in his thirties leaped up and fronted Terry aggressively, accusing him of hogging the road. He was waving his arms about and suddenly I had a fight on my hands, both men accusing the other of forcing them off the road. Now they were pushing and shoving each other around the Radisson grounds. *This is bloody lovely*, I thought, and jumped in between the two men, telling them to grow up. They were not to be stopped so quickly, but after more shoving and pushing and accusations, I demanded of Terry that we walk away, and we did. But the incident left me with a new uneasy feeling about my future. I liked a man to know how to handle himself, to be able to contain his aggression and not get drawn into unnecessary fights.

We checked out that afternoon and drove the three hours to Perth to watch Terry's horse race at Ascot. It came in second, which was good enough for Terry, and we celebrated that night, laughing and happy together. And that was the end of our honeymoon. The next morning we caught an early flight back to Broome.

Terry needed to get back to the caravan park. He was a man in a hurry: in a hurry to get married, and now in a hurry to get back to work. He had purchased an additional ten acres of land next to the park and was racing to develop it. This was 1999 and Broome was bursting at the seams with tourists and visitors. I could understand that he would want to capitalise on this, and I was more than happy to support him.

When we got there, there was plenty to do, and the most pressing thing was to clean — everywhere was dusty and dirty. Terry didn't want me cleaning, but I couldn't sit around doing nothing. Heck, I told him, I'd been covered head to toe in cattle dung — what was a bit of dust to me? Contractors were working on the new land, and Terry would take me with him as he drove around to check on the progress. Nights we often dined out — there wasn't a proper kitchen in the house — and when the rest of the staff had left, Terry would put on loud music and dance me around the room. He was such a party animal, even when it was just the two of us.

I had three weeks in Broome before going back down to Perth for my second operation. It felt strange at first, being there as Terry's wife. A lot of the holidaymakers came regularly to the park and were on friendly terms with Terry, and there was a constant stream of well-wishers. I felt like I was on holiday too, a temporary sojourn, as I was practically living in Terry's bedroom and all my things were still in my bags.

I was feeling quite proud of myself that I was able to deal with the lack of space and privacy. I liked to think that I could live just about anywhere — I had never needed to be surrounded by beautiful objects or expensive furnishings. The gifts of nature were what turned me on, and Broome had plenty of these. Once I returned from Perth I could think about making myself more comfortable — finding somewhere to hang my clothes would be a start! By then, surely, the house would be ready for us to move in, though I had some doubts about that. Terry had been strangely quiet on the subject.

Robby was in a tiny room, though, a hastily cleaned junk room, and he certainly needed more space. He was coming south too, and I'd sort him out when we got back — in more ways than one. In so many respects, Robby was a typical teenage boy. He wanted to leave school, make a bit of money, go surfing and ride motorbikes. I wanted him to go to agricultural college, but he thought he could learn better by experience. Terry had taken him for a drive and talked about how good Broome was, and that he had any amount of work for him if he wanted it.

Two weeks before leaving for Perth, something rather disturbing happened. I found some photos of a skimpily dressed Lauren on a sideboard in our living space. I assumed Terry had put them there, or Lauren, but he denied any knowledge of the photos, and was emphatic that it could have had nothing to do with Lauren.

'Well how did they get there then?' I asked.

'People are always coming and going, anyone could have just put them down for a moment,' he said.

That didn't seem very likely to me. I had to know what this was about. If it wasn't him or Lauren, then it looked to me as if someone was trying to tell me in an underhand sort of way that Terry was having an affair with his receptionist. It was hard to see what else it could mean. I told him what I was thinking, and finished, 'Terry, is there something you need to tell me?'

'If I was having an affair with the wretched girl, do you think I'd be leaving evidence of it around for you to see?' he said.

I admitted he had a point, but it didn't solve the puzzle. I stood looking at him, hoping he would say something, and was disappointed when all he said was, 'I don't want to discuss it any further — you're attaching a lot more importance to it than it deserves.'

I wasn't so sure. I accepted his word that the photos had nothing to do with him, but I couldn't drop the thought that someone had left them there on purpose and wanted to upset me like this. That left a horrible feeling.

Then one night the doorbell rang very late. Terry flew out of bed to answer it and soon returned to the bedroom, rummaged through his pockets for some money, and then went back out. 'Who's there?' I asked him when he came back to bed, but he just made some vague allusion to camp business, and when I tried to pursue the matter, crossly told me to let him be.

It happened again a few nights later and this time I followed him to the door — and there was Lauren. I left them to it. When he came back to bed I asked him what she wanted. He muttered something about cigarettes, how it was no big deal for her to come to the shop when she needed something.

After that, Terry would simply let her in and she would make herself a coffee, heat up a pie and help herself to the shop's cigarettes before going back to her own caravan.

Were they having an affair? He swore blind they weren't and, despite the odd appearances, I thought he was telling me the truth. Terry was fifty-seven and she was twenty-seven — a far bigger age gap than between me and McCorry. And though Terry could be charming, and wasn't bad looking, it was hard to believe that she would find him attractive. But even if they weren't lovers, she seemed to be more comfortable in my marital home than I was.

There was nothing I could do about it; Terry made that quite clear. So I tried a different tack. I assumed she was a troubled soul and I made a point of acknowledging her and showing her warmth. But it was always awkward between us: she never had anything to say to me in return, and she continued to use the space as her own.

Terry kept saying he was going to terminate her employment, and that I should trust him to do it at the appropriate time and place. And when I persevered one night, asking him if there was something wrong with her that he needed to give her this special treatment, he told me I was the one with the problem. In fact, he said worse than that. 'You're mad in the head the way you keep on,' were his words. We had been married less than three weeks. I felt sick. While courting me Terry had said that his first marriage had failed because his wife had been mentally unstable (much later I learned that this was far from the truth).

The warning signs were glowing like a neon light. But I had other things on my mind and I decided this nonsense must wait until I had had my surgery. I wished my new husband was more solicitous and careful of my wellbeing, but since he was not, I needed to concentrate all my energy on my health. I was going to stay cancer free.

CHAPTER 4

Anstey House

The operation at the Mount Hospital would be followed by six weeks of radiotherapy as an outpatient at Sir Charles Gairdner Hospital. I flew to Perth alone, leaving Robby with Terry at the park — they would come down the following day.

Leisha collected me from the airport and drove me to the hospital. My girl was in a worse state than I was, terrified to leave me and scared her mum could be riddled with cancer. Ready for theatre in a back-to-front hospital gown, I did my best to put on a brave front for my daughter. 'Leisha, I'll be okay, love,' I said. 'I am quite sure of that.'

'I know, Mum,' she replied, and then raced off to the bathroom to throw up again.

I considered myself very lucky to have one of my children with me. Just to know Leisha was there calmed my nervous tension considerably. After the operation I woke to find her by my bedside, just as she had been before. She looked relieved to have her mother back, but anxious. I groggily assured her I would be okay, that I was just terribly tired.

My doctor came in and told me the operation had gone well

and he'd have detailed results in three days. Then I spotted a large and beautiful flower arrangement on my bedside cabinet.

'Who are the flowers from, Leisha?' I asked.

'I don't know, they were here when I came back from the recovery room,' said my girl.

'Have a look, there'll be a card somewhere.' I wanted to hear words of assurance and encouragement from my husband. He had told me the night before I left that he loved me and all would be well. Leisha looked amongst the flowers until she found the card. '*Get well soon . . . Heath*,' she read aloud with an awkward smile.

'They're not from Terry?' I was astonished on two counts. How the hell did Heath know I was in hospital?

Once again, it was Leisha who had told him. 'I'm sorry, Mum, he rang the Shiralee. He was really upset, and wanted to know how you were. He seemed genuinely concerned.'

'It's all right, love, you were right to tell him. He's a good friend,' I said, realising I was disappointed that it wasn't Terry. I suddenly wondered where my new husband was. It was late afternoon, almost tea time, and he and Robby had come in on the early morning flight from Broome. They'd gone straight to the house of Terry's son, where Leisha was staying. Leisha telephoned the house, to discover that Terry had left Robby there and gone off to parts unknown. He'd not come to the hospital at all as far as Leisha knew, and meanwhile Robby was alone at the house, watching television.

I didn't know what to think, or, more accurately, I suppose I didn't want to *let* myself think — it would have been too humiliating to acknowledge that he couldn't even be bothered to see if I was okay or not. And I certainly didn't want to reveal any of this to Leisha. She was showing signs of strain and exhaustion as it was, and didn't need to be worried about my marriage as well as my health.

'Go home and rest, my girl, I'll be fine,' I said. 'I'm strong, love, and you must be too. You can bring Robby back after tea.' I hoped my words carried more strength than I was feeling. The truth was, I felt very flat.

Some hours later I woke to find Terry standing over my bed. I was glad to see him, but when I smiled in greeting he attempted to sit on the bed and immediately got himself tangled in all the tubes. I yelped as I felt something pulling from the wound under my arm. He got off the bed and started picking at my leftover roast dinner until the plate was clean, then sat down on the bed again and tried to stretch out beside me.

'Terry, you can't do that,' I said. 'I'm sore and I can't risk something coming adrift here.' He got up again, and now I registered that his body reeked of alcohol. He still hadn't expressed a scrap of concern about my health, or asked me how I felt or if there was anything he could get me. I asked him where he'd been and he told me he'd spent the day at Subiaco oval watching a football match with a mate.

I couldn't even begin to try to put my new marriage into any context that made sense. I felt angry and hurt and asked him to leave since he seemed unable to stay awake anyway. 'If that's what you want,' he said and left. As soon as he was gone I reached into my locker drawer for my perfume and gave the room a good spray of Coco Chanel to mask the sour smell of alcohol.

I could no longer hold on to my calm, strong persona and I let the tears flood as I tried to untangle the mess I was in. Why had I married someone so selfish and uncaring? Was I that afraid to be alone? God knows. I was in a state of deep distress that I'd rarely experienced before. What on earth had I done?

*

My test results came back two days later. Leisha and Robby were with me; I hadn't seen Terry since his first visit. Robby was sitting there quietly, composed, but I could feel my daughter's anxiety. I myself was quite calm, ready to face whatever was thrown at me.

Just after seven in the evening, Dr Ingram and a nursing sister came to my room. I sat up and looked at my doctor and waited. The few seconds of silence before he spoke might as well have been hours. 'Hello Sheryl, how are you?' he asked in a tone of voice I found impossible to interpret. 'I'm fine,' I answered, never taking my eyes from him.

'Do you want the good news first, or the bad news?' he asked.

I didn't have to think about it. 'The bad,' I said.

With a big smile on his face Dr Ingram said, 'There is none.'

I must have looked baffled. 'There's no bad news,' he repeated.

'You're sure?' I asked, hoping I really had heard him correctly.

'Yes, I'm sure,' he replied. 'Your cancer has not got away. We got it all and it hasn't spread any further.'

Leisha and I hugged each other in relief, tears of happiness rolling down our cheeks, we were so overjoyed at the news.

'But,' my doctor said, 'you must still start radiotherapy as soon as you are out of hospital.'

'Yes, of course, yes,' I replied. I knew this was coming, but I'd have agreed to anything he said, I was so relieved.

I moved in to Anstey House for the six weeks of radiotherapy. This was a residence for cancer patients from country Western

Australia, situated in the grounds of Sir Charles Gairdner Hospital where I was to have my outpatient treatment.

I didn't want Robby going back to Broome with Terry, and so he went with Leisha to join Kristy at the Shiralee. Kristy was still working for the Redmond trainer, Leisha was looking after the farm and cattle, and Robby went back to Mount Barker High School.

There was a frightening number of men and women at Anstey House, all suffering from one form of cancer or another. The building was old, a relic of the sixties, and though the place was spotlessly clean, a heavy smell of sickness hung in the air. It was the smell of cancer and I hated it; actually, to me it was the smell of death. Every time I came back to the building I was hit with a stab of anxiety and my stomach became a tight knot.

The regimen at Anstey House was the same, one day after another. Each morning I would wake early, shower and dress, have a quick cup of tea, then make a mad two hundred metre dash along the covered walkways for my treatment. I liked the morning's first appointment, to be able to get in and out before the waiting room filled with other cancer patients. Although in some ways it was a comfort to know I wasn't alone, I found it terribly confronting to see so many people with cancer. The experience was a real eye-opener for me; I'd had no idea, never given it any thought.

The radiotherapy treatment itself was quick and simple. The nurse would hand me a gown and I would lie on a hospital stretcher under a huge machine suspended from the ceiling, half expecting the darned thing to fall on me. The radiologist then lined up the beam with the blue dots that had been permanently tattooed on my chest and under my right arm. Some days I came away feeling like my breast was badly sunburned. Most days after my treatment I'd return to my room and sleep much of the day away — the treatment made me so tired I would often battle to stay awake with a book. It was a quiet and lonely time, and when my isolation started to get me down I'd go and look in the Subiaco shops or cross the road to walk in the peace and tranquillity of Kings Park.

I discovered from my radiotherapist that I had the weekends off, and I decided to spend them at the Shiralee so I could be with the children without them having to come to the gloom of Anstey House. Leisha and Robby both wanted to come and stay there with me — they had worked it out between them that they could come each week — but I persuaded them to let the idea go. With its smell of death it was no place for young healthy people — or anyone for that matter. I rang my mother most days, to stop her from coming to the city to see me. We talked, and that was good for me, but I didn't want her in this environment either.

The kids were delighted to have me come to the farm. Leisha would have come and fetched me, but I was sure I could drive myself down. And when after the first week I'd seen nothing of Terry, I decided to get my car trucked back down to the city. I had several weeks of radiotherapy to go yet, with no sign of the support he'd promised me when he was persuading me to go ahead with the wedding. I wasn't sure I'd be going back to him in a hurry. So I rang a freight company and had the Landcruiser delivered before the second weekend.

These breaks away did my body and soul the world of good. In the city I was constantly tired and worn out, but just to breathe in the clean crisp air of the south-west made me believe that soon I would be free of the treatment and cancer forever. I felt so peaceful there, just sitting on the back verandah watching the birds nesting, the young honeyeaters taking their first flights from their nest in a geranium-filled hanging basket into a patch of grevillea nearby.

Sometimes I'd walk in the back paddock through the bit of bush I had left untouched, looking for early spider orchids. One of the children might be with me, and there was always a lot to talk about. I also slept a lot, but I easily found the energy to check up on how well the cattle were, and the other work the children had been taking care of. Kristy and Leisha were doing such a good job of looking after the place, and they were happy to all be together. My neighbour Richard O'Connor was always available to them if they had a concern they didn't know how to deal with, but that hadn't happened yet.

Many of the other women at Anstey House had husbands or boyfriends who shared their journey with them. I had never spent a lot of time in the company of women and I envied them the warm embrace of a husband's arms. For the first three weeks Terry didn't come at all. I even had a visit from Heath before I had one from my husband. I appreciated that, and believe he was genuinely concerned. We talked, and the funny thing was, we talked more deeply than we ever had in the time we were lovers. I told him about the mess of a marriage I seemed to have made, and he listened like a true friend.

Over the weeks at Anstey I talked to some of the other women who had breast cancer. Many of us had been taking hormone replacement therapy (HRT) drugs. In the late eighties, while I was still working in the Kimberley, I had been put on Premarin to help control a problem I had with bleeding out of my cycle. As soon as I was diagnosed with breast cancer in Perth, my doctor had told me to stop taking this. I had to wonder if the drug had played a part in my breast cancer — there was no history of it in my family.

One day I was sitting talking in a group of six or seven women, and I decided to ask if any of the others had been on HRT. I couldn't believe it, we had *all* been taking Premarin. On my next visit to Dr Ingram, I asked him if Premarin could have given me breast cancer. I didn't get a clear answer one way or the other, and I'm still wondering.

Lying on my bed most of the day, I found myself too often grappling with the problem of my marriage. My philosophy about difficulties was, where possible, to let them be — with time, most things sorted themselves out, and trying to control things usually did more harm than good. I figured that despite our whirlwind courting and marriage, we hardly knew each other. Why would Terry care about me when six months ago he didn't even know me? I'd talk to myself in this vein and soon I'd start feeling warm and understanding about him again. And that would make me reach for the phone, magically thinking that he would be feeling the same way.

Broome was in full swing with the racing season (and Terry never missed a race day); the park was overflowing and running on overload. Invariably Lauren answered the phone. She spoke to me as if I were any other caller and I followed her lead, maintaining a cool politeness, even when she left me hanging interminably. She did this more often that not, coming back on the line with, 'Oh I am so sorry, I can't seem to find him anywhere.' Sometimes the line would simply be cut off. She was hardly more than a kid, yet she had it all over me. I felt she was playing with me. There was a faint air of self-satisfaction in her voice that made me wonder why I bothered. I have my faults, but guile isn't one of them, though I was determined I would not let her see how badly her games were affecting me.

One day Rachael, the other receptionist, picked up and put me through to Terry straightaway. I told him, 'Do you realise Lauren isn't putting my calls through to you?' He had no answer for me. Maybe he knew what was going on but was too gutless to do anything about it. Or, for all I know, he was standing there signalling her to disconnect me. Either way, I got the feeling I was no longer a very important part of his life. Maybe he couldn't handle my cancer; often he didn't even ask me how I was. He would tell me about his day, I would listen and let him finish, then we said our goodbyes.

After my third beautiful weekend at the Shiralee I made the decision that I wasn't returning to Broome. I'd had a visit at the hospital from a stockman called Mick who had worked for McCorry and me for thirteen years. He came to see how I was coping and catch up on all my news. Actually, he was the one with the news. He had bumped into Terry and Lauren up in Broome — in a compromising position in a dark car park behind the Divers Tavern. Terry knew who Mick was, and that he'd been close to me, and Mick told me that my husband had put both hands into the air saying, 'I'm not here, I'm not here!' When I told Terry this, he denied it, just as he'd denied having anything to do with Lauren. But I could find no reason to doubt Mick. He wasn't trying to stir up trouble, I was sure; he just didn't want to see me made a fool of.

Although I wasn't sure I was ready to call it off completely, I knew that once I was convalescing after the radiotherapy I wanted to be in a safe and peaceful place. And that wasn't the caravan park. Terry obviously had Lauren in his life; for all I knew, she had never left it. I didn't know why he had married me. I was feeling terribly low at the time, and my tiredness wasn't helping me think straight, but then again, this wasn't something I could think my way out of. Emotionally I was a mess. My hair had begun to fall out — every day my comb was full of it — and I cried for the loss of it.

No sooner had I resolved that I was finished with the marriage than I received a phone call from Terry. He had booked a room for the following weekend at the Kings Park Motel, just down the road from the hospital, and wanted me to meet him there.

When the day arrived I put all my effort into looking my best, not for him, but for myself; it helped me feel stronger. With cunning styling, I managed to make it look as though I had more hair than I actually did. I drove to the motel feeling sick as a dog, still suffering the effects of my radiation session the day before.

It was four weeks since I'd seen my husband and, feeling so fragile, I wasn't sure if I was up to telling him it was over. At the same time, I was wondering just how much more of this pantomime I could take. I was the first to get there, so I picked up the room key from reception — and opened the door into a roomful of lilies. They were gorgeous, a truly beautiful sight, but the perfume was overbearing, it made me feel even more sick, and I had to move most of them into the bathroom in order to breathe freely again.

An hour or so later Terry arrived, bearing a gift of pearl and diamond earrings, very proud that he had selected them himself. He greeted me more warmly than he had since we married, and insisted I put them on immediately for him to admire. Feeling somewhat like a stranger in my own marriage I greeted Terry with as much affection as my exhausted body would allow. I tried to show some enthusiasm, to show I was grateful for his gifts, but I was confused. And Terry, of course, remained true to form: the next day he left me resting at the motel while he went to Belmont racecourse.

CHAPTER 5

Back to the Shiralee

The days at Anstey House drifted by. If it hadn't been for the support of my children, it's hard to say what direction my life would have taken at that time — I could barely see it through what seemed a thick layer of fog. I was kicking myself that I had walked into this marriage. Despite the ardour with which he had given me the pearl and diamond earrings, it was hard to believe my husband had any love for me at all. Certainly, he did not appear to feel for me in the way he had when he begged me to marry him only a few weeks before.

Still my calls to him were blocked when Lauren answered the phone. And if I did get put through to my husband, after a few words to me he would get drawn into a conversation with some other person in the room and simply forget I was on the end of the line. As often as not, that person would be Lauren — she would call his name, and then they'd both be laughing and chatting about nothing very much, and there seemed to be nothing I could do about it.

I had gone from being a strong and confident woman who had motivation and direction in her life to someone who seemed to be going round in ever-decreasing circles. It was an effort to make any decisions, but I decided I would not call Terry any more. If he wanted to speak to me, he could call me.

Towards the end of my radiotherapy I had a visit from Jean, Terry's sister-in-law. Her husband Jim had only recently died, and she had taken over his role as Terry's business partner in the caravan park. She was on her way back to her farm in the south-west and came to see how I was. We had not known each other long, but I liked Jean and we respected each other. Over a cup of tea at the hospital cafeteria, she asked me whether I would be going back to Broome. She wasn't blind: she could see for herself how it was for me.

The floodgates opened. I had not realised how much pent-up emotion I was carrying — or how strongly I felt about the prospect of returning to Broome.

'No, no,' I got out between sobs. 'I'm not going back, not while she's still there.'

When I had control over myself again I asked if Lauren was still there. Jean confirmed she was. I don't know why I'd asked. Of course she would still be there. Why wouldn't she? Feeling a total fool for crying in front of Jean I begged her not to worry on my behalf. It wasn't that long since she had lost her own husband to cancer and she had enough to cope with. But I was grateful for her visit. Though I tried to discourage visitors — I didn't want to see them when I was so worn out — it was good to see someone I knew.

After six weeks my radiation treatment was complete and I was free to leave, though I had not been given the all-clear from cancer yet. That would take a bit more time. I couldn't get out of the city fast enough. I just wanted to go home to the Shiralee.

My body was racked with tiredness, my breast burned from the radiation treatment, but nothing was going to stop me driving the four hundred kilometres home to my Shiralee. My first glimpse of the purples and mauves of the Stirling Ranges, followed shortly by the profile of the sleeping princess lying peacefully along the rugged Porongurups, told my heart I was nearly home, and I felt the familiar calmness descend over my body, the weariness almost vanish. This time the joy was not shadowed by the certain knowledge that I had to go back in a few days to resume my treatment. It was over. It would be months before I got the official all-clear, but in the meantime I felt completely positive. I was home. The Shiralee was my real home and my haven.

I pulled in just in time for afternoon smoko — tea and scones — with the children on the verandah. It was a glorious homecoming.

Leisha, Robby and Kristy had mustered the cattle up into the house paddocks so that I could look at them from the back verandah while enjoying a cup of tea. Here Prince, a chihuahua and the latest addition to our household, lay curled up peacefully on my lap, while Sally never let me out of her sight. For several days I rested, letting the rhythm of life in this little southern paradise flow back into me. I could sit for hours, gazing at the tiny blue wrens that dominated the bird feeders surrounding the house, and the colourful parrots that fed freely from the orchard.

Robby and Leisha had recently purchased fifty steers for the farm, and in the weeks that followed I helped the children work the cattle through the yard, administering preventative measures for lice and worms, and delivering mineral boosters via a metal tube down each animal's throat, then finished them off with a B12 injection in the neck. They were good quiet cattle and looked fine specimens by sale day — a day I was beginning to hate.

Little Blue, our blue-black quarter horse (a horse that is fastest over a quarter mile), was worth her weight in gold, she was such a calming influence on any flighty young steers. When the new steers arrived on the farm, sometimes weaned, other times not, we would hold them in the cattle yard on hay and water for a few days to give them time to settle into their new surroundings. Then we released them into a paddock with Little Blue. This strategy greatly reduced the risk of a rush of cattle, which could end up in a trail of destruction several properties down the road — not to mention aggrieved and hostile landholders. This was not an idle worry; it didn't take much to get a rush started, as I knew from the Kimberley.

I was thinking of a muster I did with an old Aboriginal stockman called Alex while I was managing Louisa Downs. Australian Land and Cattle, the company who owned the station, was well and truly broke and it had been three months since I'd had any money to pay the stockmen's wages or buy fuel to keep the power plant operating. As it was, I would crank the old Lister engine over, but could only afford to run it long enough to keep the freezer cool, but not icy. That was sufficient to stop the meat from going green, but I needed a better solution.

I called old Alex to meet me on the back lawn of the homestead, and he came along with two younger stockmen, Ringer and Frank. We all sat down on the ground under the ancient jacaranda for a discussion, which progressed along typically formal lines.

'*Yumun*,' old Alex said, 'that Ringer and that Frank fella here, them ready to talk.'

'Thank you for coming,' I said. 'This mob I work for are broke.' I placed my hands out in front of me, palms open.

'They've got nothing, no money, so I need to do a muster to get some money. What do you mob reckon?'

I looked at all three men for an answer. They took their time, had another chew on their plug tobacco, then one by one spat the excess over their shoulders, placed the wad of tobacco behind an ear, and got down to the business of discussing the muster between themselves. Eventually Alex said, '*Yumun*, we muster them *yarriman* (horses) piccaninny daylight, draft em, start that muster next morning.'

'Good, old man, thank you,' I said, shaking his callused hands. He was perfectly right. As soon as we had mustered the stockhorses from the horse paddock, we could begin the cattle muster. And he was offering to work without pay, though I would not let them do that — they would be paid out of the proceeds of the cattle muster. I felt fortunate to have such good people working with me.

The morning after the horse muster the stockmen selected saddles, blankets and bridles from the saddle room. They saddled up and we started the cattle muster along the Mary River, below the homestead. The little black native bees were giving us hell as they battled for our ears and noses in search of moisture. Throughout the long day the men picked up small mobs of cattle and ran them into the 'coaches' (the quiet and steady cattle used to help hold wild or unruly cattle). I sat patiently behind the wheel of the bull buggy, keeping a watchful eye on a moody rogue bull that wasn't too keen on remaining with the new mob we were mustering.

Different groups of stockmen were taking it in turns to make mustering runs further afield. We would hold up for a time, wait for the fresh cattle to settle, and then move on again. With a good mob in hand, old Alex turned his sweat-covered brown gelding around and rode over to me, gazing back at the cattle as he placed his plug of tobacco behind an ear.

'*Yumun*, we turn and yard up?' he asked, pointing with his chin in the direction of the homestead.

'Yes, let's go old man, let's go home and yard up,' I replied, nodding my head in agreement. It had been a good day.

We had yarded the cattle and most of the stockmen had unsaddled their weary horses and begun to wash them down when old Biddy, Alex's wife, called out at the top of her lungs, 'Coooo-ah, coooo-ah!'

'Coooo-ah, coooo-ah,' the other women and children took up the call, and I looked over to where they were pointing. The cattle yard gates had swung open and the rogue bull that had been giving us a hard time all day was leading the mob of cattle towards the river and freedom in a heavy cloud of dust.

Stockmen in saddles and stockmen riding bareback came to the rescue, riding out of the yard as quick as their horses would carry them, galloping in a wide half-circle towards the river to try to put a bend in the wayward mob and herd them back.

When I heard them cry, 'Yull, yull,' I knew they had the cattle in hand and were hunting them back again. Then cries of 'Yull, yull,' came from within the heavy dust cloud, and soon the cattle emerged into the open and were pushed back into the stockyard.

Somehow the chain on the yard gate had come undone and I wasn't about to risk that again, so I took a head rope (a rope with a noose in it for slipping over the bull's horns) from the bull buggy and tied it around the yard gates for added security. The dollars were on the hoof and the money was as good as in the bank!

*

Having Little Blue down on the Shiralee not only helped settle the cattle but also kept a smile on Leisha's face. Leisha really is a marvellous horsewoman. Ever since she was a little girl she has broken in and handled her own horses, and Kristy has done the same. Robby, on the other hand, though a natural horseman, prefers his farm bike.

Being so confident and in control on horseback helped keep Leisha strong through the time I was having my radiotherapy and she was holding the family together. That confidence had not been won without cost, however.

Back at Kimberley Downs, while I was away from the homestead transferring a trailer load of gear to our new station, Fairfield, fourteen-year-old Leisha took a fall while training her new horse, Cavalier. She had purchased Cavalier — a big bay gelding, eighteen hands, a purebred quarter horse — against my better judgement. I had put all of the child endowment money I'd received for the children in their own passbooks. Leisha had about $10,000 in her account at the time. I told her that if she wanted him, she would have to buy him with her own money.

Cavalier had already earned himself a formidable reputation by putting two good horsemen in hospital with busted ribs and other broken bones. This knowledge alone was enough for me to give the bay the thumbs down; however, my strong-willed daughter purchased Cavalier after I had walked away. Leisha loved a challenge, and I am sure this was what pulled her towards the horse in the first place. No sooner had I left Kimberley Downs with the trailer than she chose to work her new giant between the stables and the homestead.

The horse had a very determined disposition and the dangerous habit of throwing his head back, each time very nearly whacking Leisha in the face. It was probably too soon, but she attached a loose, full-length tie-down that allowed the big bay to get his head up, but not far enough to smack her in the face. Then she got into the saddle and began working wide circles. When the horse next tried to throw his head back and realised he couldn't, he panicked and reared. When that didn't throw her, he launched himself backwards to land on top of Leisha, pinning her firmly to the ground. Had she taken the time and known her horse better she would have realised it wasn't in his nature to be so restricted. The big bay tried two or three times to rise, but because of the tie-down was unable to get his head up and repeatedly rolled back down on top of her.

A panicking Kristy was trying frantically to flog the horse off her sister, but luckily Leisha still had her senses about her. She could see the fear in the horse's eyes and called out for Kristy to stop. Eventually, with Kristy's help, Leisha was able to get herself out from under Cavalier. Shaking and trembling, her body bruised, she then helped up the frightened animal. Apologising to Cavalier, she rubbed him down as best she could, checked him over then jumped back on and rode him bareback around the paddock.

Thankfully this was the end of a tempestuous relationship and Cavalier calmed down. Leisha now knew she could deal with anything the gelding threw at her, and this helped give her a sense of her own power and strength. She would call upon this strength when she needed to hold things together for me.

I had three months of complete relaxation on the Shiralee, with only the occasional phone call from my husband. Then one day he arrived out of the blue. I was sitting in the lounge room when I caught a glimpse of him belting around the house towards the back door. He let himself in and embraced me passionately.

'Hang on a minute. You don't come waltzing back into my life just when you darned well please,' I said.

'What are you talking about?' he demanded, the picture of wounded innocence.

'We've been married less than six months,' I said, 'and I've had a major operation for cancer — people die of cancer, you know Terry — but how often did you visit me? I think you went to the races more often. I wanted to put off the wedding, remember, but you insisted we go ahead, you promised me you'd support me. Well I've never felt so alone as I have since I married you.' I hadn't realised how angry I was.

He stood there gaping at me, this was obviously not how he thought things would go. And I wasn't finished.

'You've lied to me. I don't know what's going on between you and Lauren, but it's not right, whatever it is. You shouldn't be letting a young girl come between you and the woman you married. In fact, this isn't a marriage, and I want you to leave now.' He tried to protest, but I didn't want to talk about it further then.

'Take some time to think about what you are doing,' I said to him. 'You can return another day if you really want to.'

The children wondered why I left the door open at all. Leisha came in when she saw Terry leaving and sat down next to me. 'I can't tell you what to do with your life, Mum,' she said, 'but it's hard on Robby and me seeing him make you so unhappy.' She put an arm around me. 'Just remember, you have your own farm, you're not broke, you don't need him.'

She was right, but there were many reasons for my not wanting to walk away from this marriage, despite Terry's behaviour. I was a strong and modern woman in many respects, but I also had some deeply traditional views. When I married Terry, I expected to be in it for the long haul. I was of the era that, once married, I had to try to make it work! I felt a responsibility to at least give it a chance. I had already walked away from one marriage, my first, and I was determined not to do that again. Because on top of all that there was my pride. It was my downfall. I wanted to prove — to myself as well as my family — that I hadn't made such a bad decision after all.

So when, after several more visits from my husband in the weeks that followed, he asked me to come to his mother's house for the haymaking season, I went with him to try again. I still had a fantasy that we'd help each other with our farms, even though he'd never lifted a finger on the Shiralee, I thought if I shared his load with him, sooner or later he'd reciprocate. When I was growing up I read *The Water Babies* and was struck by the character Mrs Do As You Would Be Done By. That had always seemed like a good ethic to me, so I went along with him. Robby refused to come; he was no longer comfortable with his stepfather, and he stayed behind with the girls to help with the hay on the Shiralee.

I was very fond of my mother-in-law Molly and got along well with her, but it was her house and I felt some-what awkward living there. Other than doing a share of the cooking, there wasn't much I could help her with in the house — I couldn't knit to save myself and thoughts of dressmaking had long gone out the window — so I offered to help with the haymaking.

The field grass had been slashed and I was to drive an old Ford tractor with a ten metre rake on the back of it while Terry followed behind in a much newer Chamberlain, rolling the hay. By the end of the day, every joint in my body ached. I was black from head to toe with paddock dust; my hair had gone from blonde to brown and looked like last year's bird's nest, and my eyes were bloodshot. With no power steering and the metal seat hard and rough as hell, I might have been riding an iron horse all day. At sundown I literally fell off the thing and battled to stand up straight.

By the third day on this antiquated beast I'd had a gutful. I suggested to Terry that we exchange tractors and, would you believe, out of the woodwork came another Chamberlain with a cab and power steering, so I remained on the job. It occurred to me that Terry was just testing me to see if I could stick it out in the paddock with him. It was a lot easier in the Chamberlain, though, which was just as well for these were long days, getting up early in the mornings to cook breakfast, pack the tucker box for lunch, and prepare the evening meal ready for Molly to pop it in the oven come late afternoon.

It was exhausting, and I was not really physically well enough to work the long days. I was trying to pull my weight by my husband's side while ignoring my health and trying to forget about the cancer. And this was a new experience for me, as here we were working far more acres than on the Shiralee.

When the hay season was over, Terry was returning to the caravan park, and he asked me to go with him. He told me Lauren was no longer there and that he was ready to make a real go of our marriage. I wondered if I could ever really trust him, but in the end I said yes. All the hard work had done me good; I was in fine health, and had come through my first six-monthly check-up with flying colours. I felt I had the energy now to try again.

I decided I would try to make the park my home. And yes, the park, not the house in Broome that Terry had told me he'd bought before we married. That had proved to be a slight exaggeration. But the park would not be forever; this time it really would be for a few months only. There was a million dollar house on Cable Beach which he could put an offer on if I would join him. I realised if I was going to get a real home, I'd have to meet him halfway. So I agreed in principle, dependent on seeing the contract.

I wanted Robby to feel he had a solid base, so we took the dogs with us. Robby's blue heeler Sally and little Prince the chihuahua. Leisha was already in Broome. She had gone up after the hay season was completed on the Shiralee. She had accepted an offer from Terry to work in the park's reception — I think he operated on the principle of 'keep your friends close and your enemies closer,' for there was no love lost between them. She moved into one of the old units that was lying empty and waiting for renovation.

Kristy, too, had left the Shiralee, moving to Albany to work for another trainer, and I came to an arrangement with Richard O'Connor to move into Robby's room on the farm so he could better keep an eye on things for me. It suited him perfectly, as he'd just sold his house in Narrikup and was building a new home on his farm. I didn't even contemplate leasing the Shiralee. All my possessions were there and I needed to be able to come and go as I pleased.

Terry, Robby and the dogs and I had just set off when weather forecasters announced a predicted cyclone in the Kimberley region. As we headed north beyond Geraldton, heavy clouds brought some relief from the muggy build-up that came with the cyclonic conditions, and we decided to continue on up the highway to Broome. But once Carnarvon was behind us, the countryside became a sea of water. Once-dry riverbeds had come to life, flowing with foam and pindan-coloured water. Everywhere the country was blooming as heavy rain washed the river gums and spinifex clean.

It was the middle of April, which seemed rather late for a cyclone, but Cyclone Rosita was coming in anyway. I wondered if I was fated to run into a cyclone every time

I drove to Broome. Kilometre after kilometre of highway went under water, while tiny silvery fish rained from the heavens on the Anna Plains flats — unbelievable but true. As we pushed on slowly through the flooded plains I spotted tiny silvery flashes darting through the floodwaters. Then I saw what looked like two fish caught in a leafy saltbush. I asked Terry to stop the car and got out to find the water was teeming with little fish.

I had seen floodwaters like this many times before, back on Kimberley Downs. Once I was driving with the children and the new 'govy' (the governess, who supervised the children at their schoolwork) to get stores. Homestead Creek was running a banker at the foot of Homestead Hill, and that was just the beginning. The road and flats were under water. On Tombstone Flat only the tops of the anthills were showing and the water was still rising.

I got out and tucked the mail bag onto the front grille to reduce the chance of water pressure pushing the fan into the radiator, then entered the water slow and steady. There was no obvious current. The clear water of the floodplain stretched out as far as the eye could see on both sides of the vehicle. It was an awesome sight, almost surreal, as little grey pythons curled themselves around the very tips of the anthills. The new high rise additions were darker than the rest. I saw one snake wrestling for control of the safe haven with a young goanna, only to lose to the goanna.

The gurgling sound of the engine half underwater gave way to a choking noise and I felt the vehicle lift slightly. We were momentarily floating. There were sounds of panic from the govy, a city girl, and I thought she might be going to open the door. 'Don't open the door,' I said. 'We're all right.' But in fact it was deeper than I'd estimated and I decided to reverse back out. The govy was near to hysteria now, but the children were calm. This was our way of life. We understood our wet seasons and what they could throw at us, but I was never stupid enough to risk a life. We could wait another few days for the waters to recede.

Terry and I finally crossed Roebuck Plains, which was a sea of water, to arrive in Broome in the early afternoon. The staff were running on overdrive. Cyclone Rosita was constantly changing course and obstinate tourists were refusing to move out to the designated safety areas around Broome. I filled water containers with fresh water and changed the battery in my torch. I looked for a battery-operated transistor radio, and when I couldn't find one I told Terry I was going out to buy one. 'What for?' he said. 'We don't need another radio.'

'Look, I'm not asking for a Mercedes-Benz,' I said. 'How else are we going to keep track of the cyclone if the power goes off?'

Terry ignored me and began swinging around on his office chair while tapping his desk with a ruler in each hand. I might as well not have been there.

Standing like a schoolgirl waiting for him to speak, I asked him, 'Is that your answer?' He didn't reply, except that the rapping of the rulers became louder and faster.

The cyclonic cloud mass sat like a huge mushroom over Broome. Winds ripped palm fronds right off the trunks and wrapped them around neighbouring trees. The glass rattled in our bedroom window and I knew it was time to tape it up for added safety. I was halfway through this when Terry walked in. 'What are you doing now?' he asked me, in a tone that implied I was a complete idiot.

'Taping the window,' I replied, swallowing my anger. 'It may stop the glass from shattering and blowing in on us if the winds get any stronger.'

He walked out of the room shaking his head as if he couldn't be bothered with me.

Sundown came and went, and it was pitch black outside. The constant roar of the wind rattled my nerves as it thrashed trees about, tearing limbs off and hurling them wildly about the park. The elements would not give up. The tree outside our window was uprooted and landed on the roof, branches and debris slamming against the corrugated iron walls. The noise alone was enough to arouse fear in the toughest individual.

I thanked God for Robby and his young mate Darren. Tipping out old boxes of lost-and-found gear on the back verandah, they discovered a battery-operated radio in reasonable order. With new batteries, and holding the radio to my ear, I could just make out the hourly cyclone update. At midnight it seemed Rosita had changed course slightly, so that Broome was no longer in line for a direct hit. But the situation was still very serious — the Echo Resort just south of Broome was completely wiped out — and I remained worried. Terry thought I was overdramatising and went to lie down in the bedroom where he was soon out for the count, oblivious to the wild wind playing out its fury.

Leisha was spending the night with her cousins John and Ben, the pearl divers. She assured me she was safe, that they were 'keeping an eye on the storm', which probably meant they were partying the night away.

The boys' safety was my priority, and I got them to help me drag mattresses from the bedrooms into the laundry. We set up camp on the floor there. The town's generators had shut down at 10 pm and the park was in darkness. The boys eventually fell asleep, and I lay there listening to the angry howl that rattled the doors and windows. It stopped another hour or two later, and the noises gradually settled until there was an eerie silence about the place. The static had died from my radio and I realised it had gone off air. I moved towards the window, parted the blinds and shone my torch out into the darkness, but I could see nothing. I returned to bed and fell into an exhausted sleep.

When I woke a few hours later the sun had risen. Outside it was still eerily quiet, there was not even a bird about. I parted the blinds and couldn't believe my eyes. I opened the door and just stood there staring. The park looked like a disaster zone, it was a wasteland. Trees and caravans were uprooted everywhere. I woke Terry, who staggered out in his underwear. In shock he started climbing over tree trunks and branches trying to get an idea of how much damage there was. He was mesmerised by the devastation, and I couldn't blame him. It turned out wind speeds had been recorded up to a hundred and fifty kilometres an hour.

The park was fully booked for the high season and the caravans would start rolling up in a few weeks' time. It was going to be a massive clean-up job. But no one was hurt, there was only material damage, and for that I was grateful. My brothers' mango farms suffered only slight damage, though Bruce, my oldest brother, who lives on the edge of a lagoon just off Cable Beach, had the sea lapping at his front door. Leisha and her cousins brought a team of pearl divers and friends to the park to check on us. For this they needed police permission — power poles and powerlines were down, such was the state of emergency. Under Terry's supervision they worked as a team with chainsaws, axes and the park tractor to clear away debris. On our gas burner I made steak sandwiches and hamburgers by the dozen for the helpers. We also gave ice creams to one and all. It was not entirely an altruistic gesture — we had no power and were going to lose the lot anyway.

It was an interesting way to return to Broome. It was months before life at the caravan park returned to normal, and in some respects Rosita was good for me, as I bonded with many of the park's residents as we worked together to get it back into shape. I was talking to people I hadn't spoken to before. We swapped our Rosita stories and had some good laughs together. It was a lot better with Lauren gone. In fact, she had still been there when we arrived back. But not for long. I felt that Lauren and Terry were still far too familiar and secretive with each other, and I always felt like the intruder when around them. Then one day in the office reception I decided to check the park rental slips and found that Terry was providing her with free accommodation. I told him that this arrangement didn't exactly impress me.

It didn't exactly impress Jean either; as Terry's business partner, she was keeping Lauren too! I gave Terry an ultimatum: it was either Lauren or me! I told him I was prepared to leave him. He was angry as all hell, but within a week she was gone.

Looking back I don't believe they ever severed their contact with each other entirely, though. And things still weren't any easier living in a small room with Terry. Each morning I would wake at five, dress and have a quick cup of tea, then take myself for a walk while it was still relatively cool, psyching myself up to facing the pressures of life in a fishbowl. Our tiny kitchen, dining area, laundry and bathroom were shared with staff during the day, and my only privacy lay in shutting the doors that divided our sleeping quarters from the shop. In the middle of the day it was too hot to be outside.

One day I had been lined up for a teleconference with Pastoral and Graziers Solicitors who wanted to discuss Kimberley land claims with me. I found the situation almost laughable: they wanted me for my knowledge, experience and expertise, and there I was, sitting in the bedroom for privacy with my mobile hot against my ear.

I tried my best to relieve some of the pressure under which Terry worked. Part of the problem was he insisted on doing everything himself; he found it very difficult to delegate. He didn't have faith in those around him. I took on the advertising for him, but in the end he couldn't leave it to me.

It was clear to me now that Terry had no interest in us having a proper home. The million dollar house near Cable Beach had turned out to be another dud. Midway through the deal I realised it wasn't to be our home at all — as he had encouraged me to believe — but an investment property. Luckily I had done my homework before signing any contract. I considered renting a place in town, but Rosita had put accommodation at a premium. Anyway, I knew Terry well enough by now to know he would be unhappy about that: how people saw our marriage was important to him.

Physically, I was feeling quite strong; there was no more sign of cancer. Once or twice a week I would mix a bucket of kerosene, linseed oil and dark floor polish to clean and buff the old wooden floors of the reception area and shop. It was hot and sweaty work, but it felt good to keep the place clean and looking cared for. It was good for me to stay busy too, and I filled my time with stocking the park store, looking after the park laundry and picking up the slack in the cleaning. I rarely went off for coffee with friends; I didn't want to. My life had changed so much, it wasn't easy to relate to people from my earlier Kimberley days. My friends had stopped visiting me as there was no privacy in which to sit and talk. And Terry's rudeness and arrogance made them uneasy and discouraged them from visiting. My friend Joanne could not understand what was happening to me. She could not bear to see his dominance over me. Slowly he seemed to be isolating me from my friends and I think I was gradually falling into the early stages of depression.

I had been back in Broome about three months when Kristy telephoned from Albany with some bizarre news. Someone had somehow managed to sell Little Blue, over our heads. I owned Little Blue and had the paperwork to prove it, and I certainly would never have dreamed of selling her to anyone. She was far too valuable in her new role of calming cattle. In earlier days this would have been called horse stealing and someone would have hung for it. I decided to investigate, and called my friend Brian Singleton, one of Western Australia's best criminal lawyers, to look into the matter for me. I first met Brian when he successfully handled a cattle case for friends in Broome in the early eighties, and I called him in over McCorry's case of indecent assault, the circumstances of which very nearly destroyed my happy young family. But Brian helped to keep us strong and positive. We saw a lot of him then, and after that he always dropped in to see how I was going whenever he was in the Kimberley.

I had lent Little Blue to a young niece of Heath's named Penny, so that she could learn to ride on her. Later, when Penny's family moved from their small farm into town, there was no room for Little Blue, and at that point the mare should have been returned to the Shiralee.

Somewhere along the way, however, Penny's farrier got hold of Little Blue. First, without my permission, he put her in foal to a quarter horse stallion. Then he sold her to a girl from an area north of Perth. Brian Singleton called the farrier and asked if he had proof of ownership. By the end of the conversation the farrier was apparently a little worried. 'Who are you, a lawyer or something?' he said.

Brian laughed as he told me he replied, 'I'm a QC.' And when the farrier said, 'What's that?', Singleton responded, 'I reckon you best find out!' Hearing that gave me a good laugh too.

It turned out that the farrier was married to a young woman I had known since she was a small girl. As much as I wanted the return of Little Blue, I could not bring trouble on this young woman. With a heavy heart I let the matter drop.

At about this time, Kristy moved and took up riding track for Bart Cummings's racing stables. This was something she'd had her heart set on since she was a little girl. I was proud of her for sticking to her guns and following her dream.

Shortly after this I decided to sell McCorry's old place, Sleepy Hollow. I didn't want to let it go, but none of the children wanted to work it or live there, so we sold it to some horse breeders. At the time, Leisha wanted a place of her own. McCorry had basically left it to me to decide how to settle his estate, but with the stipulation that I wasn't to hand over large amounts of cash to the children. So we sank the money into bricks and mortar, and I bought her a house in Albany.

The cows and calves on Sleepy Hollow were sold and Terry put his hand up to purchase our Blonde d'Aquitaine bull, promising to pay the price others had offered, which was $2400. This beautiful bull had produced magnificent calves on Sleepy Hollow, and we had him trucked to the Wildwood farms where he worked the following two seasons, still producing excellent calves. In his next season, however, the bull damaged a foot and Terry sent him to the meatworks. At this point he had still not paid for the bull, and at the end of the day he gave me only the meatworks' price of $900 — and it took a lot of persistence and one hell of an argument to get that.

My smooth-talking husband had prevailed once again — but not completely. If he had had his way, the Shiralee would have been sold as well, but I wasn't having that. The proceeds would probably have vanished into the park, never to be seen again. Terry loved money and hated parting with it, to anyone. Once I entertained the wicked thought that if he died before I did, I would fill his grave with bucket loads of his money so that he could carry on partying, drinking and gambling to his heart's content.

One day Robby asked if he could move into an old caravan that was lying empty in the park. It wasn't fit to rent: it was so old, the power shorted out when it rained, and it leaked like a sieve. I was worried he would be electrocuted, but Terry grudgingly let him use it. Robby was fifteen, and the tension between Terry and I made it so uncomfortable in our household that I thought he'd be better off in the caravan, even with the risk of it going up in smoke! Besides, like me, he had no privacy in the house. I fully understood his need for a place of his own.

It wasn't only the tension between his mother and stepfather that was difficult for my boy. Robby was working for Terry in the caravan park, and Terry delighted in playing mind games in front of the other workers and humiliating the underdog, which, I discovered all too late, turned out to be my son. Robby was reluctant to burden me with the hard time he was having with the men in my life, and I am still angry with myself for not seeing it much earlier and making a stand on my son's behalf.

There was one very bright spark in my life at this time — I picked up my mobile one day to a call from Leisha. 'Hello Mum,' she said, her voice bubbling with happiness. 'I've got some news for you.' There was silence for a moment, then she blurted out, 'It's good news, I'm pregnant!' I hesitated for only a split second as I counted up the months that she had known Adam — four — then said the only words I could in response to her joy. 'That's wonderful, you've really made my day. I'm the happiest nan-to-be.'

I was going to be a grandmother!

In December Leisha had returned to the city, where she had met a Adam, country boy from Moora. He was a tradesman working for a big steel company, a very decent boy. They had moved in together pretty quickly, and now their first child was coming. I prayed it wasn't too soon and that they'd treat each other well.

'And I'm the happiest mum-to-be,' she enthused. 'I'm going to have the baby in a natural-birth clinic, no drugs, no interference; Adam will be there. It's due in September. I've already booked the clinic. Now what about you, Mum, how are you?' She finally paused for breath.

I wasn't going to tell her I'd been feeling flat because I was living in a shoebox at my age. And I didn't want to pour cold water over her plans to have a drug-free birth, though the idea made me uneasy. I wanted every possible measure for her safety and wellbeing, and that of my grandchild.

'I'm great,' I lied, 'and I'm so happy for you both. And I definitely want to be with you when the time comes.'

Kristy wouldn't be around; she had accepted a three-month job riding thoroughbreds in Malaysia. When that was over she would be relocating to Victoria to resume working for Bart Cummings.

I was so pleased that the girls were happy, that they were fulfilling their dreams, but it also reminded me that somewhere along the line, I had lost sight of my own dreams. In fact, my life was turning into something of a nightmare.

CHAPTER 6

Things Turn Ugly

*I*t was 24 April 2001, Kelly's birthday, and nearly twenty years since he had died. He would have been twenty-five, and I still felt his loss so painfully that it could have been yesterday. This year the contrast between that time on Louisa Downs when he was a bright five year old, and the life I was living now, hit me hard. My new marriage wasn't remotely what I'd hoped it would be, and I was no longer sure that anything could be salvaged.

When Terry was under pressure I copped the rough end of his moods. One humid April night it was suffocatingly hot and I turned the bedroom fan on very low. I'd have turned it up higher, except that Terry was strangely intolerant of moving air. The room was so small there wasn't room to swing a cat, and the only window was bolted shut.

Suddenly Terry was standing beside the bed ripping off the sheets and covers and throwing them to the floor, yelling fucking this and fucking that — I felt sick with anxiety trying to make sense out of what was going on. I sat bolt upright in bed, saying, 'What's happening Terry, what's wrong?' but he didn't answer me, he seemed out of control, he was so angry.

He slammed around the foot of the bed, shut the fan off, then got back into bed and turned his back to me. Soon he was snoring.

I sat there wondering whether it was my putting on the fan that had made him so angry. It looked like he was throwing a tantrum, but if this was just a childish outburst of temper, I wondered what might be next. I was afraid to move, fearful of what might happen if he woke again. I listened to Terry's heavy breathing until it sounded like he was in a deep sleep, then I moved quietly from the bed and crept out to the tiny spare room that Robby had recently vacated. It was small and dusty, but there was a bed in it and a lock on the door. I locked myself in, opened the curtains — the window was bolted shut — and lay on the bed, willing my breathing to settle back to normal.

As the early morning light came through the gap in the curtains I battled to find the energy to get out of bed. I was not just exhausted from a disturbed night — for the first time in my life, including the worst effects of the radiotherapy, I felt no motivation to get up and meet the day. That upset me more than Terry's bizarre behaviour.

I did get up, and when I saw him I wondered if it had even registered with him that I hadn't slept the night with him. If it had, he made no comment, and I made none either. But later that day I said to him I needed my own bedroom, since we had completely different needs for air and it was suffocating for me in his bedroom. I wanted to spruce up the spare room and use it as a little den where I could entertain my friends, but he wouldn't hear of it. 'Stay in our bedroom,' he said quietly, 'we can make it work.'

'Terry, can't you see I have no space, no privacy? You married a grown woman, not a child.' He looked at me as though I was speaking another language. 'And on top of all that, I don't want to wake up in the middle of the night ever again to you swearing at me and ranting and raving. You've got a foul temper.' Again, he just looked at me as if I was the one who'd lost it. And he refused to budge. If I wanted to do anything with the little room, there'd be no help from him.

What was I to make of this? On one hand he seemed to despise me, and on the other hand he couldn't bear it if I were away from him. He didn't want to talk to me, but if anyone was with me he would be constantly in and out, needing to discuss this or that. With the benefit of counselling I now know that this is a common pattern in abusive partners, but at the time it made no sense to me at all. Some men have to keep you on edge. With McCorry, once he became depressed, I was often walking on eggshells, not wanting to upset him, but with Terry it was so unpredictable that the most ordinary thing might set him off. I don't know if he did it on purpose, but the effect was to keep me on edge all the time.

He seemed to need people around him all the time. Most nights he would be partying with whoever would join him, mixing red wine with shooters and rum. That was a lethal combination, and when his friends were gone he began more and more often to turn on me.

Perhaps only someone who has been through a similar situation can understand why I didn't just pack up and take my boy back to my beloved Shiralee. At the time, I didn't understand it myself. It was as if I'd lost my will, my motivation. It was no longer a case of wanting to prove my sticking power to myself or my parents; now I simply didn't have the courage to leave. My confidence had vanished so fast, I didn't know what had happened to me. I was like a lemming heading for the cliff, passing sign after sign saying, 'Wrong Way, Go Back!'

I didn't know myself any more. I'd lost the strong and proud person I'd been when I was managing stations in the Kimberley. Even though I owned my own farm and had a good sum of money invested, something made it impossible for me to leave my husband. I really didn't believe I'd survive alone. I was frightened, though if you'd asked me what I was frightened of, I wouldn't have been able to say.

My recent brush with cancer was probably a factor in my depressed state. And feeling so low, it was not so easy to maintain my faith that I would remain cancer free. I wanted to be cared for, loved, nurtured, and the man I married was running in the opposite direction. If anything, my health was a source of irritation to him, as if he resented the fact that I was due some TLC. I was doing my best to take some of the weight off his shoulders in running the park, to make him happier; I tried to solve his problems, fix things where I could; if I saw something that needed doing, I'd step in. I just wished he wanted to support me too.

And the cancer medication wasn't helping. I had been taking Tamoxifen for eighteen months but now was suffering stomach pain and sometimes internal bleeding. Dr Ingram gave me a new prescription, for Femara, and the pains and bleeding stopped and slowly I began to feel better.

But in the meantime, I felt vulnerable and frightened and my only real happiness was to receive a phone call from my children or parents — and if it was on the office phone, Terry would be standing over me while I tried to talk, urging me to finish up quickly so he could make some important business calls. He wouldn't put in a private line for me.

If I ever challenged him, even mildly, he would invariably respond by challenging my sanity. 'You're mad in the head!' he'd say. 'You should get out of here, and don't come back until your head is right.' No one had ever said anything like that to me before. I wish I could have just laughed at such a crazy line, but I couldn't. Not then, even though I knew he'd used the same line on his first wife. I had never met Terry's first wife, but I didn't believe his nasty comments about her. He constantly put her down to me and told me how much he disliked her. Once he blurted out that she had taken out two restraining orders against him, something he seemed to find quite amusing. Warning bells should have rung for me then. Looking back on it as I write, I feel my temperature rise in fury that he should have tried to convince me I was mad — and that I should have fallen for it.

It was around this time that I was seeing my doctor about the Tamoxifen, and he asked me, 'Are you suffering any problems in your marriage?' I couldn't bring myself to answer him. But I wondered how he knew. It hurt my pride to think he could tell just by looking at me. If he knew, how many others did too?

I remembered myself as such a strong and competent person, but I didn't know, and it had never occurred to me, that if someone is constantly telling you there's something wrong with you, then a part of you actually starts to believe it. Maybe if I'd talked to a friend about what was happening I would have realised this, but there was no way I could tell anyone, friends or family. I didn't want people thinking I was some pathetic victim. I didn't see myself that way at all.

I had confided in my old friend Joanne, and my mother. But then I had to deal with the fact that they worried terribly for me and for Robby, and so it was better to try to convince them that I was all right. When Joanne or any of my brothers dropped in, we all acted as if everything was fine. I would watch this happening, and it was almost as if we were in a play, acting roles, keeping everything nice. I didn't know what else to do.

When it came to arguments, I stood up for myself less and less. Arguing back only made him worse, and it never brought me anything I wanted. One night I was standing my ground about his drinking — we were about to go out and I couldn't bear the thought of another evening ruined by his overindulgence, getting loud and foul-mouthed — when he raised a clenched fist and said, 'You need a kick up the arsehole, should've had one when you were a kid.' I hated the gutter way he spoke, but this was something else. I had never felt physically threatened by him before.

Strangely, and in spite of all this, I often felt a kind of sympathy and sadness for Terry; his father and brother had both died fairly recently and I think he felt a huge weight of responsibility for keeping the family farms and the newly purchased caravan park out of the hands of the bank. In this he was successful, and it is probably a large part of the reason he was so mean about money with me.

During this low time of my life I found joy where I could. My greatest pleasures have always been in the simple things in life, like crabbing. My younger brother Eric would take me to his secret spot to catch the huge mud crabs that thrive in the mangroves around the Broome coastline. We would collect our crab hooks and buckets — dingo flour drums with handles made from fence wire — and off we'd go. The tide would be out and we'd trudge through oozing, knee-deep mud that constantly fought to suck your boots down with each step you made. The sun would have enough heat in it to boil a billy, but gentle sea breezes would keep our sweating bodies cool.

One day we were making our way through the mangroves, covered from head to toe in grey mud, my flour drum feeling like a lead weight from the three big crabs it carried. Eric was in front and sang out, 'Keep your eyes open, a huge croc has been here.' He was pointing out the tracks to me. I thought he could have picked a better place and time to tell me this. I clung tightly to a mangrove tree and had a good look around, noting that the tide had turned and the sea was rushing in. This would be a terrible place to come face to face with a big croc in its own territory. I've lived in the north all my life and have nothing but a healthy respect for the saltwater crocodile, so that dampened my enthusiasm for catching any more crabs that day.

When I was a girl in Arnhem Land one of the family's favourite fishing haunts was Dalywoi Bay near Cape Arnhem. It was a picture postcard kind of place with its clean white sand, aqua blue water and one sturdy casuarina. Every time you dropped a line you caught a fish, and at that time we were the only white family on the bauxite plateau other than the people at the Yirrkala mission. The isolation made it especially tranquil.

In the tidal river where we fished, a gigantic boulder rose out of the water. One day we motored out to our favourite spot as usual, my father at the outboard motor, my brother Bruce in charge of the anchor at the bow, and Eric and I sitting in the middle. No sooner had Dad stopped the motor and Bruce dropped anchor alongside the rock than out of the water lunged a four metre croc, sending our aluminium dinghy into a dangerous roll. Despite our shock and terror, we remained still and silent while the water around us was in turmoil. I was sixteen, but it never entered my head to start screaming or crying: it was something we just had to deal with, and as calmly as possible. Eric was ten, and appeared to show no fear at all, but I whispered to him, 'Hang on to the seat, Dad will deal with it.'

I watched my father level his rifle and fire as the giant salty rose high out of the water for its second assault. It seemed unreal, it was so huge. Fear gripped my body and the blast from the gun deafened me, but my faith in my father shot up even higher. In my young eyes, he was our saviour. I felt that nothing really terrible could happen to my brothers and me as long as Dad was by our side.

Moving quickly, Dad threw a rope around the beast and strapped it to the side of the dinghy, started up the outboard motor and towed the croc to shore. We needed the power of the Landrover to tow it up onto the beach and there Dad skinned it, planning to distribute the meat among the Aboriginal people camped around the bay. We kids were given a leg each to hold while Dad did the dirty work. Occasionally his knife hit a not so dead nerve, and the tail would give an almighty whack, sending me flying up the beach, convinced the croc was coming back to life.

'Come back and hang on, it's dead!' Dad roared when the tail sent me tearing up the beach for the third time. But I'd had enough of that, and flatly refused to help any more. My ears had picked up the murmur of voices somewhere beyond the wall of tall spear grass, and soon a group of people came out into the open — they'd heard the shot from their campsites and come to investigate. With their help, the task was quickly done and they all disappeared again with their fresh meat.

My father was a tough hard man of the outback, fearless and fit, and I wanted to be just like him. He brought up my brothers and me to survive in even tougher conditions. It didn't matter what was going on, my father was in control and protecting us; we felt safe with him. By contrast, it seemed to me that my husband looked after no one but himself.

Days crabbing with Eric were a rare relief from the sorry thing my life had become. I slowly slipped into a dark tunnel, isolated from family and friends. There was never a real home for people to visit me at the caravan park, and I felt less and less like going out to see them. My life seemed to be contracting into smaller and smaller circles, and I was worried about the effect all this was having on Robby. He seemed to be withdrawing from everyone, cocooned away in his dingy caravan. He hated Terry's aggressive moods, and seeing me so miserable. How I wish I had been able to act decisively then and take him away from the damage it was doing to both of us.

The straw that broke the camel's back was quite meaningless. It came during a dinner with one of Terry's friends. The two of them were as full as boots and were telling me how lucky I was to have Terry for a husband. You'd think we lived in different universes.

I don't know why, but this particular night I snapped and let them have my honest opinion for the first time. It was almost worth it for the look of utter shock on their faces. 'I'm sick of hearing how bloody good you are,' I yelled. 'You think you're god's gift — well I'm here to tell you, mate, you are *not*!' I was so mad. But when the friend had gone, Terry brought out his old refrain. 'You really are mad in the head.' He almost sounded as if he felt sorry for me. 'You really need to get that checked out.'

The next morning I packed my bags and Robby and I left for Perth. I felt an enormous sense of relief on leaving Terry and the park behind. Once I realised I could breathe freely again, without the pent-up tension that had been part of my life for so long, my body wanted only to shut down and sleep. I battled to keep going; I wanted to get the greatest distance between me and my husband as I possibly could.

I was driving on nervous energy, and I hit two kangaroos between Karratha and the Fortescue roadhouse. These were the first roos I'd ever hit while driving, and I doubt I would have hit them had circumstances been different. There was no damage to my trusty Landcruiser, but the deafening whack of the second animal against the bullbar shocked me.

'Stop Mum,' Robby pleaded. 'You're way too tired to keep going tonight.' He was right. But I was glad we had got beyond Karratha. I don't know why I was so worried; I didn't really expect Terry to try to follow us. When I told him I was taking some time out in the south, he had nothing to say, only stood staring at me as though he hadn't got a clue what was happening — and couldn't care less anyway.

We stopped at the Fortescue roadhouse and got a room for the night, and the next morning kept travelling until we arrived at my parents' house in Northampton, just north of Geraldton. The further south we drove, the more we found ourselves relaxed and smiling. I had no need to explain to my parents why we were there; they knew. Only a few weeks before I had unburdened myself to my mother after a nasty outburst from Terry, and she had encouraged me to take some time away to think.

That evening I received a phone call from Terry. He was ringing full of gentle concern to make sure we had arrived safely, and told me he loved me.

'Why are you telling me this after months on end of insisting I was mad in the head?' I said. He had no response. I was thinking, *If you want to say something, why not say sorry?* This was a word I never heard my husband use.

After just two days away from him, in a place where I was loved and supported, I could see my husband's behaviour for what it was. Unpredictable, except that predictably it always left me unsettled, distressed and quite often physically unwell.

I listened to him speak, feeling almost nothing at all, only sadness for the mess my life was in, and sorrow that it had also affected my son.

I wasn't blaming Terry for everything, or for what my marriage had become; I blamed myself for not having my eyes fully open at the very beginning of my life with him. The signs had all been there and I had chosen to ignore them. I thought it would be different. Well I had made my bed and I had to lie in it! I told him I needed some time out.

Robby and I spent four happy days with my parents. My mother packed a picnic box and in my father's car we all drove to Port Gregory and Kalbarri. Robby loved listening to his grandfather's stories of buffalo and croc hunting, and I talked quietly to my mother. She reminded me that I must not let my marriage harm my health, and that my children needed me. These few days of quiet gave me back some strength and serenity, even a little of my confidence. I realised just how much I had doubted my every move, to the point of even having trouble reading a road map — the very map I had read and followed many times before with complete confidence.

A few days later Robby and I arrived at Leisha and Adam's unit in Bentley. We would stay with them until Leisha had her baby, then Robby and I would go home to the Shiralee. Adam was at work, and a heavily pregnant Leisha ran out to meet us. It was a pleasant shock to see my daughter this way, though she seemed huge and looked as if she really needed to bring her baby out into the world.

Leisha and Adam were on cloud nine waiting for the arrival of little Brock McCorry-Smith. They had known their baby's sex for some months and had named him already.

In the early hours of Saturday 1 September 2001 Leisha's waters broke and we all did a mad dash to the Subiaco Natural Birthing Clinic, Robby included.

'Are you sure you want to do it this way, love?' I asked my girl.

'Yes, Mum. No drugs.' She was very sure.

'What if the pain becomes too much, do you want something then?' I asked, not knowing whether she had thought about this.

'No, Mum. I've told Adam that even if I ask for drugs he's not to let them give me anything,' she said.

I had been unable to give birth naturally — all my children were Caesarean deliveries, I had no choice. I'd had to have one with my first and was informed that as a result I wouldn't be able to give natural birth to any subsequent children. So watching my girl suffer the natural pains of childbirth had me suffering with her. Robby couldn't handle her cries and tried to get out of the building, only to discover he was locked in due to heavy security procedures. Adam seemed to be the calmest of us all. At one point Leisha's pains became so unbearable for me, I had to get out of the birthing suite, if only for a few minutes. I had been helping Leisha with the oxygen mask, and before leaving the room I instructed Adam on how to use it.

As I paced the corridor with Robby, who was still trying to find a way out, we couldn't help but hear Leisha's cries of pain. Frustrated, I charged back into the room and saw the oxygen mask was not being used. 'For god's sake, Adam, put the mask on her,' I urged. You didn't get a medal for being brave, not around here anyway.

Adam ignored me; so, grabbing the mask, I placed it over Leisha's face, saying to her quietly, 'Breathe, darling, take big breaths, nice and steady,' hoping like hell the baby would hurry up and come, not only for Leisha's sake, but for mine as well. But I could see no effect at all, she wasn't getting any relief from the oxygen. 'What's wrong with this thing?' I said to Adam in frustration. 'It's not working.' It turned out the mask was more or less useless — this was a natural birthing clinic. I felt like wrapping it around Adam's neck, thinking, *You've done this to my girl, you got her pregnant*. Of course I knew it wasn't his fault. I was a frustrated mother who hated to see her girl hurting.

Nine and half hours later Brock was born. From the very moment Leisha held him tenderly in her arms, lovingly admiring her new baby, I knew that every scrap of pain was well and truly worth it. Though I wasn't sure I wanted to watch my daughter give birth again — it was just a bit too traumatic for me.

Robby and I spent a week in Perth with Leisha and Adam. I had to have some mammograms and ultrasounds for my cancer check-ups, and after that we were able to travel home to the Shiralee. The results were all fine and I had only to keep on taking my daily medication.

Overflowing with happiness, a wonderful calmness came over me as I walked in through the door of my house. This was my home, and I thanked God for getting us back there safely.

CHAPTER 7

Lift the Bloody Plank Yourself

*T*here was work to be done on the farm, checking fences and drenching cattle for lice and worms. Richard, who is an excellent farmer, had been taking very good care of the Shiralee since Kristy had left. My cattle looked good, and Robby and I were free to take care of that side of things again.

We were fattening steers, but there was also time to relax. It was whale-watching time on the southern coast, when mothers and their calves were journeying north. I listened to the local ABC radio station and each time there was news of a pod in the Middleton Beach area Robby and I would jump into the Landcruiser and head down to the coast. We spent several weeks enjoying coffee on the beachfront while watching mothers and their calves frolic in the bay. It was just what we needed to blow away the miseries of the past.

Feeling much better after our idyll in the south, we returned to Perth in October to see Leisha, Adam and the baby. Terry was due to fly into Perth too. It was haymaking time again, and he was coming south to work on the family farms. He'd rung to tell me Molly was unwell and had asked me if I'd come and see her and help out with the haymaking. When it came to working together, I always wanted to say yes. I needed something constructive to do. I understood the pressure on the household with meals and smokos during the haymaking season. This was my chance to spend quality time with Molly too, I liked her and we got on well. The Shiralee was under control, so I drove up to the city to collect him from the domestic terminal and we booked into a motel while Robby stayed with Leisha and Adam.

We both trod carefully, and I felt Terry was trying to make an effort. We had a few days in the city, then left with Robby to stay in Molly's house. We would cart cattle to Harvey meatworks and then start on the hay.

I didn't feel great about Robby coming to Wildwood, and I was torn about what was the best thing to do. Robby was sixteen years old and it was difficult for him to work with his stepfather. 'I don't want to stay here, Mum,' he said. 'I'd rather go back to Broome while he's down here. I can't stand his yelling and screaming, and he always picks on me, just like he does at the caravan park, he's never game to pick on the other workers, he knows they'd just knock him down.'

He'd have preferred us to return to the Shiralee, but at this time in his life I worried about the isolation there. At least in Broome he had his uncles and aunts and cousins. Bruce and Eric made a point of being there for him. In the end, he decided he would return to his job in the caravan park for the time being. At least he wouldn't have Terry to torment him up there. I had tried many times to speak to Terry about his treatment of Robby, but he never listened. He would just scoff, throw his head in the air like a mad stallion and charge off. But Terry was also cunning enough to never let me catch him intimidating Robby — just as he made sure he was never caught abusing me in the presence of my family.

A lot of farmhands refused to work alongside Terry. His yelling, shouting and abusing was not confined to me or my son.

Astonishingly, it was doing farm work that we worked best together, though it still almost always ended badly. With Terry, the offsider inevitably copped it. Early on in our marriage, when all the other workers had walked off the job, I helped him replace an old cattle yard. We were going very well until the moment I did not have the strength he needed from me. 'Lift it higher,' my husband demanded as I battled to keep a heavy timber plank level above my head. The muscles in my arms were screaming and there was enough heat in the sun to fry an egg on a shovel.

'Higher!' he yelled at me furiously. 'Higher, and hold it. Hold the fucking thing steady!' But I couldn't. Dropping the plank to the ground, I swung around to face him and said, 'Lift the bloody plank yourself!' I waited until I could draw a deep breath and said more calmly, 'Can't you see I'm trying to help you and I'm doing my best? No one else can work with you because you're always so full of anger.'

Infuriated, I turned and headed for home. The yard was close to completion anyway. I was hot and perspiring and covered in black dust that irritated me almost as much as the hundreds of flies I was battling.

Back at the farmhouse Molly came out the front door and wrapped her arms around me, cattle dust and all. Which straightaway brought on the tears. Small, frail, white-haired Molly was tenderly taking care of me. I pulled myself together over a cup of tea and said, 'Molly, I reckon you must have jumped the fence to have Terry.'

Molly, standing in the kitchen with the teapot in her hand, burst out laughing.

I'd often heard Terry say, 'There's only one of me.' He meant it in a self-congratulatory way, but how true, I thought, because he and his brother Jim were as different as chalk and cheese.

Molly wasn't well. She had an unnatural drowsiness about her and I took her to the medical centre. Within minutes of her seeing a doctor I was asked to go home and collect a few of her things and to return with them to Busselton Hospital.

Molly was diagnosed with leukaemia. The prognosis wasn't good. Terry had arrived by now and when he and I left her in the care of the medical staff, it was with a heaviness in my heart that I walked with my husband down the long corridor and out of the hospital. Only the echo of our footsteps broke the deep silence. I had grown close to Molly. She was very like a mother to me. She told me I was the daughter she never had and confided in me, telling me some very personal secrets and giving me a list of things she wanted me to do if anything happened to her.

That evening when we went back to the hospital, Molly had been given a blood transfusion. The sight of her lying listlessly in her hospital bed, pale and lethargic, brought back painful memories of old McCorry. Pulling my chair close by the bed, I held her frail hand.

'How are you feeling, has the blood transfusion helped?' I asked.

'Dear,' Molly said, 'I don't feel very well at all.' She didn't look well, and her hand was very cold. Then she said, 'Would you mind if I don't have any more transfusions?'

This hit me like a smack in the face. Molly was asking *me* to help her make a life-and-death decision, not Terry. Without further transfusions, she could go downhill fast, and I am sure she knew that.

Hay season was in full swing. Everyone was working from dawn to dusk to get the hay in. I was working flat out with Terry but every evening I would go to town to visit Molly.

She didn't have another transfusion, but five days later she was sitting up in bed doing crosswords, her favourite pastime. I was so happy to see her stronger, but alas, it didn't last long. Over the next few days she gradually drifted back to the state she'd been in when she was admitted.

On Thursday, 8 November Molly was again sitting propped up in bed, working on her crossword, and I decided I would stay. I could spend the next day and night with her to keep her company. With my lounge chair stretched out beside her hospital bed, I dozed off while holding Molly's pale and delicate hand in mine. Twice through the night I woke to check on her, then fell back to sleep. The third time I woke, her hand was quite cold. I sat bolt upright in my chair, and cried softly, 'Molly, Molly, wake up.' I couldn't find a pulse. Her hand seemed too cold. Dear Molly had passed on and I didn't know exactly when.

I stood by her bedside and my vision blurred with tears as I thought how much I admired this woman who had gone without for most of her adult life to help build up a family farming empire. Molly's death brought back unresolved feelings of emptiness and loneliness from McCorry's death. Now I was feeling even more isolated. But I did feel grateful to have had her in my life, and still feel Molly was the only gift my marriage really brought me.

I stood there and thought of another death, on Louisa Downs years before. Kaye, a slightly built, always quiet Aboriginal girl, had been absent from the station for three weeks. Asking after her whereabouts, I was informed, 'She was kidnapped by some Balgo boys, Missus.'

'Kidnapped?' I echoed in astonishment. 'They can't do that; people can't just take you away against your will.'

Their replies were vague and I let the matter rest, presuming she was visiting people, though Balgo men had a bad reputation in Halls Creek. Then she was back at the station and not at all well, and three days later she passed away. I understood that she too had leukaemia, similar to Molly's. She had had no treatment.

Another grave to dig with a crowbar and shovel. Filling the forty-four-gallon drums with water we dampened the ground and dug, early morning and late evening in the cooler weather. It was hard going, the ground was so rugged and stony. I worried about a small boulder that protruded a third of the way down at one end of the grave. I pointed it out to the men who were helping to dig the grave. 'We should get this out,' I said. 'Nah, him right,' replied one. Sacred, superstitious or lazy, I don't know. I could see they wanted the job completed in a hurry.

Aboriginal people gathered from surrounding camps and communities to pay their last respects to Kaye. Katie asked for calico, and I gave her a sheet which they tore into scarves and wore to show they were in mourning. Coolabah performed the service.

I was standing on the rim of the grave, swaying with the movement of the people while they gripped onto each other and to me for support, mourning and wailing. The men began to lower the coffin. I was feeling emotional myself, my eyes misty with tears as I thought of another coffin, a much smaller one. Suddenly, the coffin stopped, jammed on a terrible angle, and so did everything else, hymns, wailing, and crying. I looked about me at all those eyes peering over each other and into the grave. I was torn between laughing and crying.

'Everyone leave now, burial finished,' I called, shooing everyone away from the grave. The men pulled the coffin out, knocked out the boulder, then lowered the coffin successfully and filled the grave. I retired to the kitchen for a pannikin of tea. How many more deaths?

CHAPTER 8

A Dark Shadow

Molly left about seventy years' worth of personal papers and letters for me to dispose of. The afternoon before her passing she had held my hand and looked at me with pale and distant eyes and asked me to do this myself. I promised her I would. I began the work of sorting through them, but had trouble settling into Molly's house after her death. Out of the corner of my eye I sometimes glimpsed a dark shadow passing through the family room as if heading towards the carport. This happened to me three times, but it really got to me when Leisha, visiting with Adam and their baby, saw it as well. Is it possible that Molly had come back into our lives? Could she be a ghost now and visiting me? I was ready to freak out. Should I pack my suitcase and get the hell out of here? Then another day my young grandson Brock was playing with his toys in Molly's bedroom doorway, he then started laughing and giggling while holding his toys high. Was Molly's ghost playing with him? I believe that our lost loved ones are constantly around us. This is how I have come to terms with my beloved son Kelly's death and McCorry's death. I've convinced myself our loved ones live in another place, so in my mind this shadow had to be Molly and the fear left me. Despite these events though, the house was peaceful and after a while I managed to get the job done.

Terry jumped on his tractor and didn't get off it until all the firebreaks were completed. I wondered if that was his way of grieving his mother's death. I never saw him cry.

The next job was drafting the last of the Friesian steers out of the paddocks to be sold to the meatworks. This was some draft! These tall, leggy steers were new to me, some were as high as I am tall, but they were reasonably placid. Terry was trying to draft out the heavyweights in a round yard that had a three-way draft — meaning he could draft out steers and heifers separately, and bush the rest. He was dancing from one foot to the other and never left off shouting abuse, whether to the cattle or to me, all the time waving a lump of poly pipe about his head.

'Push them up!' he bellowed while performing what looked like a Maori war dance. 'Push the fucking things up!' He was waving the poly pipe, dancing and swearing at the top of his voice. He seemed quite out of control.

I stopped in my tracks and watched him, amazed. The cattle were stirred up too, and the animal closest to me kicked out with its left hindquarter and came close to wiping my face from my head. Worse, I was now covered in yard muck that was a mixture of urine and shit. Dodging cattle while trying to wipe the putrid mess from my face, I had another close call as the steers rallied around the yard.

'Push the fucking things up!' Terry yelled again.

That was it. I wasn't risking my life for his rampant incompetence, getting the animals unnecessarily — and dangerously — wound up. 'Push them up yourself!' I yelled, then turned and walked away. *If I was running this show you wouldn't have a job in a cattle yard with me*, I was thinking as

I pulled out my thermos and sat on a log under a shade tree for a cup of tea.

During the haymaking Terry loaded the truck while I carted it to the fenced-off hay site for stacking. One day amongst the hay rolls I was bitten by a spider on the back of the neck. In no time the bite was the size of an egg and I felt as if I had a sudden bout of flu coming on. All hot and cold with fever, I should have given myself a rest until the poison had left my system, but I was angry with my husband, who was sitting in the air-conditioned comfort of his tractor listening to the horseraces, oblivious to my reaction, and so I kept on at my job, determined to show him how a person pulled their weight.

Leisha and Adam were still in Perth with their beautiful baby, and we all had Christmas together, Terry too. Robby stayed in Broome, which bothered me. I understood why he preferred to be away from us, but still it hurt me, not least because I realised that if I left Terry there would no longer be a barrier to seeing my son. It was in my hands.

In January and February, when the hay was done, we were preoccupied with cows having trouble calving. Calves were being born with some sort of deformity, their front quarters buckling under towards the body, leaving them unable to stand or suckle. Talking to other farmers, we discovered we were not alone with this problem. Presumably it was some sort of mineral deficiency. We dosed them with everything we could think of, and after a month or two most managed to gain sufficient strength to be able to stand and drink from their mothers.

That summer I was quite unwell with nausea and stomach pains. I was bleeding internally, and after many blood tests, bone scans, a colonoscopy and a trip to the operating theatre, they had come up with zilch. As a last resort, my breast cancer medication was changed. Within hours I was suffering an excruciating headache. The light was intolerable to my eyes, and the pain was so unbearable I could feel every follicle of hair prickling on my scalp. Even so, that afternoon I was at a heifer sale, right back in the thick of it again. It was totally self-destructive of me; but I told myself I had to pull my weight beside my husband. He wanted me with him at the cattle sale, so I would be there, even if it killed me. I knew Terry well enough to know that he hated being alone, so as his wife I felt it my responsibility to be by his side and help him if needed. I'd made my bed and I had to lie in it. In retrospect, it is clear that I had lost all confidence in myself and was no longer able to see things in perspective. I was losing my will to stand up for myself, it was easier to simply follow. I was following him in the fog.

On the other hand, I was getting really angry over the way Terry used my Landcruiser on the farm. The mats were full of cow shit, the car filthy inside and out. It wasn't as if there were no other vehicles available on the farm — there was an old Commodore and a Statesmen, both in excellent condition, yet he chose to drive my Landcruiser through the mud and slush around the farm. I hated the thought that he was running my vehicle into the ground for no good reason. He said he would pay the difference on my next trade-in on another Landcruiser, but I had no reason to believe that he would keep his word. He never had on such things before. It seemed he could always find money for racehorses and to gamble, but he could never play fair with his wife.

It was costing me money being married to Terry — and it seemed I was getting a lot less return than he was. I could not farm the Shiralee the way I wanted to because

I wasn't there. My own operation was going backwards while I helped my husband with his empire. He advised me to sell the Shiralee and buy a farm closer to Wildwood so that I could run my own cattle and not rely on someone else to do it for me, but I didn't want to sell the Shiralee. It was my sanctuary, a place to rest and heal when my marriage became too difficult for me to deal with.

Somewhere in the middle of February 2002 was such a time. After a day at the Wildwood farm, mentally and emotionally exhausted and pig-headedly working my guts out by my husband's side, I was suddenly tired of the anger that surrounded me. Terry's house on the farm was rented out so whenever we were at Wildwood, we would stay in Molly's house — it had always been that way. In anger one day he told me if I wanted a home of my own I would have to sell my farm and build one myself on his farm. *Not bloody likely*, I thought. Molly's house was solid brick and sturdy enough, but the inside had never had any work done on it. I tried to express to Terry my frustrations over living with perished curtains and water-rotted carpet, but that was useless and in the end I gave up.

I packed my suitcase, put the dogs in the Landcruiser, and three and a half hours later I arrived at the Shiralee. I went straight to bed and slept until ten the following morning when I woke to the little blue wren tapping on my bedroom windowsill. I felt calm and at peace. If only my life could always be as free of stress. Nothing I had ever done before made me feel so insecure and constantly uptight as my marriage did.

But on the morning of my third day back at the Shiralee Terry telephoned. He wanted me to come home to him and, just as I had done before, I left the same day and returned to Wildwood. I don't know why. I wasn't happy and it seemed as if I was being led. Terry needed a helping hand so I would oblige. When I was down and very low, it was just easier for me to follow. I never had the energy to argue or the will to stand up for myself. I couldn't see what was happening to me.

If part of me had believed in the bed of roses he promised, I had no excuses for my delusions! The following morning I was Terry's stockhand again, doing the dirty work of trucking new steers in to the dairy yards. The farmhand wouldn't have a bar of it. The Friesian and Hereford steers were as wild as chicken hawks, having had little handling — in the Kimberley I would have said they were feral. The cattle yard was made from weld mesh and left a lot to be desired, and the yard posts were not secure in the ground.

'Block them up, block them up,' roared Terry as the cattle pushed each other about the flimsy cattle yard. 'Get around the back, block 'em!' he yelled. I was already putting every ounce of effort into the job, bar running around on all fours and biting the cattle on the heels. It was obvious to me the cattle yard could not hold these big steers if they really wanted out, and want out they did. The Friesians took the lead of the mob and one attempted to jump over the yard but got caught on the top rail, then fell to freedom. Another, pushed by the mob of rallying cattle and full of fear in the confined space, jumped clean over the top of me and the yard, hitting the ground heavily, and escaped. By this time Terry had worked himself into an absolute rage and was screaming, 'Block the fucking things up!'

It was exactly the same story as before. I was in danger of getting my head kicked in by crazed beasts in their frenzy to escape, and Terry still couldn't see it. Several more jumped the yard before the weld mesh was pushed over and then the whole lot got out. It was far too dangerous and I got myself well and truly out of the way. I was livid. Weld mesh I considered suitable only for penning in chooks. It was so frustrating to suffer the consequences of bad decisions I had had no part in making.

The gut-churning experience of being leaped over by a bolting steer brought to mind a memory of a young Leisha on Kimberley Downs. She spent every free moment she could down at the stables with Lady and Little Blue, and was preparing their feed bins one day when she was disturbed by a frenzied barking coming from behind the workshop.

Spider the dog (who belonged to Craig, the husband of our new governess) had bailed up a cow by the overhead fuel tank. The poor animal was unable to escape, with Spider hanging off its nose one minute and swinging from its ears the next.

Feeling sorry for the cow, Leisha raced through the yard and grabbed the dog by one hind leg. But while she kept a firm grip on the dog, Spider kept a firm grip on the cow's nose. The three of them fought it out doing circles in the dust. My daughter's love for animals had put her all alone and in a rather tricky situation, since the cow was now furious as all hell. Spider, who was hanging from the nose of the cow, was off the ground at this point and suddenly let go, leaving Leisha to take the full fury of the berserk cow. It hit her with an almighty kick to the head and knocked her out cold.

When she came to, she was confronted by a close-up view of the cow's udders — the beast was standing over her. She panicked. The cow was shuddering with fury, snorting and blowing snot everywhere. Luckily Becky, our Thursday Islander cook, had heard the commotion from the kitchen and arrived at the scene in the nick of time. Thank God for her long legs: she raced in and pulled Leisha out from under the cow, literally threw her at the gate and simultaneously grabbed a lump of wood, belting the cow on the head with it. Then, before her luck changed, she joined Leisha on the gate. The cow attacked the gate, blowing and snorting, but Becky was able to help Leisha down on the other side, shocked but with no real damage suffered.

Towards the end of the calving season Terry suggested a week's break in Albany. I jumped at the idea, thinking it would do us both a lot of good and would give me a chance to check on the Shiralee. In fact my function was simply to be the driver to get us home safely from dinners with Terry's friends.

We didn't get to the Shiralee at all and it was not a pleasant trip. On a visit to the Mungrup horse stud, whose owners, Jan and Gray, are good friends of mine, I got to talking with Jan about the Kimberley as we usually do, and after a while Gray and Terry came in. Gray joined in the conversation too, until suddenly Terry began talking very loudly over the top of all of us, describing my father in quite horrible terms. Our conversation came to an end in an awkward silence and I sat in shock, ashamed that he had behaved so badly in the house of my friends.

With the benefit of time and distance and the wisdom of some expert counselling, I now know that the use of criticism and humiliation are part of an abuser's pattern, but I didn't understand that then. His behaviour was simply incomprehensible — that, or he was the one who was 'mad in the head'. Certainly he did not seem able to control his ranting, he was practically yelling over us.

I wish I could say things ended there, but some weeks later I returned with him to Broome where once again I sank into despair and ill-health.

Robby was working at the caravan park as a groundsman and he was still vulnerable to Terry's jibes and ridicule. This was the worst thing, what was being done to Robby; I tried but I couldn't stop it. Terry took no notice of me at all. For the sake of Robby alone, I should have left. He had the classic symptoms of depression, starting with not wanting to get out of bed.

Some days I, too, battled to get out of bed, but I felt I had to put on a good face, even though I had a constant headache and was feeling very unwell. I wanted to be strong for Robby, though he must have known that I was hanging on by a thread. It was too much of a burden for a young man who should just have been having fun with his mates.

In the end I went to my doctor, I felt so unwell. It turned out I had Ross River fever, which explained all the aches and pains. The virus is contracted from mosquitos, though, according to my doctor, stress and a hostile environment also play a large part in determining how badly a person will suffer from it. He asked me if there were problems at home. I was amazed. For the second time a doctor had picked it when I thought I wasn't giving anything away. This time I decided I would speak. He was calm and courteous, and treated me seriously. It was a relief to be able to talk my fears through, and he assured me that I certainly was not mad in the head and that I would probably find it helpful to talk some more. If so, he would be pleased to recommend a counsellor to me. He didn't urge me to leave Terry, as I thought he might. I think he realised that it was more than I could manage at that stage.

One evening, while giving my breasts a routine check in the shower, I found another small, pebble-like lump. I wasn't particularly worried, but I made an appointment to have it checked out. I was sent to have X-rays at Broome Hospital to make sure that the cancer was still in remission. I began to worry when they told me I needed to see my specialist in Perth for further tests. I thought, *Bloody hell, that's all I need in my life right now, the cancer back in my bones.*

It was a tense time down in the city, waiting for test results, but after four days I got the news I had been hoping for. Dr Ingram rang me to say I was free to go. He explained the tests had confirmed a benign cyst that was 'likely inspissated material within a duct.' Benign was the word I understood, and I was grinning from ear to ear.

For all the chances I gave him, Terry only got worse. At his request I organised a big party for his sixtieth birthday, and he ignored me all night until finally someone else asked me to dance. No sooner had I begun to relax in my partner's arms than out of the blue my husband appeared, trying to cut in. Yet after only a few minutes dancing, he led me off the dance floor and went back to his friends. I was just a possession to him. He was happy if other men admired me, but he didn't want them to touch.

Then in July, at the wedding of his cousin Alan on the lawns overlooking Cable Beach, Terry was knocking back shooters, wine and rum, his laughter getting louder and more raucous. He began openly flirting with a young married woman whose husband was also in the party.

As the evening began drifting out of hand I leaned towards him and whispered, 'Do you think we should go? Alan looks so tired.' Alan was a wonderful man, tragically battling a brain tumour, and he probably did not have very long to live.

Loudly and nastily, Terry answered, 'Urgers are worse than bludgers, urgers are worse than bludgers.' He repeated it again and again. I had to wonder if he had some sort of brain tumour himself, which might explain why he behaved so badly. There was such a hostile expression in his eyes, it was as if he really hated me.

Burning with humiliation, I sat for a little longer, trying to work out how best to deal with this. It was rare that he let this side out in public and I had no idea how much further he might go.

I leaned towards the wedded couple, wished them happiness and health and told them I was leaving. As I rose from my chair, I saw the flash of anger in my husband's eyes. 'Wait, I'll have one more drink,' he said. But I'd heard this too many times before. I said my goodbyes and suggested he stay if he wished.

Walking through the resort in the dark I suddenly felt sure someone was following me. I stopped for a moment. I knew he was behind me then because he stopped too. 'I know you're, there Terry,' I said.

'Urgers are worse than bludgers,' he started again.

When he came home, he got on his push bike and said, 'I'm going to check the park.' But he left the door wide open, something he never normally did, particularly at night. As he set off on his bike I pushed the door shut then returned to the pile of clothes I planned to iron.

I had my back to the door and didn't even hear it open, but I suddenly froze in fear as I realised I was not alone. There was a thump, thump, thump across the timber floor, and I didn't even have time to turn around before I was grabbed from behind. Struggling, I turned around to face my attacker. It was my husband.

'What are you doing?' I asked, almost laughing, thinking it was some kind of joke. But his hold on me tightened as he shoved me towards the glass coffee table. 'Let me go, what are you doing?' I cried. His face was set in a frozen, twisted smile and I was suddenly afraid for my life. Thoughts of my children finding their mother bleeding to death on the floor flooded me.

'Get off me, let me go!' I yelled at him, using every scrap of strength I had to get out of his grip.

'See how strong you are now,' he said, pushing me backwards across the coffee table. I landed smack up against the TV set. The more I fought, the more spaced out became the look in his eyes. I kicked him as hard as I could, but to no avail. I twisted and turned my body to break free, only to cop a hit across my shoulder and breast that almost floored me with pain. I screamed, but it was as though he had no off button, he had become another person. He pushed and shoved me across the floor. Then the most stupid thing blurted out of my mouth, but it definitely saved me. 'I'm calling the police.'

He immediately let go of me, put both hands in the air and said, 'I never touched you, I never touched you.'

When he let me go I was ready to run, but I stopped, unable to believe my ears. I looked down at myself. Red welts and bruises were already appearing on my arms. I stood and looked at him for a moment. 'You've done this before, haven't you?' I said. He knew what to do. It was as if he was remembering some lawyer's advice.

I moved further away from him. 'Yes, you've done it before.' He said nothing. I was free to go. I moved into the tiny spare room and locked the door, then the shaking and trembling started.

I got up early the next morning, my body stiff and bruised. Terry had disappeared and I took advantage of his absence to begin packing. I was going home to the Shiralee. I organised removalists to load my boxes on Friday and arranged for new tyres on the Landcruiser that day. Leisha and Robby dropped in as they did most days, took one look at me and demanded an explanation. Upset and angry, my girl demanded, 'Mum, how much more are you going to take? He has no respect for you — he couldn't marry you fast enough, and now he treats you like shit! You're just a possession to him, Mum, can't you see it?'

At that moment it seemed like she was the mother. I just looked at her dumbly, struggling not to cry.

'You've got to leave, Mum, you can't let him talk you out of it again. We're quitting! We're coming with you.' She was on fire. She and Adam were separated at this time, and he had gone back down south. They were handling things well though, and both managed to keep young Brock's welfare firmly in top priority.

They left the room when Terry arrived with an enormous bunch of flowers. Not that he thought he was in the wrong — there was no apology, there never had been — but he wanted me to stay. He had plans to meet a friend at the Fitzroy River rodeo and wanted to take the Landcruiser.

'Are you coming?' he asked in a rather subdued manner. 'No,' I muttered, mistrusting him, but trying to hide my feelings. I did not want him flying into another rage. He stood there looking so lost, I came close to feeling sorry for him — until I reminded myself of the look in his eyes the night before. 'No,' I said again, more strongly.

'A lot of your Aboriginal friends will be there,' he said, trying to persuade me.

'No,' I said again, thinking of Katie, Jeanie, Alma and the old elders. I could almost hear them saying, 'Him no good for you, *yumun*, him no good,' their pain for me showing in their eyes. I didn't want to see it; I was ashamed and embarrassed to be caught in this web.

I had been strong once, I reminded myself, watching my husband's temper rise again. How quickly the hang-dog look was replaced by a set jaw, unreadable eyes and clenched fists. I was terrified of him hitting me again.

The situation felt tense and volatile, and I returned to my little room to finish packing as he took himself off to the rodeo. Leisha came back with my Landcruiser fuelled and packed and Robby's farm bike and gear in our trailer.

Terry arrived back from the Fitzroy rodeo just as we were about to set off the next day. He looked pale, sick and sorry for himself, and I told him I wasn't leaving him for good, but that I needed time and space to think things through. I was feeling muddled and was frightened that the slightest little thing might cause Terry to grab me and nail me up against the cupboards again. I was fearful of his strength and wondered just how far he would go. Would he or could he kill me? I honestly thought he might. I was far from rational myself, but I was trying not to enrage him before we left. I had packed everything and I had no intentions of going back to him.

'Are you ready, Mum?' Leisha called out, worried that I might be talked into staying again.

'Yes, love, I'm coming now,' I said, then turned to my husband. 'Are you sure you want to be married to me? Because a lot of the time I don't think you are. We are not exactly on the bones of our arse, yet I have no privacy in my married life with you, and I live in a room here at the park and a room at your mum's house. Please think about this.'

I said goodbye and walked out the door. I was not a punching bag, I still had enough strength in me to realise that.

CHAPTER 9

Back to the Shiralee Again

*W*e reached Carnarvon that night and early the next morning we left Perth and just powered on through to the Shiralee.

Refuelling on our way through the city, I had expressed to Leisha how surprised I was that we were all so wide awake, considering the miles we'd covered. 'It feels like Daddy and Kelly are travelling with us,' I said, 'making sure we get home safely.'

A few days later I called my mother. Before I could give her my news she said she had something to tell me. She had had a dream three days earlier, in which a little blond-haired boy appeared saying, 'Tell Mum to go home.'

'Mum,' I said, 'I am home. I'm at the farm.' At first she hadn't been sure what to make of the dream, but I think we both understood now. Kelly had been looking out for me.

Looking back, the past seemed blissfully simple, and I often remembered funny old stories to cheer myself up and remind me of the way life — and I — used to be.

When we were living on Oobagooma station, a hundred and fifty kilometres north-west of Derby, I felt I was in the middle of a million acres of freedom. I never had a care in the world — well, I thought I hadn't.

I have a sharp memory of a cool Kimberley night in the stock camp when I really wanted to bathe and wash my clothes, but the spring near our camp had an icy edge to it. So I walked back to camp to collect my bath tub — a forty-four gallon drum cut in half. The quickest way to get it down to the spring was to roll it clean off the top of the bank. I did this, and the tub came to a halt right at the water's edge, just as I'd intended. This was my bathroom. I collected three good sized rocks, sat my tub on top of them, made sure it was balanced, then filled it three-quarters full with spring water. Once satisfied with the water level, I collected wood and piled it high around the sides and jammed what I could under the drum, then lit the fire. I climbed back up the river bank to my camp, grabbed my shampoo, towel and a clean change of clothes and returned with a keen sense of anticipation.

Tonight's bath was going to be the best — and, most importantly, warm! On my return, the fire had died down somewhat. I threw a few more logs on and decided I couldn't wait any longer. Stripping off my dust and sweat-covered clothes I sank into the warmth and luxury, adding shampoo to make a bubble bath. With my knees up around my chin and my hair lathered in shampoo, I gazed up at the clear night sky, alive with a hundred thousand twinkling stars. It was hard to imagine there could be a better bathtub on earth.

My paradise was short-lived, however. Soon my bath time was interrupted by the grunting, rooting and squeals of feral pigs moving up the spring in search of vegetation and roots to eat, or maybe just to check me out. In the golden glow of

My father, Mr Snow, keeping watch for crocodiles while the film crew were shooting a movie in Arnhem Land, 1967.

My mother, Mother Wallis, holding her darling grandson Kelly, 1980.

Old McCorry in deep thought, late 1980s.

Right: Kristy giving the orders from the bull buggy: she was good at that! 1989.

Bottom: Kimberley Downs station: the last muster, early 1990s.

Top: Old McCorry strapping a bull, late 1980s on Kimberley Downs.

Left: Leisha barrel racing on Little Blue, 1995.

Bottom: Oobagooma station in 1995.

Top: Leisha castrating young weaner bulls with the help of her father, Old McCorry, 1996.

Right: Leisha, Robby and I at the Sheraton in Perth for Christmas 1998.

Bottom: Old Bob McCorry and his girls: Leisha and I, 1998.

Top right: Leisha and I in 2002.

Left: Robby with a mudcrab he caught in Broome at his secret spot, 1999.

Kids on the job: I believe in educating them early in the cattle game! Here, they are along the banks of the Lennard River, Kimberley Downs, chasing bulls in 1988.

The new steel cattle yards we erected when we moved to the Shiralee, 1996.

The view from the Shiralee towards the Porongurups.

Summer at the Shiralee, 2001. The farm was my refuge from my marriage. (I haven't showed any photos of my ex here as I'm now in a happier place.)

Leisha and Brock in 2004.

I travelled all the way to Yiyili on Louisa to hand my dear friend Katie a copy of my book *Diamonds and Dust*, 2007.

Leisha in 2007 with another of her quarter horses, Mio. Without a horse Leisha is not complete.

The front entrance to the Shiralee, the place we all call home.

Dust rising in the background of a yard full of cattle, 2008.

Top: The Shiralee in its old world splendour, 2008.

Right: The beautiful view from the Shiralee, 2007.

Bottom: The back of the Shiralee homestead with flowers in blossom: little blue wrens' heaven.

Looking through the cattle yards at sundown: we were all buggered, but what a beautiful sight, 2009.

The Porongurups in all their glory look like a sleeping princess lying on her back, 2009.

Robby and Tara giving Michael a hand mustering his cattle in late 2008.

Leisha getting ready to saddle her quarter horse, Joe, early in 2008.

Another day, another muster: great fun and enjoyment for all, late 2008.

Right: My grandsons, young Brock (left) and Cohen (right). Cohen is still smiling, even after four hip operations.

Bottom: From left to right: Robby, his fiancée Tara holding Cohen, Leisha, Brock and her fiancé Nigel. This photo was taken after another day's work in the cattle yard in 2009.

From left to right: Robby and Tara, Michael D holding Brock, Cohen on my lap, and Leisha and her fiancé Nigel. This is our tight-knit family. The bunch of twigs is stronger than ever.

Me in the cattle yards among the beautiful Angus; I found them to be very placid compared to the cattle I was used to working with in the Kimberley.

Top left: Robby and me after a day's work in the yard: still smiling, 2009.

Top right: 'They're ready to go, Nan. Sell 'em,' says Brock in 2007.

Centre: Young Cohen, ready to go to work, 2008.

Right: Tara and Robby having a well-deserved break after handling cattle on the farm, 2009.

Robby in deep thought at break time, 2009.

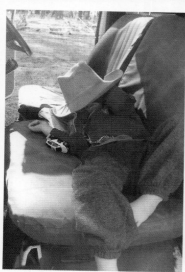

Cohen: Nan's off-sider is buggered and chucks in the towel, 2009.

Tara and Buddha: this shot was taken by Robby on the back lawn of the Shiralee in 2009.

Michael D in the cattle yards, he has a tonne of patience while working cattle, 2009.

My dear friend Michael D and myself on the back verandah, 2009.

the fire it looked like a large family, most of them covered in coarse black hair and some with white markings. There was one huge male with a broken tusk, probably the daddy of them all since he seemed to be pushing and shoving the others around. They advanced towards me, rooting and snorting, the piglets squealing as they flipped my clean clothes about before burying them in sand. I froze. I wanted to keep my dignity but I was terrified of what they might do next. I sank myself down into the tub of water as I wondered just how inquisitive they might be before moving on.

It eventually occurred to me that the pigs wouldn't get going before I boiled myself alive, so I swallowed my pride and called out to McCorry for help. This sent the invaders wild. All hell broke loose, and clothes, burning logs and coals were scattered in all directions. Wild boars and sows were fighting, piglets squealing and running amok, and my tub had become a carnival ride. Within no time they had uprooted everything and disappeared into the night.

McCorry eventually put his head over the bank. He had walked down from the stock camp where he had been repairing a saddle in the firelight. 'What's wrong?' he called. 'Nothing,' I answered, trying to keep some dignity. 'But come down to the spring, the wild pigs were rooting around.' I was still submerged in my tub.

'They're gone now, they won't be back,' McCorry said, as if wondering what all the fuss was about. He was rolling a cigarette. 'Find your clothes, I'll be here.' Grateful to have him close by, I flew out of the bathtub, dodging bits of burning wood and glowing coals to find my clothes. They were filthy, but I was grinning. This was a way of life for me and I never saw anything unusual about it, in fact I loved it.

When we arrived back at Oobagooma with the cattle, I left the stockmen to yard-up on the banks of the Robinson

River while I returned to the station homestead to let Silver the cook know we were back. 'Silver, we're home mate,' I sang out loudly, not wanting to spook him and set off a heart attack. There was no answer. 'Silver, Silver!' I yelled, walking from room to room, thinking, *You old bastard, what have you got up to now?*

I was starting to feel uneasy, and checked all the rooms again, just in case he was slumped in a corner and hidden in the shadows. Maybe he'd gone fishing down on the river . . . had a saltwater crocodile got him? I was still running around the homestead, calling out for him, when the stockmen and working dogs arrived back. I should have had the billy on; they were looking for a pannikin of tea. Then the sound of laughter and cattle dogs barking came from the new laundry thirty metres up the flat.

'Missus, come,' said one of the men. 'Come an' look at that old man Silver.' Well, at least it sounded like he was alive.

I followed the man up the path to the new laundry, which was now surrounded by the stockmen and their wives, laughing and ribbing each other. As I approached they moved aside to let me through. The laundry reeked of alcohol. Sporting indecent red jocks, Silver was out cold and badly sunburned — he was shedding skin like a lizard. The old bastard was surrounded by watermelons he'd obviously picked from my vegetable garden. He'd cut the tops off them, then fixed them back on with my meat skewers. There was what looked like a bung in the bottom of some of them and a straw poking out the side of one.

I sent the stockmen away and turned the hose on Silver until I had woken him up. He looked pretty sorry for himself, and I told him I hoped he'd suffer a headache for pinching my watermelons. I helped him to his room and left him to sleep off the grog, then turned my thoughts to dinner. I was the cook now until Silver recovered sufficiently to take over again. I stoked the wood stove on the verandah, then sliced up a huge rump, knocked the shoots off some old potatoes and put them in a pot with some onions and a dozen shrivelled carrots. I found a packet of dried green peas that would enhance the appearance of the dilapidated carrots and had just begun to grill the rump when the dogs started going berserk outside. As the barking closed in I could also make out the squeal and grunt of pigs.

Pigs again. I suddenly realised it must be mating season, that's why they were on the roam. All of a sudden a very large agitated black pig burst onto the verandah followed by seventeen barking dogs and a tangle of squealing boars, sows and piglets. They all met in an aggressive dance, ploughing right through the old homestead. With a firm grip on the sizzling pan of steaks, I clambered up onto a flour drum and balanced myself with the other foot on the wood stove as the dogs and feral pigs fought it out below. The noise in the corrugated-iron homestead was painful, but at least it caught the attention of the stockmen, who soon came roaring and hollering. They got the dogs penned up again while the feral pigs scattered into the scrub in the direction of the billabong. Calm settled back over the homestead and I was able to get on with cooking tea.

I didn't have the worry of feral pigs on the Shiralee and, for a while at least, I could leave behind the trauma of my marriage and work on regaining my strength in a place of beauty and contentment. On our return Richard moved back to his own farm. He'd done a good job. Paddocks looked lush and green with feed in abundance. The cattle looked good and the fences were up and tight.

It was time to buy steers for fattening again. It was so good to get back into what I loved doing. Cattle were plentiful at the saleyards, though in July the prices had jumped — good for the seller but not the buyer. Robby helped me with the cattle, moving them about the farm and keeping an eye on the fences. He was his old self back at the Shiralee, happy to step back out of his shell. By unspoken agreement, we never talked about Terry.

Once Leisha had seen me settled back home she sold her house in Albany. She and Adam were giving their relationship another go and they wanted to try Cairns. In part, Leisha needed some distance from me, since I could not promise her that I wouldn't get back with Terry and that really upset her.

She and Robby and I were sitting out on the back verandah when she told me this.

'Please, Mum, Robby and I can't handle watching him destroy you in front of our eyes,' she said. I could understand how they felt, and it made me feel terrible that I was hurting them so much, but I still couldn't see myself leaving my marriage. I'd worked everything out in my life up till this point, and I figured I could also work this out. I tried to tell them that.

'But Mum,' Leisha entreated, 'each time you go back to him it always ends with him drinking and getting into foul moods. How is that ever going to change?'

'I don't know, love, but each time he wants me back it's an opportunity for us to work things out. I've got to be able to meet him halfway.'

But even as I said that, I knew the chances of him meeting me halfway were slimmer than the Second Coming. I was caught between two hard places, and I felt my eyes brim with tears. Robby came over and gave me a hug. 'It's all right,

Mum, I'm staying here with you. But right now I'm going to check on the cattle in the back paddock, okay?'

When he was gone, Leisha asked me if I loved Terry.

'Love him?' I repeated. 'I don't think I know what love is any more.'

'Yes you do, Mum,' said my incredibly wise daughter. 'It's trust, togetherness, wanting to do and create things as a couple. It's not feeling like you're all alone in the world.'

She had hit the nail right on the head. I had never felt so alone in my life as I did with Terry. There was no trust or togetherness, and the very thought of these things made me realise that *was* what I wanted in my marriage. Was that asking too much?

Did I have a fear of being alone? Is that why I couldn't leave him? One thing I knew, I didn't want another divorce. I'm a woman who can work well on her own — most of my time managing cattle stations I was on my own — but all the time I was being the independent manager, I knew McCorry was there for me. I didn't want to be completely alone and I didn't want to be looking for another partner at this time in my life. If that sounds desperate, or pathetic, well I didn't have a lot of gumption left in me at this point. It seemed a long time since I'd been the strong and confident woman who could deal with just about anything life threw at her.

'Mum —' Leisha started, and then paused.

'What is it, love? You can say anything you want to me,' I replied. 'I am strong, you know.'

'That's just it,' she said. 'As soon as you're away from him, you're far happier and healthier than when you're with him. You really are better on your own.'

I didn't have any answer to that. I felt like I had become a downtrodden wife. I hardly felt like a grown-up woman any more.

'Mum, I know he *can* be a good person, but what's a man of his age doing hanging out in nightclubs when you're not around? Handing out money to girls to say he wasn't there?' This was something she'd witnessed herself in Broome.

'I know, I know. Everything you say is true. It's only . . .' But I couldn't finish. There was no argument I could make in his defence — nor in mine.

'It's your life, Mum. I know you'll make a decision when it feels right for you. Just be careful. Take care of yourself. We love you.'

How did my daughter get to be so wise and compassionate?

It was hard parting from Leisha, and I did a lot of soul searching when she was gone. I knew she was right, but I couldn't walk away. Maybe that meant there was something wrong with me, but I couldn't afford to think about that. Just the thought of going down that road made my brain feel like it was overheating. There were times when I truly did doubt my own sanity, though I've talked to enough people to know that this probably won't make sense to anyone who hasn't been through something similar. Old friends told me I was one of the sanest people they knew, yet still I doubted myself.

Certainly, when someone passed on to me the rumour they'd heard that I had attacked Terry before leaving Broome I had to laugh. I'd done no such thing. When I finally sought counselling I came to understand better the characteristics of an abusive personality. Shifting the blame is one characteristic, and Terry was projecting onto me the very things he did and could not acknowledge about himself. As for myself, I was a prime avoidance case. I did not want to seriously look at what I was doing — to myself or to my children.

It was during this period on the Shiralee that I first decided I was going to write. With Leisha gone, I realised how much I wanted to tell my story for my children — and to reconnect with the woman I knew I was deep down. The fact of my breast cancer spurred me to stick with it, even when I felt quite out of my depth. I rarely let myself consider that the cancer might kill me, but there was a little part of me that was looking ahead to a time when I would not be there for my children, and I wanted to leave something real of myself for them if it happened while they were still so young.

I had no thought whatsoever that what I was doing would ever become a book that strangers might read. I certainly didn't feel like a writer; once I began, it was more as if I was just writing a very long letter to my children. I wrote longhand in pencil, in exercise books. As I wrote, the whole process became cathartic — I would feel happiness, anger and sadness.

The writing comforted me. Going back over my past in the Northern Territory and the Kimberley helped ease the pain and turmoil I was feeling about my marriage. I'd start from the journals I kept during those years, until something would spark memories so real I could smell the dust in them. Like this one.

I could plainly see the dark clouds buffeted across the sky on the stormy afternoon I was working on a fence line on Kimberley Downs. My Aboriginal crew of Jackie, Yardie and Churchill were helping me construct a secure paddock to move the cattle into after they had been tested for TB. As the men pounded the metal star pickets into the hard dry earth and strained the barbed wire tight, I followed along tying the wire off on each picket. Leisha, who was ten, and young

Richard, Jackie's son, were with me, while Kristy and Robby were in the care of the govy back at the homestead. Our camp was by the windmill on police camp bore, two hundred metres from where we were fencing.

I had dinner cooking in the camp oven and sent the children to check that the coals were still warm, and if not, to shovel hot coals from the fire around the camp oven. Both Leisha and Richard understood cooking in the bush; they had grown up around it.

The sky was becoming darker, and the winds were picking up, whipping up the red dust into the air. Every now and then the wonderful aroma of the rain-wet pindan dirt was carried in on the breeze.

'Come on, let's finish before the storm gets here,' I called to the stockmen. I looked to the horizon, which was now black, and then noticed with horror that the windmill was turning. It had been tied off earlier in the day as the tank was full — there was a wire rope attached to the mill head, which was wound tight by means of a handle to stop the blades rotating. Somehow the handle had been released.

Running towards the camp, I never took my eyes off the huge blades — Leisha and Richard were each hanging onto a blade as they slowly rotated ten metres above the ground. My body was screaming in fear but I remained silent. With the stockmen hot on my heels, I lunged for the handle of the windmill and started turning it as fast as I could.

'Jackie, Yardie,' I called to the men. 'Climb up to the head and grab them two.' Inside I was praying, *Don't let them fall, Don't let them fall, please God, don't let anything happen to the children.*

As the mill came to a stop the storm was whipping up around us. Yardie grabbed Leisha as Jackie took a firm hold of his son, and they brought them both carefully down the metal steps of the huge Southern Cross windmill. 'For god's sake, what were you two doing up the mill?' I asked Leisha. I was upset that I hadn't seen the children climb the windmill in the first place and I was terrified of what might have happened.

'We were just having fun, swinging from the blades and they just took off,' answered Leisha.

'Did you release the blades?' I asked my girl.

'No Mum, honest, they just started going round in the wind.' These mills were over twenty years old.

'I believe you, but don't ever climb a windmill again unless I tell you to,' I said. Wind slashed at the tarpaulin shelter, ripping it to shreds as Leisha reached the ground. I scooped her up and put her securely in the vehicle. The men jumped in with Richard, and we were off back to the station. It would be safer there.

Life on the Shiralee kept me busy. I would not let myself fall down in a heap. In the evenings when I wasn't writing, I was reading, or dressing porcelain dolls in long tasselled gowns and old-world hats, pearls and feathers. I'd make and glue on the clothes as I sat there chuckling — I'd never thought myself capable of sitting still long enough for any form of craft work. More than that, I had spent half my life belting around a paddock covered in mud, and here I was dressing dainty dolls! But maybe there was a part of me that longed to be cosseted and cared for like a doll.

In the mornings I would ramble around the paddocks and walk through peaceful remnants of bush. There was still a lot of natural timber on the property. I was also planting native trees around the farm, and these attracted the birds.

Little by little the body pain I had suffered in Broome left me, and I found myself feeling ease and happiness again.

Did I really want this marriage? I questioned myself. I hadn't taken a single Panadol since leaving Broome.

It was wonderful to feel alive again, to want to work, to laugh and feel free of tension and stress. I am sure the writing played an important part in this. As did the cattle work. Robby and I were buying steers in small lots from the Mount Barker saleyard. We would get them home and process them through our new cattle yard, sometimes with the help of Richard O'Connor, but other times by ourselves. We worked well together, pushing our beautiful steers up into the forcing pen, from where they would move steadily along the cattle race into the crush. Here Robby would pull the lever of the head bail, which pinned the beast in a standing position so that we could administer minerals and supplements.

As Robby worked the head bail I would battle to ear-tag or dispense hormones. Since the breast surgery I'd lost a fair bit of strength in my upper right side, which made cattle tagging frustrating, although somehow we always managed to get the job done between us. The odd one would bellow and yank its head from side to side as I struggled to get a tag in its ear and for the next week I'd be covered in band-aids, looking like I'd just stepped off a battlefield.

The new cattle would have a night in the yard on water and hay to give them time to settle in their new surroundings, and in the morning we'd sit on the top rail of the yard to admire them and discuss the difference between our Kimberley cattle and these southern beasts. It was good for Robby to connect back to a time when he was just a boy and life was far less troublesome.

We had been back at the Shiralee for nearly three months when I rang Terry at the caravan park and discovered that he was in Perth. We'd only had occasional phone calls since my leaving, in the course of which Terry had continued to assure me that he did want to make a go of our marriage. Mind you, I had also heard from various folk at the caravan park that Lauren was back, haunting the house late into the night again.

I called him on his mobile and asked if he'd been planning on coming down to the farm. Silence. It appeared not, and I had a quiet giggle to myself. 'I'm here for the races,' he finally said, rather cautiously.

'With Lauren?' I questioned. Again, there was silence on the line. 'You're not fooling me, Terry,' I said. 'People have been ringing me from the park, telling me she's visiting you at night. So I suggest you don't waste my time or yours. I'm sick of the bullshit.' And I hung up, feeling very angry and disgusted about it all.

This had been such a revitalising time, why did I even ring him? I should have known it would be like waving a red rag at a bull. Perhaps that's what I wanted. He arrived early the next morning in a hire car.

We went to lunch in Albany, at a restaurant overlooking Princess Royal Harbour. The bay was like a huge pond, uncharacteristically smooth and glassy. Way in the distance the slowly rotating blades of the wind turbines made a picture of peaceful serenity. It felt like a good place to talk. Terry told me he loved me — and then confessed to having rekindled his affair with Lauren. Even though I had heard the rumour, his confession shocked me. It was the first time he'd told me the truth. And it was the first time he didn't ask me to return to Broome with him. Yet he still wanted me, he said. What he wanted me for, I wasn't sure. He didn't want to build a life with me, and he certainly didn't want me for sex — I had long ago in Broome found a leaflet for Viagra, which obviously was not for my benefit. I hadn't seen the old fella for years. *Well*, I thought, *watch out you don't bonk yourself to death, Terry*.

Old McCorry has been dead four years now, and how my life has changed from the Kimberley days. Despite this confession, despite my growing strength and wellbeing, when October came around and Terry came south again, I joined him at Wildwood farm. I don't quite know how to explain this, but I still felt that if only I worked hard enough at it, I could save my marriage. I wasn't yet prepared to accept that no matter how hard I worked I could not make a success of the decision I'd made — even if I had made it out of grief and loneliness and insecurity. I wasn't prepared to face my own failure.

CHAPTER 10

Hitting the Road

I spent Christmas 2002 in Broome with Robby and Terry. For all the grief Terry gave him, Robby had his mates and cousins up there. He loved the heat and sunshine and the atmosphere. I missed him. My children had been my closest confidants since my marriage. I had divulged too many problems and fears to Leisha and Robby — and worried that I had loaded them with too great a burden.

With Robby back at the caravan park Richard helped me run the Shiralee again. He would live there and I could come and go as I pleased, knowing my cattle and the farmhouse were safe in his hands. Terry didn't like this arrangement, but his opinion about how I managed my farm no longer mattered to me. My relationship with Richard was a purely working one, I could speak to him over the phone and he would organise the buying and selling of cattle for me.

Then Terry and I returned to the Wildwood farm to prepare for a trip to Tamworth in January with Terry's friends and fellow farmers Bert and Jan. It was a risky thing to go travelling with him — the close quarters and no escape was asking for trouble — but the country music festival really appealed to me, and Bert and Jan seemed to have a positive effect on Terry.

In many respects it was a good holiday. We even had some fun. There were no set plans and we were never sure where we would end up each night. We just travelled until we found a town where we could get a room, and often ended up absolutely bushed.

Tamworth was packed with cowboys and cowgirls looking for a country weekend. I enjoyed the music tremendously, but there was too much red wine and before long Terry was being hostile and crude again. But he kept his aggression carefully buttoned when our friends were in hearing range, and with them he was always charming and fun. Later, I realised what this meant — that he was, in fact, in perfect control of his behaviour. It wasn't that he lost control and didn't know what he was doing, as he often claimed; he was calculated enough to keep up the pretence in front of our travelling companions.

He was clever, too, with his refrain of 'Urgers are worse than bludgers', which he would slip into the conversation at unpredictable times. The others had no idea of the significance of this, but Terry knew the effect it had on me. It reminded me that he had assaulted me once and got away with it, and he would do it again if I wasn't careful. I was in the horrible position of being in the company of other people yet feeling terribly lonely and alone. I yearned for someone really strong and understanding to talk to. Yet the Landcruiser was mine; I was free to pick up the keys and drive away. But in fact I was not capable of doing that, just as I was not capable of confiding in Jan, who knew, I'm sure, that things were not great between Terry and me. I doubted myself and my confidence was low and I was afraid. There was a constant knot of anxiety in my belly. I was tiptoeing through a minefield, yet somehow it felt too hard to change things.

We met up with Kristy in Melbourne, and Bert and Jan flew home the next day. Then Terry and I headed north again, to visit Leisha in Cairns. Travelling up the Queensland coast we stopped at Maroochydore so Terry could visit a Big 4 caravan park. Tension had been building between us ever since Bert and Jan had left, and it reached boiling point that night when my husband referred to me as a 'dog' because I hadn't shown enough interest in the caravan park's clothes-line construction. His attitude changed in a split second. The terrible look in his eyes, the set jaw and aggression, frightened me and I suddenly felt sick, the pit of my stomach churning.

In Cairns I tried to hide my state of anxiety from Leisha, but I needn't have bothered.

'Mum, why are you still with him?' she asked. 'Can't you see what it's doing to you?' I couldn't answer. 'Mum, we love you very much,' she said. 'I hate the way he speaks to you and treats you. He has you in tears all the time. Please think about your health. You need someone who cares about your health, not someone who makes you feel worse.'

I couldn't say anything to that. She sat beside me and said, 'Look at me, Mum, you're the strong woman who told me never to allow a person to dominate me, physically abuse me, intimidate me, manipulate or humiliate me — can't you see he does all that to you and more.'

Leisha had bought a new bedroom suite and curtains especially for our arrival, but Terry wanted to stay in the old Tropicana Motel that was managed by his cousin John and wife Robin and he thought it would look bad if I didn't go with him. I saw Leisha every day, but we were torn apart by Terry's anger. In the end Leisha said, 'I'd rather you stayed at the motel with him than have him here and angry and you in tears. I can't handle that.'

From Cairns we travelled over grass-covered plains that reminded me of Fairfield station, my last cattle station in the Kimberley.

We travelled through Longreach and Boulia to Alice Springs, where I went looking in Aboriginal art galleries. I found a good piece for my wall, but at the same time I felt disturbed by an old Aboriginal man I saw sitting on the polished floorboards of a sterile room as he produced a dot painting: the lines on his face could tell a thousand tales but his eyes were distant. It felt wrong. How could this old man of the land draw inspiration within such sterile walls?

We left Alice Springs in the early morning, heading for Halls Creek in the Kimberley by way of the Tanami Desert and Wolf Creek crater. Coming through Ruby Plains station brought a flood of memories of Mick and Cherrie Quilty, both of whom were now deceased. Mick had been one of those hard-working outback characters who are a special part of the wild west. Mick was wild all right. One day Cherrie and I were making home-brew ginger beer in the kitchen at Ruby Plains when Mick arrived home from a day at the Halls Creek pub with a two metre python inside his shirt. He'd had a bit to drink and came through the door with a handful of snake while the rest of it was trying to wrap itself tightly around his girth.

He was doing his best to scare the living daylights out of me and Cherrie, and he was succeeding. When he tripped and lost the snake Cherrie grabbed her .410 snake gun. That was enough for Mick. One look at Cherrie with the gun in her hands and he found that snake pretty fast. He tied it up in a hessian bag, ready to release it out bush the next day. I went to bed and bolted my door for safety.

We arrived back in Broome in the middle of March 2003 to face the last of the sweltering heat and humidity. Giant thunder heads were hovering high over the horizon, building up the energy to give the red pindan and spinifex country of the Kimberley one last burst of rain. The corrugated-iron roofs and walls of Broome would be washed free of dust for the new tourist season. The giant green bullfrogs that kept us awake through the hot nights with their bellowing would vacate the toilet systems they blocked during the wet season and head for greener pastures. And out on the cattle stations people waited patiently for the wild and woolly knock–'em-down rains to come and flatten the useless spear grass so the stock camps could get out from the homesteads, cross the bugger-bugger plains and move into the magnificent valleys to begin the mustering season.

I was happy to be back in the Kimberley, and I also felt pleased to have done the trip, for all the unpleasant behaviour and nasty comments. There had been moments of behaving almost like a normal couple, and I held on to these memories rather than the unpleasant ones.

Robby was still working at the caravan park and being back near him made me very happy. I decided I would stay a while. Robby was flat out spraying weeds in a new section of the park, and then he and his cousin Michael, the son of my elder brother Bruce, started on repainting the bay numbers. I joined them; the numbers needed to be bright and clear for the tourist season.

Making a store run with the boys to restock the shelves of the park's shop, which had been near empty through most of the wet season, brought to mind a shopping trip I'd made from Oobagooma station. While McCorry and I were away mustering, visitors from Broome set up camp under a boab tree on the banks of the Robinson River, planning to spend a couple of weeks fishing for the plentiful barramundi. After drafting and trucking the last mob of cattle from the old wooden cattle yards, McCorry and I were heading for Derby on a mail and store run to replenish our supplies. The visitors from Broome — Mary and Tom and the Pom — called at the homestead asking if I would pick up some stores for them. Mary's order went like this:

1 bottle Brandy
1 bottle OP Rum
1 bottle Gin

'Any food?' I asked. 'Yes,' replied Mary, 'I'm coming to that.'

4 cartons Emu Export
1 column Log Cabin Tobacco

A column is ten tins. 'Is that it?' I asked.

'Yeah, that'd be about right,' said Mary.

'You don't want to order something to eat?' I asked, and she got me to add five pounds of spuds.

'And that should do it,' she said, and went off to collect her toiletries in order to use the station's shower. *Bloody hell*, I thought, *I hope they don't drink all this alcohol and fall into the crocodile-infested river*.

I was on the back verandah lighting up the wood stove when all of a sudden the Pom let out a blood-curdling scream. Then came Mary's voice. 'What's wrong with you, you bloody Pom, whinging about the water now, are you?'

'No,' was the Pom's reply. 'I was damned nearly electrocuted.'

Mary could hardly speak for laughter. Between gasps she wheezed out, 'Who would have bloody believed me if I told them a Pom had got electrocuted in the shower.'

In fact the Pom probably did get a shock and the cockatoos were to blame. They often chewed on the power line's insulation between the generator and the homestead; I had experienced the same shock myself.

The days were long at the park, and the humidity wasn't disappearing in a hurry. I was becoming very tired, which I assumed was because I was putting in a lot of effort oiling the office floors, painting location numbers and tripping into the bank, post office and the local supermarket, sometimes three times a day. Then one day I found another marble-like lump in my right breast. This was the third.

I went to my doctor, who promptly referred me to my Perth specialist again. I didn't need this, I thought, I was just too tired to go through it all again. But I pulled myself together and Robby accompanied me to Perth where I returned to my specialist for the necessary tests. I felt prepared for whatever lay ahead of me, though I really did believe I would be all right. My only worry was my children, but I told myself they were close enough to one another to draw strength from each other if it should prove the cancer had returned.

The next day I called my doctor for the results, to hear him say, 'Sheryl, I'm happy to say you're free to go home.' It was another benign cyst. I immediately called Leisha, then my mother to relay the good news, then phoned Terry in Broome. He was happy for me, though I think he was mainly glad there would be no demands on him for support. Back at the caravan park I learned how he gave everyone the impression that he worried terribly about me. I just wished he would show that concern to me sometimes!

The day before my fifty-fourth birthday on 13 June, I sat waiting for Terry in his Statesman outside the bank when

I saw Brian Singleton. I jumped out of the vehicle to greet him and was flabbergasted when he looked at me strangely and said, 'What are you doing here?'

'What do you mean?' I said. 'Why wouldn't I be here?'

Brian looked at me as if weighing up whether to speak, and then said, 'When I saw Terry the other night he told me you two were separated. I understood you were down south. But he said there was a chance you'd get back together.'

I laughed, if somewhat half-heartedly, and said flippantly, 'That would be Terry, keeping the back door open.'

Brian laughed too, then said, as he turned to leave, 'Don't let him affect your health, that's most important.' I told him I was okay.

I gazed towards the doors of the bank thinking, *I've been in some tough situations in my life but this marriage has to be one of the toughest*. At that moment Terry emerged and got into the car. I sat for a moment wondering what I wanted to say to him, then simply came out with, 'Why did you tell Brian Singleton we were separated? You might at least have told me.'

'No, it's not true,' he said, without much conviction, though he was looking rather grey. If he had a motto it would surely be 'Deny, deny, deny'.

'Well, I tell you what,' I said, 'I'll believe Brian Singleton QC before I'll believe you,' and left the conversation at that.

He was quiet for the rest of the day, and the following day went shopping and presented me with a pearl necklace for my birthday. I might have been glad to receive it under different circumstances.

CHAPTER 11

Bad to Worse

Kristy flew in from the city for a week with me in Broome. She had recently left Melbourne to return to Perth but still missed the Kimberley. She was twenty-five now and had found work on the outskirts of the city riding thoroughbred racehorses and was over the moon as Hide the Halo, a horse she rode track on regularly, had won three races in a row.

It was a relief that one of my girls was in good shape. Over in Cairns Leisha was having a tough time. She and Adam were not getting on well and on top of that she was stressed out with working, renovating and taking care of Brock. Around midnight one night she called me in deep distress from a park bench, crying as she battled to make the right decision for her son's future. To be so far away and unable to take care of her was more then I could bear, but I knew she needed me to be stronger than that.

Once I'd established that Brock was at home with his father, I said, 'Leisha, I will get off the phone, then you must call a cab and go home. I'll give you a few minutes, then I'll call you back.' I hurriedly made myself a cup of tea to help calm my nerves, then called Leisha again. By now she was in a cab and we talked about everything and nothing until the cab driver delivered her home, much calmer, and determined to think things over a little more. Adam was a decent man and they really loved and cared for each other, yet it seemed impossible for them to make it work.

Soon after that, in May 2003, I had what I thought were two minor skin cancers removed from my shoulders, but a few days later I received a call from my GP. 'Sheryl, we need to take more from your right shoulder, it's a little larger than I originally thought,' said Dr Edmond, not giving away too much on the phone. I readily agreed to go in to the medical centre as soon as possible — at least I didn't have to make a trip down to the city — but what he had discovered was a malignant growth, a melanoma.

My fair skin had taken a beating over the years in the outback. I'd always covered my face in sunscreen and now I wished I'd done the same for my shoulders and arms. And yet I had always gone out fully covered. When I was a child growing up in the Northern Territory, my mother always made me wear long-sleeved cotton shirts.

Dr Edmond was satisfied that he had removed all the cancer and there was no need for chemotherapy. I was shocked at first to find that I had cancer again, but at least it wasn't breast cancer. But it was the fourth time I had faced the possibility of cancer, and the second time I had faced cancer itself. I promised myself and my children never to become blasé about it and to keep my cancer checks up-to-date.

I then flew to Cairns. Leisha and Adam were by now living separately, on amicable terms thankfully; both were mature enough to make their young son their main concern. Leisha had no particular plans, except a vague yearning to study, perhaps psychology, when she and Brock were settled. For now, she would come back to Broome with me. Adam was assured that he wasn't losing his son, and I drove back west with Leisha and two-year-old Brock.

We had not been back long when one evening Terry came home after several hours at the local tavern. He was going into the office to deal with customers, which I thought was a bad idea, since he smelled strongly of alcohol. I made the mistake of saying so, and in a moment he had me slammed up against a wall cabinet. Then straightaway he was holding both arms out on either side of his body saying, 'I didn't touch you.' I willed myself not to crumple. 'Just get away,' I demanded, and tried to push him off me, but he fastened a vicelike grip on my right arm, while threatening me with his clenched right fist.

'You're kinked in the head,' he said, over and over, shaking his fist in my face.

We were doing this crazy shuffle around the dining room when I heard the back door open. Terry instantly released his grip and stepped away from me. It was Leisha. With a look of horror, she stood for a moment surveying the situation. 'What's happening here?' she demanded. 'What was all the commotion about? I could hear it outside.'

Terry spun around and rapidly left. 'Did he touch you?' she asked me, leading me towards the bedroom. 'Mum, you really have to get some help or you're never going to get out of this.'

I was shaken, more scared than I'd ever been. If she hadn't walked in at that moment, I don't know what he would have done to me. The next morning I gave in to Leisha's concern and visited my doctor in Broome. I talked openly to him and, like the other doctors, he assured me I was far from insane. But he thought I should leave Terry. 'For your own sake, you need to get away from this situation, otherwise your health will go downhill fast,' he said. He gave me the card of a counsellor he recommended. I slipped it in my purse, thinking I would call the number when I got home.

But I did not call the counsellor, and I did not leave. Over the months of writing this book and reading old diaries I have sat at my writing table and shaken with anger at myself for staying. When I finally did seek counselling I began to understand why, when I was in the middle of the abuse, I was unable to take care of myself — or my children — and seek help at that time.

There were many reasons. First, there was the simple fact that when I first knew Terry he was a fun, bubbly, happy man who loved my company, and I was still waiting for that man to return. I thought that was the real Terry, and I did everything I could to relieve his stresses and pressures so that the real, relaxed man I met could emerge again.

But it seems there might also have been a part of me that believed I deserved all the punishment I received. When the counsellor first suggested this, I laughed, it sounded so completely ridiculous to me. It still sounds ridiculous. But for all my wonderful uncomplicated, outback childhood — where my brothers and I were nature's children, free to roam where we pleased — I grew up to make three very difficult marriages (not to mention the dramas with Heath). But if I'm honest with myself, I have to admit that every step of the way since Kelly died has been a battle. I think I felt responsible for the loss of our son. I have blurred memories of McCorry, in the long dark days that followed Kelly's death, asleep at the dining table, his head resting on his arms, gazing intently into the dry distant paddock accompanied by only the deep dark silence that he used to shield himself with. He wouldn't talk to me. When he did, his answers were short and sharp and full of anger. Because of his anger I always thought it was my fault. I now realise he dealt with our son's death in a very destructive way and that I dealt with it differently, but in an equally destructive way, by putting on a brave face. Though I truly loved old McCorry and know he loved me back, he had a very dark streak, and after we lost Kelly he retreated into a terrible sadness that, fuelled by alcohol, became bitterness. Although McCorry's anger was primarily turned on himself, anyone in range was going to cop it, and ultimately that was the reason we had to separate. He wouldn't come back from that dark place to be with me and the children. And that upset me more than I let on at the time. I didn't say it, because there was no getting through to him, but if he had let us try to work it out together, I feel sure we would have come out the other side stronger and happier.

But he wouldn't, or couldn't, and in our own ways we somehow survived, if separately. And even McCorry's resentment of my successes never stopped me from functioning well in my work and as a mother. But with Terry, it was as if I became a completely different person. What I *could* manage, in all but the worst of times, was to put a bright face on for the world, my polished shell, and *appear* to function well. I suppose from the start I'd done this for the children, to protect them from McCorry in his depression. But McCorry at his worst was an angel compared to the way Terry tried to destroy the spirit of my son.

I can never forgive myself for keeping Robby under his stepfather's roof. A person who dominates and ridicules a younger person until their spirit is broken is about as low as you can get. I tried but I could not protect my boy from my husband's scornful and humiliating games. I should have left and never come back. And I did not.

Now all that is finally behind me, and counselling is giving me a way to understand what happened, I can see the tactics that are used by abusers in order to dominate others — in some animal species as well as by certain human beings. And I realised I had observed all this long ago in a contract horse breaker when I managed Kimberley Downs.

Roy was a lean six foot two and covered in freckles and an assortment of skin cancers. A shock of red hair jutted from under the brim of his dusty Akubra — and he had a temper to match!

Roy had finished handling the station colts in the round yard — reining and breaking them in — and was shoeing in the open lean-to off the adjoining shed. Now that he was done with the round yard, Leisha and Kristy had taken it over to handle their foals. The children always broke in and handled their own horses. Little Robby was sitting on the top rail of the yard, giving the girls his two bob's worth.

Then I heard Robby calling. 'Mum! Mum, the girls want you! Now, Mum!' I hurried to the horse yards. 'What's wrong?' I asked, and all three answered with their eyes, glaring at the horse breaker. As I turned and followed their gaze I saw Grey Boy shivering and shaking in a lather of sweat. The gelding was cut and bleeding up the flank, across the hindquarter, from under the belly to across the neck, and it copped another blow with the rasp while I was standing there. 'Stop it!' I screamed. I was shocked and furious; this was the first case of horse bashing I'd ever seen, anywhere.

'This horse needs a bullet,' Roy muttered. 'So do you, mate,' I said. It seemed he'd been trimming feet and shoeing horses all afternoon with no incident, but for some reason he and the grey fell out. Maybe the horse kicked out once too often, but that was no excuse for what he did, no excuse at all.

I told Roy to forget the shoeing and release the gelding; he was on a one-way ticket off Kimberley Downs. I paid him out and watched as he rolled his swag and headed for the road.

Meanwhile the girls led Grey Boy away to wash him down. Robby fetched the vet box from the homestead, and between the three of them they doctored his cuts and wounds with purple paint. A week later the children and I watched him limping around the airstrip paddock. Most of his wounds had scabbed and he was showing excellent signs of recovery.

There was another incident of wanton violence against animals on Napier Downs station some years before that, this one fuelled by arrogance, I thought.

Maria, a young friend from a neighbouring cattle station, had just suffered a very sad loss and was spending a few days with me. We were taking it easy and had just settled on the front verandah with our pannikins of tea when an ear-splitting explosion echoed down the range, destroying the peace and tranquillity. The blast hit us like a whack in the chest, it was so close to the homestead.

I checked on baby Kelly who had begun to murmur in his cot. Another blast rang out, even louder. I was pretty sure someone was close by, shooting a high-powered firearm. Wondering who it could possibly be, and where they were shooting from, I nervously checked the front and side verandahs for bullet holes. I pictured an unstable gunman who might nail any one of us.

Unable to work out the direction the shots were coming from, I crept back to Maria and said, 'Crouch down and let's get the hell out of here.' I figured we could make a run from the homestead to the shelter of a large water tank, then to the old men's quarters, and from there make a dash for a cave a little way up the hillside behind the homestead — the same cave where our pet dingo used to camp. I wrapped Kelly in a light blanket from his cot and we moved silently towards the back door. We were just at the door when it burst open, nearly hitting us. We both screamed, but it was only Jeffery, my head stockman. 'Missus missus,' he called out, trying to calm me down.

'My god, Jeffery, what's going on?' I asked him.

'You all right?' he said.

'Yes, we're fine. What about the camp people, are they all right?'

He nodded his head.

Now Charlie arrived from the camp and came and stood beside Jeffery.

'Missus,' Jeffery said, 'Charlie and I, we track 'im.' I was worried for their safety but they were good trackers and smart men.

'Be careful then, this person has a very powerful gun,' I said. 'And if you find him, tell him I want to speak to him, or else it will be a police matter.' Maria, Kelly and I would join the other stockmen and their wives in their camp until they returned.

We waited at the camp for an hour and there were no more shots, and no sign of Charlie and Jeffery, so I decided to go back to the homestead. Another hour and a half later I picked up the sound of the bull buggy coming down the corrugated track. Running out to greet the men, I was pleased to see they were unharmed, but taken aback by Jeffery's sombre mood.

'What's wrong?' I asked.

'That fella shot your pet donkey, missus, in the front gateway, butchered and taken her hindquarters off,' Jeffery said. 'And that good pack mule too.' The pack mule wasn't quite dead when they got there and blood was still pumping like a fountain from its side.

The stockmen had tracked the vehicle up the dusty Gibb River Road and into Mount Hart country, through scrub and gullies until they came face to face with the vehicle's occupant. The driver was a young Aboriginal fellow from Derby.

The driver flew out of his vehicle and abused Jeffery and Charlie for tracking him up. And when they delivered my message that I wanted to see him, he said he would get into me as well. He reckoned he was doing me a favour, shooting vermin on my property. I thanked the men; they had been very brave, they did not have to be so protective of me and mine, and I was very grateful.

Well, I waited and waited. I was sure he would come. An hour later he pulled in with his 4WD tray-back. He was a big fellow, and seeing he'd had such a lot to say to my fellows, this time I decided I would have my say first.

There were four steps up to the back verandah and I stood in the middle of the top step. He had to stay at the bottom.

I said, 'Before you open your mouth and say one word to me, you produce your permit or written permission to shoot vermin on this station.' There was none of course. If there had been, it would have been me who had signed it.

He opened his mouth to speak but I held up a hand and went on, 'You shot my pet donkey and our pack mule, for god's sake.'

He said, 'Do you want them?'

I glanced towards the slaughtered hindquarters protruding from the open tray of his 4WD, then swung back to face him. 'You must be bloody joking, do you think I'd feed my dogs my pet donkey?'

He had nothing more to say, only hung his head. I was finished. The pack mule and my jenny donkey were dead, and nothing was going to change that. 'Get in that bloody car and get the hell out of here and don't ever come back again, because next time it will be in the hands of the police.'

This reminded me how strong I once was. How I never used to put up with rubbish from people.

With only a few days notice, Leisha and young Brock left Broome for Terry's Wildwood farm. Terry's son Ken had gone down there to pick up some equipment and had found the house in a terrible mess. There was a mouse plague out of control — the place needed to be occupied. Leisha was still suffering the turmoil of leaving Adam, and it was hard for her to remain in Broome and watch me battle mine, so she volunteered to go down to Wildwood to clean up.

Leisha called me at the park to say the kitchen was a total mess. The mice had had a field day in the pantry, and that was the least of it. A branch had fallen on the roof and blocked the gutters, sending the water into the house, damaging walls and carpets, flooding rooms and passageways. The house was still full of Molly's possessions. Even though she had asked me to dispose of her personal contents for her, I'd not been able to bring myself to do so. She was in everything, and the house could never feel like mine. Terry and I might live there when we were working on the farm, but it would never be our home. Terry refused to buy new curtains or carpets or furniture. His racehorses were a far higher priority.

A few months later, Leisha was travelling with Brock from the Wildwood farm to Perth to meet Adam so they could all spend a week together on the farm. But on the trip to Perth something strange happened. Leisha began to suffer blinding head pain so unbearable that she became disorientated and ended up off the track near the small fruit-growing town of Donnybrook. Pulling the car off the road she called me in tears. 'Mum, I think I'm lost,' she cried. I told her just to talk to me. Firstly I wanted to know whether

Brock was all right. Leisha assured me he was sleeping in his car seat. She told me the headache was so severe she worried about being able to take care of him. 'Please Mum, what should I do?' she cried. I suggested she get back in her car and keep driving until she found a motel to spend the night. I would call her every half-hour until she settled or found some relief from the pain.

I paced about restlessly, worried that she might have a brain tumour. Eventually she settled for the night and I promised to call her first thing the following morning.

The next morning she rang before me, in tears again, to tell me about the terrible dream she had woken from. 'Mum, don't think I'm mad, but I need to tell someone. The dream was vivid, it all seemed so real, I still don't know what's happening.' She was calling me from Williams. After feeding and bathing Brock, she had driven, dazed and muddled, in the wrong direction, towards Nannup. Realising her mistake she had turned back towards Williams.

'It was a terrible, terrible dream, Mum,' she said. 'There were two little children. I could see their faces under murky water, they were side by side. I saw them so clearly I could draw them.' She sobbed while describing the children's faces, their hair colour.

'Mum, I feel they want me to find them, it's terrible, what do I do?' she said. 'I know it sounds stupid, I know it was a dream, but I feel I can drive right to the place they are. It was so real.'

Worried for Leisha's vulnerable state, I said, 'Love, are they under the murky water?'

'Yes!' she cried.

By now I felt like a cot case myself. 'Leisha, if they're under the water I feel sure they have passed,' I said, trying to comfort her. 'There is nothing you can do now.' I don't know why I said that, but I was worried my daughter would go on a wild-goose chase on the strength of her dream.

After a while she had got her heavy feelings about the dream off her chest and she continued on her journey to Perth. The headache was over too. I watched the news across all the television channels for the rest of the day and was relieved that there were no stories of children drowning.

Then in the evening of the next day, 4 October 2003, there was a news flash: 'Two young children drowned as their parents tried to cross a flooded river in the Nannup region.' The photo of the two children that appeared on the screen exactly fitted the description Leisha had given. I called her up and told her that, and she responded very calmly, 'I know, Mum, the dream was so clear.' It was a deep knowing she had, I have no doubt at all.

Later that month Terry and I drove down to Wildwood. After a year of constant arguing I hoped to find some relief with just the two of us together on the farm. Leisha planned to return to Cairns with Brock to finish work on the duplex she had been renovating. I really wanted this time to put some serious effort into cleaning out Molly's things. My own farm I had put on hold indefinitely; one day I would go back there, but not yet. I knew it was in good hands. I had called Richard before I left Broome and asked him to do another draft of the larger steers and deliver them to market for me. I wanted to restock with lighter weight steers and try to make a dollar out of their weight gain. It was always a relief to know I did not have to worry about the Shiralee. The pastures were thriving. It was that time of the year when the grasses were strong.

Robby remained in Broome and worked at the caravan park. My one bit of good news was that a young woman named Tara, who was newly arrived in Broome, had become a friend. The two of them looked set to team up and that seemed like a very good thing to me. Tara was eighteen and worked on a pearling boat as a cook's offsider, which could be a pretty tough job. She had a quiet strength about her, and a strong determination — something Robby needed around him at this time in his life. Simply knowing the two of them were there for each other relieved me immensely.

While we were down south I had my annual breast cancer check-up with Dr Ingram at the Mount Hospital. The test results were all negative, so I could breathe a sigh of relief for another year.

From Wildwood I visited a psychic again, a mother and housewife who worked from a bookshop in the small seaside town of Dunsborough. Her hair was a mass of unruly curls that stuck to her face with perspiration and she wore a free-flowing smock. She asked me if I had a particular question. I said, 'I'm only looking for reassurance on what my gut tells me.' I didn't want to give anything about myself away. She dealt out some cards and began to read them. 'Your husband's life is based on money,' she said. 'He has deceived you and been unfaithful.'

In my bones I already knew this. But then she did surprise me, as she told me I would write a book that would be a bestseller. Reading my final card she said, 'You're a good businesswoman.' I thought if I really had any business sense I'd be on the Shiralee and working it myself, not sitting here. I left the card reader with mixed feelings, but most of all pleased that the death card hadn't come up. From there, surely life could only get better.

Driving back to Wildwood with Terry I could not bring myself to look at him or speak to him. Then out of the blue I blurted out, 'I know you're seeing someone else again.' For a moment I thought he would stop breathing and we would crash. He denied it of course, but blind Freddy would have known he was lying. The only time I had ever seen anyone go this colour was old McCorry on his deathbed.

We were to return to Broome for a fortnight to relieve Terry's nephew Jeff, and a few weeks before that I picked up the phone; it was Terry, ringing from somewhere on the farm. He said, 'Your return air ticket to Broome is nine hundred dollars.'

What was he saying? Did he want me to pay for it? Or did he want me to refuse? 'Are you telling me I have to pay for it?' I asked. There was silence on the other end of the line. 'Forget it,' I said, and slammed the phone down.

I had four hundred and fifty dollars a week housekeeping, with which I had to pay the Wildwood phone account, lawn mowing, stores, my Landcruiser services and registration, any repairs around the house, and anything else that cropped up, including my visits to the doctor.

I believe now he wanted me to leave him, that he was provoking me, for all that he always said he wanted me back. And wasn't I the same? I wanted to leave him but I couldn't go. In the end he paid my airfare and we flew to Broome for five days, leaving the Landcruiser at the airport.

Oh, the saga of the Landcruiser! In February 2004 I was ready to trade in my current model with the intention of getting a smaller vehicle with better fuel economy, but Terry, who is a big man, wanted me to replace it with the same model. He insisted he would take care of the changeover cost — nearly $33,000 — in payment for his company's constant use of it over the last five years.

As we left for the car yard to collect the new vehicle I said, 'You do have your chequebook with you?' He nodded and I chided myself silently for having doubted him. But as we got out of the car and the salesman approached, Terry turned away saying, 'I just have to grab a few things in town.' And he boldly walked away, leaving me holding the proverbial baby. I entered the sales office and wrote out a cheque for the new vehicle. Not a week later, Terry flew to Perth to buy another horse at the thoroughbred sales. He was very consistent about money, and I knew I'd never see any reimbursement — and of course my new Landcruiser was used daily in the caravan park. I could have stood up for myself, I could have insisted the Landcruiser be only for my own personal use, but I didn't. I can blame Terry for lots of things, but I can't blame him for my own inaction.

CHAPTER 12

The Wind Beneath my Wings

I found relief from my poky existence at the caravan park in writing about my life in the outback. I used the tiny spare room, sitting on the bed with my back to the window to take advantage of the natural light that filtered through. Sometimes the writing just flew. I'd be telling a story and I'd feel I couldn't write fast enough to capture the words.

Reliving my past was mostly a good thing to do; sometimes, though, it only served to make my current life feel painfully lacking by comparison. And Terry, it seemed, felt particularly threatened by this past, for he hated my taking myself off to write. When I retreated to my room he'd find any number of reasons to call on me, and when I emerged he would make comments like, 'What, airing the dirty linen?' Or he'd tell me I was wasting my time. 'Who do you think would be interested in your story?' he said one day with a sneer. But, in fact, people were interested in what I had to say, and he knew it.

If we were out to dinner with friends of Terry's, or visitors to the park, once they knew of my life in the Kimberley, they would be full of questions. We would be talking away, but within minutes Terry would change the subject, talking loudly over the top of me. I would stop talking and raise my eyebrows at the person I'd been talking to, as a signal to them not to push it.

When we were among his friends, he didn't like to share the stage with me. That hurt, because it meant he had no desire for me to connect with people. He didn't like people engaging with me. It always had to be about him.

But I kept writing; if I had little else at that time, I had persistence and determination, because at least I kept on writing.

I have always been determined, and before I met Terry I never shrank from what had to be done. I remember when I was managing Kimberley Downs and we were in need of a killer, which is when you shoot, butcher and bone out one of your own beasts (or one of your neighbour's, if you think you can get away with it) for the station's meat supply. It was 1988 and my time on Kimberley Downs was nearly at an end. The tuberculosis eradication program was almost completed and we had reached the point of shooting any potentially infected strays we had missed along the river. The cattle stations on the program were paid by the government for any cattle shot, though it still seemed an enormous waste of beef to me. I'd eaten the same beef all my life, and I believed if we cooked it well, we were safe from TB. That's the way people had managed in the outback for years.

Determined to take some of this beef for the station, I arranged with the chopper pilots and shooters to run the strays out onto a claypan flat to shoot them. Then they were to put the chopper down and help with bleeding the beasts for me. With no men about the station — they were contract fencing on Noonkanbah station — I talked Narda the cook and Leisha into coming along and giving me a hand.

Grabbing the cookhouse butcher's knives and steel, we left the homestead chasing the choppers, now minute specks buzzing in the brilliant blue sky.

As the choppers spotted a beast they would gradually work it around and deliver it as close as they could to where we were waiting on the claypan, and then drop it with a bullet. Whoever was closest to the dropped beast would slit its throat and bleed it. If this procedure was not carried out, the meat would become dark with saturated blood. Leisha and Narda covered the tray-back of the Toyota with gum and bauhinia branches, making a bed for the fresh beef to lie on, and with the afternoon sun pounding down on us and the choppers smothering everything in fine yellow claypan dust, we worked furiously to butcher the animals and get the meat to the station's coolroom fast.

We had several beasts on the ground at once and at first we battled to butcher out one animal each. Our knives became blunt from the tough cattle hide and needed constant sharpening. Leisha was running from Narda to myself, helping to lift the heavy and bloody hindquarters as we removed them. We soon decided we would be more efficient working together.

It was heavy work and tough going in among the prickly spinifex, yet in four hours we had taken off twenty-eight hindquarters between us and slung them up onto the back of the Toyota. Our backs were buggered from bending over, and hungry flies feasted on our blood and perspiration-soaked bodies. We were all three of us covered in blood from head to toe; we looked as though we'd been involved in some terrible massacre. We covered the beef with more branches to help protect it from the dust and flies, and as the afternoon sun sank towards the west I headed for the homestead with our payload of beef. More than pleased with our haul I said to

Leisha, 'This will keep us going for weeks; it saves us going out and hunting down a killer.' The enormous effort was well worth it, because it ran rings around the old salted beef we'd been eating.

I sometimes wonder whether determination is genetic, because Leisha certainly has it in bucketloads. It was this determination that made her want to work on her relationship with Adam, to be a family for little Brock, and I was so pleased when she announced the two of them were not only back together, but were planning to get married in August.

'It's not going to be a big deal, Mum,' Leisha said. 'I don't want an expensive bash. We just want to do it here in Cairns, quietly.'

Hell, I thought, *she's my only daughter and she wants a three minute wedding*. However, thinking back to my own marriage to her father, that was exactly what we did. A three minute ceremony in the Derby registry office. When it came down to it, I didn't really care how they married. What was important was that they seemed happy to be together again, and feeling so positive about the future, and little Brock was the happiest of all.

I felt I could put up with just about anything knowing Leisha and Adam and Brock were all together again, but that feeling didn't last long. Just two weeks later Leisha telephoned me from Cairns. 'Now stay calm, Mum, and don't panic,' she said, and straightaway I felt my heart sink. She explained that the doctor suspected she had cancer of the uterus. She was booked in for an ultrasound and a CAT scan the following day. 'I honestly don't think I have cancer,' my girl told me rather seriously. 'We'll just have to wait for the test results and go from there, Mum,' she said. And that's what we did, and sure enough, a few days later Leisha was proved right. She was given an all-clear and I was able to breathe a sigh of relief again. But I was left with a terrible fear that cancer was somehow stalking my family, and wondered where it would raise its ugly head next.

Health wasn't off my agenda either. Since being back in Broome, I'd fallen into the grip of another bout of Ross River fever. I had never felt so unwell, with constant fever and an aching body; all I wanted was to curl up in a ball and sleep the pain away. Once you have it, you are always liable to recurring episodes. And, as my doctor explained again, I was especially vulnerable because I was living under the stress of a difficult marriage. 'To a bully,' were his words. He advised me to 'stop putting a band-aid over the problem'.

It was up to me to leave, is what he meant, but I felt like I was under a heavy weight that held my limbs down and made it impossible for me to speak out for myself. Like those dreams where you need to scream to save yourself but you can't. You're scared to death and you open your mouth wide but no sound comes out. It was as if my health and marriage problems were slowly burying me and I didn't really care. It became easier not to care. And yet not once, even in my darkest days, did I consider suicide. I would not take that way out. I would not do that to my children.

My husband's behaviour became so bizarre, I didn't want to speak of it to anyone. If ever I crossed him, no matter how inadvertently, he'd respond full of hostility with his mantra, 'You're mad in the head.' Once he invited guests for tea; he cooked and served them all but there was none for me. I was fading into the background; it was like something out of a dark fairy tale.

Then writing in my bedroom one day, I discovered I was being cast as the scapegoat in some drama between Terry and his sister-in-law Jean, his partner in the caravan park. Terry had had an architect draw up plans for a new reception area and shop, topped with a flat for each family above. I had suggested he discuss this new project with Jean but he didn't think it was necessary. Now all hell was breaking loose in the dining room. Terry had come out of the office to find Jean with the building plans spread out across the tables and demanding to know why she had not been notified. I didn't blame her. I would have felt the same way. Only I was shocked to hear Terry tell her that I was the one who should have passed the information on! I considered going out and setting the record straight, but the heat of the exchange made me think better of it. I was too weary of conflict to go looking for it. In the end, the project was put on hold anyway.

I think Jean knew enough about Terry to realise I wasn't the one responsible for her being kept in the dark over his plans. It wasn't long after this that she came to me with a problem that was causing concern in the park office. Apparently Terry, who was well into his sixties now, was playing flirtatious games with an eighteen-year-old staff member. 'This can't be tolerated,' Jean said. 'It doesn't look good.' Of course it didn't look good. She wanted me to speak to him; she was as wary of his temper as I was. I agreed, though I doubted I would achieve anything.

I never saw it coming. I had barely got the words out when he charged at me with the full force of his body, sending me flying across the office floor to crash against the old blue lounge. I opened my eyes to find my husband standing right over me, sneering down at me that there would be no marks this time. He had no remorse at all.

When he stood there above me like that, I wish I could describe the place it put me. I was nothing, not a woman, not a person any more. The effect was to annihilate me. I was nothing and had nothing. And I truly feared that one day he would lose that last scrap of control and seriously hurt me.

Or push me over the edge so I really would be the mad woman he kept telling me I was.

I knew I wasn't mad, yet I feared I so easily could be, and the fear was stronger than the knowledge. Rationally I knew I was perfectly sane, but there was a part of me that wasn't rational, like the part that dreams and has nightmares — and I was living in a nightmare. That part of me wasn't so sure. That part of me was terrified. Terrified of Terry, and terrified of managing on my own.

And maybe I had always been afraid to be alone. Terry gave me nothing, no sense of security or worth, no sense that he even liked me. And yet I stayed. Why? Why wasn't I walking away as Leisha kept begging me to? There weren't any answers to these questions, just a hot whirling confusion. I'd see his face, with those mad eyes staring at me full of hatred, and as if I were a kangaroo staring into the headlights of an oncoming car, I could only stand there and wait for the impact.

Why wasn't I able to stand alone? I was renowned for my strength, but where was it? Had it vanished with McCorry? I always said he was the wind beneath my wings, that it was his belief in me that made me capable of flying. Without him I was scared of plummeting to the ground. It was an irrational fear, but it gripped me nevertheless. And even though I could see that it was irrational, I seemed unable to overcome it.

Was that why I had said yes to Terry when he wanted to marry me? I saw a strength there I felt I needed? If only someone had been there when McCorry died, someone wise enough to tell me, 'Sheryl, you're going to feel terrible for a year at least, you'll feel as if you're drowning on your own. But you won't drown, you'll find the very strength McCorry always knew you had, but you'll find it in yourself, not in anybody else. Whatever you do, don't go clinging to some other fellow, thinking his belief will support you.' But it was too late.

I had exhausted myself. When I saw Terry later that evening, after all the staff had left, I whispered, 'This isn't a marriage, I can't go on like this.' He was much calmer then, and said, 'Yes you can, one day we'll be finished here, and all the pressure of this place, then things will be better.' The storm had passed, there was no solution yet, only to take a big deep breath, put on that smile and keep going.

There was always something to pull me through. Robby and Tara were living together now in the old caravan. Tara's arrival in Robby's life was a gift from heaven. Their relationship was new, but they were determined to make it work. With her quiet inner strength Tara was able to help Robby believe in himself again. Certainly she helped restore his battered confidence. And she probably also distracted him from worrying about me, for which I am immensely grateful. She got him eating well again too, with her great home cooking. I was so happy to have her as part of our family.

In July 2004 it was time for my annual bone scan. We fitted in a visit to Wildwood and the Shiralee first. It was disheartening to arrive at the Wildwood farm to overgrown lawns and gardens; to open the front door of the farmhouse to that unlived-in stagnant smell. Every visit I cleaned up the sad mess, got the sprinklers going and replanted, knowing I'd repeat the whole process in six months. Nothing took root or prospered; every time I returned there, it was back to square one.

When we arrived in Perth, Terry had business to attend to, but Kristy had taken time off work to accompany me to the hospital for my bone scan. After the procedure we sat together over a cup of coffee. She let slip that the last house she had rented a room in had burned down while she was out one day — she hadn't told me before as she felt terrible about the loss in the fire of two saddles I had given her. But all that mattered to me was that she was unharmed. I did value the saddles, at least for nostalgia's sake, but I no longer ride and we both had to just let them go. I was grateful to have Kristy's presence at the hospital and in my life as a whole. I know it bothered her to know what was happening between Terry and I. But Kristy now leads a life of her own and knows where I am when she needs me. I'll always be as proud of her as I am of my own two children.

My results were fine, a small problem in the right shoulder again, another melanoma, but nothing I couldn't handle. It scarcely seemed worth worrying about. That's the funny thing about cancer. It starts off as the scariest thing in the world, but after a while you get blasé about it, especially the smaller stuff.

And then it was Leisha's wedding. Terry and I flew to Cairns and it was a real joy to see her little family happy and content. 'This is the way families should be,' I told her in a quiet moment. She was still insisting on a short ceremony without any fuss, and I half wished I'd never told her how old McCorry and I had married. She seemed set on making it a family tradition.

Eventually, after a bit of persuasion, she gave me licence to add some trimmings, just what I could pull together in twenty-four hours. I was sure I could create a perfect wedding party on a day's notice, and I did. I hired a car, and Terry drove me around Cairns until all was organised: a proper wedding cake, caterers, fine crockery and cutlery, white balloons and a white marquee. For once I spent a day with my husband without fighting or having an unhappy exchange of words, and

I experienced him in the way he often was with other people. Magnanimous, even generous. He gave Leisha a beautiful pearl pendant for a wedding present. What was the magic ingredient, I wondered. I would have bottled it if I knew.

Leisha and Adam were married the next day on the back lawn of their newly renovated house. The ceremony seemed so fitting, held under a massive gum tree which I saw as a perfect symbol of Leisha's early outback years. Young Brock, dressed in long pants, white shirt and waistcoat, walked out with his mother in the place her father should have been. I couldn't help but shed tears of happiness for them all.

We took back some of the lovely wedding vibe with us, and for a little while life was kinder than usual at the park. But it wasn't long before the violence came to the fore again, fuelled as usual by an excess of alcohol.

After a fabulous concert by Jane Rutter and David Helfgott at the Mangrove Hotel, Terry's rage towards me surfaced once again. It was rare for him to be blatantly malicious in public; it wasn't the image he liked to project, and I could see people wondering how I could be putting up with his uncouth behaviour. But we'd come in the Landcruiser and he refused to hand over the keys; I wasn't about to leave him with it in the tanked-up state he was in. So I spent the evening with a false smile on the outside and feeling humiliated and downtrodden on the inside.

In some respects I had become so used to Terry's outbursts, I hardly knew my stomach was knotted unless Leisha was there to tell me. It wasn't just the fear of violence — verbal or physical — that was getting to me, it was my incapacity to act on my own behalf. I was ashamed, and became more and more isolated from friends and relatives who might have been able to help me if I'd spoken out. I was frightened they'd think I was a nutter.

There were the odd occasions when someone would bring out the old me. At the caravan park there was a major problem with the plumbing for the park extension — instant 'springs' were sprouting all over the newly developed land, even shooting through the new bitumen roads in places! If it hadn't been a serious and expensive problem, I'd have felt like laughing. The contractors weren't fixing anything until Terry caught up on his payments to them — and they were holding out for a $70,000 payment.

Terry was jumping up and down over this, and I suggested that he get all the paperwork regarding his dealings with this company from his law firm in Broome, and I would ask Brian Singleton to handle the case.

This perfectly sensible suggestion set Terry off again. To him it was proof again that I was 'sick in the head'. It really offended him that I had an opinion and that I dared to tell him how he should operate. He had responded the same way weeks earlier when I'd suggested he take photos of the water damage as it arose.

The situation was still unresolved when we left for Wildwood and the southern hay season, so while we were in Perth I threw caution to the wind and arranged a meeting with Brian. Terry begrudgingly agreed to come, and I felt like giving Brian a bottle of the best French champagne when he told Terry he should have taken photographs of the sprouting fountains as they arose — exactly the advice I'd given. Had he done so, Brian said, the problem might have been solved without resorting to a solicitor's office. He passed the case on to another Perth lawyer and after lengthy negotiations it ended with a compromise on both sides.

Before we left, Brian said something very complimentary about the way I approached the problem, telling Terry he was lucky to have me. That gave me such a good feeling that, as we got into the car, I couldn't help saying, 'You know, Brian Singleton doesn't think I'm at all mad.' This was a big mistake of course, but it felt so good to be affirmed by someone who was completely sane and sound. Predictably, Terry's temper flared. He didn't say anything, but the vehicle lurched out onto the road in a dangerous manner and I was struck down with fright again.

CHAPTER 13

Writing the Story of my Life

I was living out of a suitcase between the farms and the caravan park, and seemed to be constantly packing and unpacking. I promised myself I would stop for a while and concentrate on writing my memoirs for the children.

Terry was selling and buying cattle, while Ken, his son, was flat out demolishing and replacing old fences. The southern race season was in full swing and every race day Terry would disappear, on one trip returning the proud owner of another two racehorses. Yet the next day, when I came home with a car load of plants for the farmhouse garden and asked for some money towards them, he ignored me. Such things had to come out of my housekeeping money. If the expenditure wasn't going to benefit him directly, he was simply not interested.

One day at Wildwood I decided I was never going to live in the caravan park again. I refused to live any longer in a single room and share my toilet and kitchen with all the staff. It was still a compromise, making Wildwood my home, but at least I wasn't packing all the time. And there were things I needed to do for Molly.

Terry was racing about the shed looking for tools to pull a cattle crate to bits. He was putting his glasses down and then was not able to find them again. Next he insisted I'd lost a registration card for one of his new racehorses. With more confidence then I was feeling I said quite calmly, 'You're always accusing others of losing or hiding things, but it's you doing it, I see you do it.' I lifted my gaze and met his eyes across the room.

Near panic took hold of me at the look in his eyes and the twist to his jaw said he would kill me if he got hold of me. He took a step towards me, his fists clenching and unclenching as if out of his control. I backed away to stand by the phone and said, 'Touch me, and I'll call the police. I mean it.' And I was totally amazed when he turned away and walked out of the house.

I sat down heavily in a lounge chair to gather myself together. *That's it*, I thought. *I am not putting up with this bullshit any more.* That night I slept with a chair wedged against my bedroom door.

The next morning I woke to the sound of him ransacking bedroom drawers and kitchen cupboards, and the slamming of doors. I went out to the kitchen to see what all the commotion was about. 'What's wrong?' I asked, afraid of upsetting him even more.

'I'm going to Perth,' he said, glaring at me as though I was clearly to blame for whatever was wrong.

I asked him if he could leave me a hundred dollars as I had no cash. He said he had none. That was rubbish, he always had money on him, and he knew I knew it. At that moment I felt like I'd been hit in the solar plexus with the most severe pain, and I fainted over the kitchen sink. When I came to he was gone.

*

From Perth Terry went back to Broome and while he was gone I cleaned out the sheds and set bait for the rats that were again on the prowl. Terry seemed more content back up north and called me twice a day, but I knew that nothing had changed. His next foul mood was only a matter of time.

On my own at Wildwood I was content too. Cleaning out sheds and attending to vermin seemed just the thing for me to be doing at this time, and I breathed a lot more deeply. It was as if I was doing on the outside what I was still working up to on the inside. But I had begun to feel positive. For me, too, it was only a matter of time. I felt it very strongly. I was sure I could trust that I would take the right steps when the time was right. It felt good to trust myself.

Writing gave me a lot of joy. Every day I wrote, and often I began over my first cup of tea in the morning. I had covered the early years in Darwin and Arnhem Land, and my long courtship with McCorry. Looking back, it still seemed romantic and I felt a warmth as I remembered how well McCorry and I worked together. Thinking about those years was like a fresh breeze blowing through all the rotten wood of my current marriage.

To cap things off Leisha rang me from Cairns to say she was pregnant. This was wonderful news. She and Adam were building the little family they always wanted. Leisha and Robby had both helped carry my load for me. I know my unhappiness had affected their lives and I was ashamed of that, but I felt so glad that they both found partners who were kind and positive and generous and who loved them.

My parents travelled down from Northampton to spend a week with me. Dad was in his eighties but he was still in good shape and he never sat still for long. He pulled down the old clothes line and erected another while mother and I got stuck into making fig jam and drinking gallons of tea as though we did this every day.

It wasn't all smooth sailing, though. My parents' visit stirred up murky feelings — of having failed in my life, of being alone on my husband's farm and marking time while I waited for the courage to make a complete break. Not that they wanted me to stick with my marriage, far from it. But to see them, still happy after 63 years together, made me wonder what was wrong with me that I could not make my marriages last.

I was determined that I was not going to let myself go under, so when they had gone I visited my doctor. 'Why are you taking it?' he asked when I described the situation with Terry. 'You need to get your own life back.' I sat in front of him feeling like a bloody idiot, wondering where I could find the strength to make a new life for myself. He assured me a happy and stress-free life was possible without an aggressive male around me, and sent me away with a prescription for antidepressants. But I promised myself I would only take them for a short time. I wanted to get myself together and I knew I needed all my wits about me. Prescription medication can be addictive and this was my biggest fear. After a week on those particular tablets I had to dispose of them. I reacted to the medication and became sombre, feeling nothing, seeing nothing. That particular medication wasn't good for me. Later I was prescribed a low dose of a newer antidepressant and found it eased the huge knot that was forever trembling in my stomach.

I had been travelling this rocky road for six years now, but what never ceased to amaze me was how, when I was feeling particularly low in myself, my mobile phone would ring and I would be talking to an Aboriginal friend from the Kimberley. Katie, Alma and Jeanie often called to check on their *yumun*. I would stop, have a good talk and laugh with them, then get back to my life again, feeling so much better about the world.

'You got a new old man?' Katie asked me one day. I would try to hide my unhappiness in my marriage from them, but they always knew. 'Yes Katie, I've got a new husband,' I said. 'What for you need old man?' she questioned, sounding worried for me. I didn't want the third degree, so I said, 'Maybe to chop the wood or something.' Katie burst out laughing. 'You should come and visit me,' she said. 'I will, Katie, I promise you,' I replied, feeling more homesick than ever for my old life in the Kimberley.

One Saturday evening I was sitting on the verandah, contemplating how good life could be when it was free of tension. The phone rang through the stillness; it was Terry suggesting I turn the television on to the ABC. 'It may interest you,' he said. Across the screen was the face of an Aboriginal man who had grown up in my stock camp on Napier Downs. Terrence Dann had murdered his two small stepchildren in the Derby graveyard and tried to kill his partner as well. I wanted to throw up.

Back in the seventies Terrence's parents had arrived at the homestead looking for work. Although they came over from Brooking Springs and had not worked on Napier Downs before, it was apparently their home country. They were a young couple in an old faded blue Holden sedan that was packed with a tribe of young children, Terrence among them.

The family settled in and the children played happily around the camp and on the homestead lawns with their dingo pups, shyly hiding behind me or a parent when a visitor arrived at the station. I remember them one corroboree night throwing all inhibitions to the wind as they pounded the soft red pindan with their bare feet to the powerful rhythm of the didgeridoo. The camp fire crackled as it burnt down, throwing the dancers' shadows up against the backdrop of the Napier Range. Bodies shiny with sweat glistened in the smoky night light, their tribal markings stark in white ochre. The kids fitted in beautifully. So what had happened to Terrence?

Only twelve months ago I had seen him at a pub in Derby. Pubs have never been my scene, but it was the only place we could get an evening meal on Derby race weekend. I was very glad to see Terrence though: he was looking great, well dressed in country and western gear. He had become a country music entertainer and sang with a slight Yankee twang. He came up and introduced his wife to me, and then dedicated most of his songs that night to me, publicly acknowledging me for treating his family right all those years ago on Napier Downs.

There was a whole mob of people from Napier Downs, many of whom I knew from when I was managing the station. There were plenty I didn't know, but those I did know were bringing the strangers to meet me, introducing me as 'the missus who grew me up'. There was a constant stream of people coming up to the table, and beyond, I could see eyes on me, fingers pointing at me.

I had not realised before this just how much I meant to the Aboriginal people I had worked and lived with. I knew Bob and I treated them far better than they were treated on many stations, but still, this was unexpected. It was lovely to see them all, though I felt faintly embarrassed at all the attention. Terry was lapping it up, which was a surprise to me, but he wasn't well known in Derby, there were none of his friends around, no one he had to prove anything to, so maybe it was all right for me to be the centre of attention for once. And I was introducing him to everyone — he was shaking their hands and having a great time. If he'd always been the way he was that night, I could have loved him.

But still, it seemed he felt he had to be the big man here, and was buying grog for all the men and women. I wished he wouldn't, and told him so, but while that didn't trigger a nasty reaction, he wasn't going to stop. I had a horror of alcohol and Aboriginal people — they just didn't mix, the combination only brought heartbreak. Which is why every station I ever owned or managed was dry. I had a blanket ban on alcohol. And still we always had the biggest stock camps of any of the Kimberley stations.

Thinking back to that night, I wondered if alcohol (and maybe drugs) played a part in bringing Terrence to the point where he could kill his own children. I don't mean that as an excuse for what he did. But he was clearly not the person I knew; he had changed.

I remembered the time when another Aboriginal family came to Napier Downs. I had been woken in the middle of one sultry night by the barking of Sally, our blue heeler. I threw on my jeans and shirt, grabbed a torch and went to the front door. Outside in the dark of night I could just make out a large gathering of people by the homestead gate.

'What's wrong?' I yelled out from the front verandah.

'Missus,' a female voice answered, soft and hesitant. I did not recognise the speaker, and walked slowly out in the dark towards the people. They stood in total silence, and close up I could see that they were strangers to me. I wondered where they had come from at this late hour. A bent, grey-haired old man walked towards me with the aid of a stick. I extended my hand in greeting and introduced myself. His name was Spider, he told me.

'We bin leave that Mount House station, missus,' he said. Mount House was a hundred kilometres north up the Gibb

River Road. It was owned by King Ranch at the time, an American company that bred horses.

'Okay,' I said, and nodded my head in the direction of the station camp. 'You can make camp up there.'

'Good, good,' Spider replied. He then asked if 'Boss' (old McCorry) would take him back to the Mount House camp the next day and bring the other old people to Napier Downs.

There seemed to be some urgency attached to this move in the middle of the night and I wondered why. As I walked towards my outdoor freezer to get some beef for them to cook up, I counted about fifteen to twenty of them, mostly healthy-looking young men and women in their late teens or early twenties, with a scattering of children.

As they distributed the meat among themselves by the dim light of the freezer I took the opportunity to talk to one of the women. 'Why did you move camp at night?' It's not something I'd known Aboriginal people to do normally; it seemed unusual to me. Hiding her face, her head down, she clearly didn't want to say anything. I let the matter rest, but went back to my bed slightly worried.

Early the next morning I woke to the rattle of the kettle coming from the cook house. Katie was leaving me in no doubt that she was up and about the homestead. I knew she would have news for me on last night's invasion.

Settling myself by her side with a cup of tea on the front step of the homestead, I asked her about the people who had just joined us. It seemed they were from a different tribal group — they were Wungundin people — and I wondered whether the two groups would accept each other.

Katie explained what had happened. 'One girl from that camp and that boss fella make big trouble, missus,' she said, scratching at the step with a finger. 'On that boss fella's table in him office, missus.' Katie burst into near hysterics, all of a sudden finding it hilarious.

'What?' I gasped, catching her meaning and pretending to be shocked.

Then her laughter stopped abruptly and Katie sat up and finished her story. 'That white missus, boss's missus, she got a pistol when she come into that office.' Now it all made sense to me, the immediate upheaval of their camp and the move to Napier Downs in the middle of the night. No shots had been fired, no one had been hurt, but the white missus had threatened the Aboriginal woman with the gun, and that was enough for her whole family group to pack up and leave.

Later that morning McCorry went up to Mount House with Spider and picked up the old people. The elders never talked to me about the incident, perhaps feeling it brought shame on them. I took their lead and didn't mention it either. As far as I was concerned, so long as they worked things out with my camp, they were welcome to stay. (They did stay, and moved with me two years later to Blina station.)

But the troubles for the Mount House people were not over. The next morning a group of them came to see me. They stood waiting at the homestead gate with shaved heads covered with white scarves torn from a calico bedsheet. I realised straightaway that this was a sign that they were mourning a death in the family, and I worried that there had been some violence relating to the incident. However, it was not connected. It was an old man, one of their elders, who had passed away in camp in the night, presumably of old age.

I left them to make their own arrangements, but by mid-afternoon the westerly breeze was carrying the acrid smell of burning towards the homestead. Worried again, I made my way out to the back lawn where I could see smoke billowing towards the heavens. It was coming from the direction of the station camp.

Bloody hell, was my immediate thought. *Please don't let there be trouble*. I didn't know what I might have set into action by my hasty decision to let the Mount House people stay. There might have been bad history between the two mobs. I was preparing myself to face whatever new catastrophe might be brewing when Katie walked up to me.

'Katie, what's happening?' I asked. I could see my job going up in smoke, too, if they burnt the camp down.

'Him not burning that camp, missus,' Katie said matter-of-factly. 'Him smoking the hut that old man died in, smoking them bad spirits away.'

'Oh, that's good,' I said, relieved. I should have remembered that this was commonly done when someone died, and I felt a bit silly that I'd thought the worst. I should have known Katie would have told me if there'd been anything to worry about.

On Wildwood farm I carted and stacked seven loads of wood in the shed, ready for the cold winter months to come. I was looking forward to the change in seasons. I had decided I would stay here awhile. I had contemplated going back to the Shiralee, but Richard was happy there and was keeping everything sweet for me. I didn't want to disrupt his life at this time. And for all my bad memories of Wildwood, I needed to see something through. I had made a promise to Molly, and I wanted to set the place straight for her. I felt her spirit still restless there, and in a funny sort of a way I needed to do my own version of 'smoking' her house so she could move on.

It was good for me too. As I slowly created a sense of order, I felt myself relax and unwind. Before long Leisha, who was not far off giving birth, came down with Adam and

Brock to join me. They had sold their duplex in Cairns and would spend some time with me at the house before finding a home of their own. Adam soon found work in Busselton, and at home Leisha and I took turns with the cooking. We had a great four weeks together.

I was so happy to have my family around me again. Life was going well and I could feel a smile returning to my face. I was proud that I was staying on my own course, doing what I felt I needed to do.

I hadn't cut Terry out of my life completely. He rang quite frequently and we didn't get into so many arguments. He'd talk about the park, pass on gossip or news from friends. For the first time in many years I felt more or less at home. I wasn't living out of a suitcase. I had somewhere to sit and enjoy my cup of tea in the morning. I could breathe deeply in the cool clean air.

Best, I had stuck to my decision of writing my story. Up until this time in my life, I'd had no experience of writing at all, but I looked on it as just another task that needed sound strategies to accomplish my goal. I worked out a schedule and divided my life into years and cattle stations; I read my diaries, placing tags on different events and making many notes. Drinking mug after mug of tea, I would sit by the fire and let my memories, thoughts and feelings flow. I wrote on happy events and sad ones, some days in tears or anger over what I thought were injustices in my life. Sometimes I was so churned up I'd be unable to sleep at night. I can't say I was analysing what I'd been through, but it seemed to get worked out just the same.

I have heard it said that writing is good medicine, and for me that was true. In some ways it was as if I had made myself, from the start, just like I had made those little dolls back at the Shiralee. In other ways, to sit alone with the time to go over momentous events in my mind was a luxury. While I was living that life, I never had a moment to sit and think about what was happening. Everything just got tucked away while I got on with the business of living: managing children, animals, stock camps, cattle stations.

Terry always kept a very clear distance from my writing. He didn't like me doing it, he hated me even being in conversation with people about my life in the outback. He told me he didn't want me to write under my married name — his name. I assumed he wanted to distance himself from the possibility of my making a fool of myself. In fact I had always intended to write as Sheryl McCorry, the person I had been, that I was deep inside — the person I was beginning to find again. The satisfaction that came with realising that, for the first time in years, I had a fierce grip on my own life only made me more determined to keep at my writing.

CHAPTER 14

Reclaiming Wildwood

*A*t the same time as I was rescuing the Wildwood farm-house from neglect, I was determined that I would not let my beloved Shiralee fall into the same state. Richard was great with the stock, but the Shiralee needed a woman's touch too. It was a four hundred kilometre round trip, but I just needed to reconnect with it. I would stay overnight and go on with my writing at the kitchen table. Then I could return home to Wildwood content and satisfied, knowing everything was fine.

Towards the end of the year Robby and Tara drove south. Robby wanted to show Tara the Shiralee, the farm he had grown to love, and they planned to be away from Broome for the whole of the wet season.

Now I had all my family around me. I felt so grateful that in those terrible years of my life I had not lost my children. I had missed a lot of young Brock's early years while Leisha was in Cairns, but now I was making up for that, taking him for walks in the surrounding bush and having smoko on the front verandah. He loved our smoko picnics. The little blue wrens found time between courting to drop in on the bird feeders I had scattered throughout the garden; it made my heart sing to see them. A couple of blue-tongue lizards had taken cover in the nearby wood heap and occasionally set my pulse racing when, with a quick glimpse, I mistook them for snakes. I was used to handling king browns on the stations but I found it hard to accept the tiger snakes in the south, particularly when they camped around the back door of the farmhouse. To me the darker colour of the tiger snake made them look more aggressive and sinister, and I would freak out at the sight of them. Yet the king browns have a reputation for being more aggressive and I have always felt I could protect myself and family from them.

One lovely spring morning with Leisha and Brock on the verandah, I was absorbed in the various bird calls when my mind was distracted by a rustle in the nearby grass. Tiger snake, I thought, and was leaping up to grab Brock when I saw the telltale stumpy leg of the blue-tongue — which brought to mind an encounter with a lizard on Kimberley Downs, a tata lizard.

It was rodeo time in the Kimberley and I had given my windmill men time off, so it was up to me to check on the boundary bore — which I did, only to find the tank was empty.

Boundary Bore was an important staging post on the way into Kimberley Downs. There was a large trucking yard, where we kept cattle in paddocks waiting on their sixty day test for TB. A worn old Southern Cross jack pump stood over the bore, black and sooty, and the surrounding ground was soaked dark with heavy black sump oil. The pump had probably earned its weight in gold for the constant supply of water it had produced over many years, but lately it had become a pain in the arse to get it started. I religiously performed all the right procedures. I'd stand over that pump and feed it a little capful of oil, a tiny sniff of petrol and crank my guts out — to no avail. Next, I repeated this strategy, leaving out the oil. I gave it an extra sniff of petrol, again cranked like hell — nothing. When my body was exhausted and my chest heaving from the effort, I lifted my head from the job, only to see a tata lizard watching me intently and revolving its arms like the clappers. It looked exactly as though it was mimicking my cranking. I'd never seen such a thing before, and I often think of that little tata lizard.

But I still had a pump to get started. Some years back Ike, a slightly built but very handy windmill man, had worked on Kimberley Downs. He never quite had the strength to crank heavy jack pumps, so a rope in the Toyota had to do. I decided to follow his example. Hooking my rope onto the pulley of the jack pump, I wound it around several times, secured it to the bullbar of the Toyota and reversed at speed. The rope broke and shot backwards, exploding against the windscreen and sending me ducking below the dashboard. On my second attempt, I pulled the rope in two. At this point I made a mental note: buy a new rope! But the third attempt was successful, and I managed to keep the old jack pump working until all the cattle were watered and the tank was full to the brim.

Terry flew down for a week to check on his racehorses and wanted my company. Of course it wasn't about me at all, but his need to use my Landcruiser to do the rounds of the stables and agistment centres that were scattered all over the south-west.

His moods were still dark and angry but I watched my every word and managed to keep from reacting and making things worse. I had realised by now that it was safer to pump up his ego than say anything that he might construe as criticism, as his frustration would easily turn to aggression. When we arrived at the airport with an hour to kill before his departure, I suggested we have something to eat together. We had just sat down in the cafe when Terry suddenly stood up, slamming his chair back in anger. His jaw set in that terrible way and his eyes bulged, and he said, loudly enough for the people around us to hear, 'I'd rather back horses than buy you lunch. I've made money from horses, but nothing from you.' These were his exact words.

I was thrown straight back to that old sense of helplessness. I thought I had managed things so well, but still it had led to this. I felt my body burning with shame. But from somewhere I found the strength to say quite calmly that a cup of coffee would do. Then suddenly he was being charming, wanting to order every bloody meal on the menu for me. I was utterly confused. I had no idea what pushed which buttons. I gathered myself together, said goodbye and walked out of the cafe, seeing nothing, feeling nothing.

Out in my trusty Landcruiser I called Leisha. My girl listened patiently as I talked and then said, 'Listen to me for a minute, Mummy. There is not enough darkness in the world to put out the light of one small candle. He doesn't have that strength. Think about it, Mum, you are our candle. He can't quench your light. And don't forget it.'

My strength flooded back to me. This was the world I preferred to live in, a world of light and tenderness. I was almost glad of the unpleasant incident — it reminded me how cold, calculating and money-hungry my husband was.

I had been back at Wildwood only a few days when I had a full-blown water crisis. For months the house water supply had been rank. It stank and not even tea or coffee could disguise its foul taste. I had been carting drinking water in from another tank further down the road in plastic jerry cans.

It was an enormous effort, heaving them into the house, and I couldn't let Leisha help, her baby was due any day.

It was a very wet and windy Thursday morning, and thunder rumbled away in the distance. The heavens seemed to open right above the farmhouse and the rain just tumbled down. But the water never made it into the rainwater tank, instead it flooded into the homestead. In no time there was water everywhere; inches of precious rainwater that should have been filling the house tanks was filling bedrooms, passageways and the family room, then lights were blowing as the water poured furiously down through the fittings. I told Leisha to take Brock out of the house and into the car parked safely in the shed. I was worried someone would be electrocuted. She put him in his car seat and fastened the safety harness, opened the windows and stocked him up with fruit juice and toys. He was happy there while we got to work, one of us popping in to check on him every few minutes.

This was the third season this had happened — it was one in a long list of maintenance jobs Terry had put off in the hope it would disappear before he had to throw any money at it — and I wasn't going to stand for it a moment longer. 'I'm going to fix this problem once and for all,' I said to Leisha as I ran to the pantry to grab a hacksaw from my tool box.

I ran barefoot out into the rain with my jeans hitched up to my knees and attacked the first downpipe that came into view, hacking it off with a vengeance. The only way to get a job done around the house was to do it myself. Why had I left it so long? But I knew the answer to that. The Sheryl of one, two and three years ago had had the stuffing knocked out of her.

I stood back and admired my handiwork, feeling a deep sense of satisfaction while standing in the ankle-deep water gushing down from the roof. At the same time I grieved for the senseless waste of good rainwater. Then Leisha came up and grabbed the hacksaw from me and started on the next downpipe, and between us we didn't stop until every downpipe around the farmhouse had been cut in two.

The water flooding into the house stopped immediately. Our next move was to clean the gutters that supplied the outlet pipes that carried the water from the roof down to the underground pipes that fed into the rainwater tanks. Tony the painter was driving down the road while I was hanging from a ladder cleaning gutters. He wheeled his panel van into the muddy driveway and jumped out demanding, 'What are you two doing?' I was not feeling particularly friendly towards any man at that moment. 'What does it look like?' I said, sounding somewhat ungrateful. Tony looked towards Leisha for support; she only raised her eyes as if to say, 'You're a bit late.'

'I wish you would get down off that roof; it's a man's job, I'll do it for you tomorrow,' Tony said. He couldn't hide his shocked expression as he surveyed the cut-off downpipes swinging around the homestead, but he didn't say another word and promptly left the scene. And as quickly as he went, the rain stopped too.

The ladder was an old heavy galvanised-pipe kind and as heavy as all hell, but we lugged and dragged it about the house until all the gutters were clean. But still the water backed up when we tried reconnecting the downpipes, so that meant the underground pipes must be blocked. We stuck down flexible tubing and, sure enough, they were blocked only metres from the house, full of stinking black muck filled with maggots.

We disconnected the inlet pipes from the rainwater tank and used a high-pressure hose directly from the bore to clean out the muck, leaves and stinking maggots from the under-ground pipes. Once we had the clean water running through the pipes we started the job of joining everything up again. Trips into Bunnings were a great laugh. 'Here come our plumbers again,' the staff said on our second visit. Our first trip had not been successful — the PVC pipe joiners were too small — but this time we were spot on with our measurements.

'No job too big or too small,' we echoed as we left the building.

'Darling,' I said to Leisha, 'Mummy might be able to become a gutter and underground-pipe cleaner now.' I was feeling incredibly good about the job we were doing.

With only three downpipes left to rejoin, Leisha suddenly buckled over and leaned against the wall holding onto her very swollen belly. I dropped all tools, ready to go into panic mode, but she said very steadily, 'Calm down, Mum, it's probably false contractions.' *I bloody hope so*, I thought. Tony the painter arrived at that moment and quickly volunteered to complete the remaining downpipes. He was astonished to see what we had managed to do between us, but he couldn't get off the farm fast enough. I guess he didn't mind giving a hand with a repair job but he wasn't about to help in a birthing suite.

The contractions went on for an hour or so then eased, so we decided to get on with the day. I hooked up the trailer and loaded it to the brim with rubbish. Leisha wasn't going to be left behind on the big clean-up and we headed to the dump at Dunsborough to unload. Halfway through unloading the trailer Leisha cried out in pain and doubled over again.

'Oh my god, don't have the baby in the rubbish dump,' I said. I was only half joking.

She cracked a smile and we left the dump for the farmhouse in one hell of a hurry. Hours later, Leisha was admitted to Busselton Hospital, where they informed her she needed to travel to Saint John of God in Bunbury to have her baby turned as he was in a breech position. The following morning she was released from the hospital — baby had changed his mind again about when he was coming into this world.

Thirteen days later, after her second natural birth, Leisha delivered another beautiful baby boy, Cohen. She had Adam by her side again, but she didn't have me there this time! I couldn't go through another natural birth with my daughter. I simply could not handle seeing and hearing her in such pain. For years I had been perfectly confident helping people out in the bush in times of need, but I battled seeing my own family in pain.

Cohen's birth bought back a flood of memories from Louisa Downs station. In my mind's eye I could still see Katie waltzing into the homestead, her arms outstretched, saying to me, 'Look here, missus, little baby belong Barbara!'

She handed me a beautiful, slippery, waxy baby girl with a length of umbilical cord still dangling from her. Questions swam through my mind as I stood there, overwhelmed but with a firm grip on the baby. Then her cry brought Leisha running from the schoolroom. She pulled up a chair for a better view, and I said she could stay and give me a hand to bath and check the little girl.

I turned back to Katie. 'Where is Barbara? Is she all right?'

'Ya, ya, she's having a shower now,' Katie said, pointing with her chin to the outside shower by the laundry.

'Where did she have this one, Katie?' I asked.

'Barbara from my Louisa camp, she was visiting family at Yiyili when the baby started. They tried to get to the homestead, but that was too far for this piccaninny. She born in a spinifex circle by the horse paddock gate.' Tussocks of spinifex often grow in a ring around an old or dead spinifex.

After bathing the baby I radioed the flying doctor and they diverted from a trip to Balgo Mission to conduct a routine postnatal check. We all walked to the airstrip, where the flying doctor pronounced both mother and daughter fine and well. Katie and I went back to the house to look for some of Leisha's baby clothes, and I said to Katie, 'You have to tell Barbara to name this baby girl. We can't have a baby with no name.'

Barbara called her little girl Maria Anne Cox Wallaby — probably the longest name of any Aboriginal child I knew! She has grown into a beautiful young woman and still lives on Louisa Downs, where she is a noted artist in the area.

Wonder of wonders, Terry engaged Tony to paint and tidy up the smaller farmhouse by the big shed. He did this of his own volition, wanting to make it attractive to Leisha — he knew if Leisha was close by, that would keep me happy. It was across the paddock from the main house, about six hundred metres away, and the old house looked as good as new when Leisha and Adam and their two sons moved in.

Soon Christmas was rolling around again. Leisha and I decorated the huge Christmas tree with help from young Brock. We ended up with gold and silver tinsel scattered from one end of the lounge room to the other. For the first time in years Christmas felt like Christmas again. Brightly wrapped presents were scattered about the tree. I was excited just to have some family around me.

Terry came down too; it was his nephew's turn to take care of the caravan park. We had his three sons as well, and Adam's sister Jody and her partner. Roast pork, apple sauce and all the trimmings adorned the table, along with lobster, prawns and cold chicken, with plum pudding and custard, and fresh fruit salad with ice cream for dessert. Leisha and I worked side by side from sunrise, having a marvellous time in the kitchen. She had put the finishing touches to her speciality, a high-powered fruit punch, and I was completing the fruit salad, when Terry walked into the kitchen to find me squeezing fresh lemon juice over the banana to prevent it from turning brown. Terry was suddenly screaming in my face, 'You've ruined it, you've completely ruined it.'

I was utterly bewildered. I had no idea what he was talking about.

'You've turned it sour!' he shrieked, and I suddenly understood that he was having a tantrum about the fruit salad. I began to shiver. The tears started and I had no control over them. I was terrified of collapsing and making even more of a scene in the presence of guests. Leisha hurried over and wrapped her arms around me, ignoring Terry completely. He stopped screaming abruptly and left the room.

'He'll never change, Mum, please don't cry,' she murmured. 'I can't stand to see you so unhappy.'

Somehow I got through Christmas lunch. I was there in appearance only, silently studying the scene. *What a sad lot of clowns we are, puppets on a string*, I was thinking. There we were, trying for Christmas cheer, trying to keep Terry happy when most of us probably wanted to be elsewhere now.

Leisha was downing glass after glass of her famous punch, becoming slightly intoxicated as she took over as hostess, cracking jokes and waltzing around the table, encouraging everyone to eat. I had a glass of wine myself, snapped out of my gloom and reminded Leisha of the Christmas on Kimberley Downs when she was thirteen.

It was Christmas Eve and we were bouncing around in the Toyota as we crisscrossed the bugger-bugger flat looking for a Christmas tree; after much discussion we decided to chop down the large and very thorny mimosa out in the middle of the bullock paddock.

With a blunt axe and a great deal of effort I called 'Timber!' as the tree hit the ground, spraying white-winged flying ants high into the air. The children helped as much as they could to load the butt of the mimosa onto the tray of the Toyota; the rest we dragged along behind the vehicle, leaving a trail of red bulldust. We wanted to get the tree home and decorated before McCorry came back from Kilto (our own station) where he had been fencing.

Jack and Alma, my Aboriginal friends, were there with their children Rodney and Stephanie as we pulled up in front of the homestead dragging the Christmas tree behind us. Jack stood back in admiration. 'This proper big one, missus,' he said smiling. I was pleased he thought so.

Four years after I had lost Kelly, Jack and Alma lost their son Jeffery in a bull-buggy accident. Jeffery and Kelly had been mates. I felt I had a lot in common with Jack and Alma; we understood each other. I wanted this Christmas to be a happy one for all of us, particularly our children.

With everyone's help we pushed, shoved and grunted until the thorny mimosa was wedged in a twenty litre drum filled with rocks on the front verandah of the homestead. The children would be able to see the tree from wherever they were playing on Christmas.

Dragging a large box of decorations from the dormitory I gave the children a free hand in decorating this monstrosity of a tree while Jack, Alma and I sat back to enjoy a pannikin of tea as the evening cooled down and the sun drifted behind the blunt plateau of Mount Marion. We watched Rodney and Stephanie dress the tree with Leisha, Kristy and young Robby. 'That Christmas fella coming tonight,' I said to the kids. 'There's no Christmas fella, missus,' said Rodney. 'Yeah, right, Mum,' said Leisha, not really wanting to spoil it for her little brother Robby.

'That Christmas fella and that Jesus fella are the same, aren't they, Mum?' asked Robby, reckoning he had it all sorted out.

'I'll have to think about that, love,' I said, not too sure what Father Lawrence had explained to him about the Jesus fella question.

Later Leisha helped me pile the presents about the tree. There were gifts for everyone; Christmas in the Kimberley was always like that: on the station no one was any more special than anyone else.

Very early the next morning, well before the golden rays of sunshine spread their soft glow across the homestead, I heard the camp children playing and talking excitedly by my bedroom louvres, Rodney and Stephanie among them. Next minute Leisha, Kristy and Robby had joined them and soon there was the crunching and tearing of wrapping paper, whistles and horns blowing, and a football being kicked about on the front verandah. It was time for me to get out of bed.

Soon Alma and Jack arrived to join the festivities. Jack got the barbecue going and cooked the spare ribs (the kids' choice), fillet steak and *cherabin* (something like a yabby) caught in the river below the homestead. This was our Kimberley Christmas lunch, accompanied by a huge salad and baby potatoes.

Once the novelty of new toys and clothes had worn off, the children disappeared over the bank into the creek with their horses, Lady and Little Blue. After an hour I became concerned and headed towards the creek, only to find Leisha skiing off Lady's tail, being towed up and down the creek on her belly in fine style. Before I was in shouting distance, Kristy was skiing one-handed behind Little Blue. They were showing off, but all of them — right down to the smallest ones — seemed to be having a very good time.

CHAPTER 15

More Homecomings

I didn't know whether my family was peculiar in this, but health never seemed to be off the agenda for me or my children. Up in Broome, Robby was in a bad way with a collection of symptoms that had the medical profession stumped: he had stomach and chest pains, trouble breathing and he even blacked out every now and then. At one point his stomach pains were so severe he was unable to walk, and Tara had to near drag him to the Broome hospital — no mean feat since he's a lanky six foot three and she's tiny. He nearly collapsed on the front entrance floor, only to be told by a doctor to go home and blow in a paper bag. That was as good as telling Robby there was nothing wrong with him and it was all in his head. When I heard this I was so angry I felt like flying to Broome with a huge paper bag and tying it tightly over that doctor's head — except that I've spent enough time around hospitals to know how pressured and under-resourced the entire medical profession is. So I cooled down and let the matter rest and instead flew Robby and Tara to Perth in search of more specialised medical attention.

Eventually he was diagnosed with a leaking appendix. This had apparently been affecting his health for nearly two years, slowly poisoning his body until he had become very ill. It had played a big part in pulling him down mentally and emotionally too. Once his appendix was out, Robby was a changed person. His health zoomed ahead like never before, and my happy son was returned to me at long last. It was another lesson to me about how important our health is, how illness changes everything.

As soon as Robby's health settled down I found myself having some serious talks with my daughter. Sadly, her marriage seemed to be balancing precariously on the rocks again and had been ever since little Cohen was born. It felt terribly sad to me that they couldn't stay together. I thought of them as star-crossed lovers. Each time they parted something brought them back together again, yet once together they could never sustain it. This was the final parting, though, a heartbreaking but mutual decision to end their marriage.

Leisha and I took long walks with the children while she agonised over what she should do. In the end she decided to study psychology by correspondence through TAFE. Adam moved to Busselton and the two of them remained good friends; I was proud of them for that.

One day in this period, I had another call from the caravan park staff in Broome; they were ringing for Terry, believing he was on a trip home to visit me. This pattern had been going on for years, but this was the first call I'd had in a while, and it reminded me how much I hated being lied to. I hated finding out he was at the races in the city when he'd told staff members he was visiting me on the farm. I knew I should just get over it, though. The man I had married was practically incapable of telling the truth; it was simply a question of whether he was caught at it or not.

I remembered an incident at Wildwood in our first year, when both his parents were still alive. His mother and father and I were in the kitchen when Terry pulled the cattle truck up in front of the farmhouse and came running through the kitchen saying, 'I've won the lotto, I've won the lotto!' He grabbed something from the fridge, returned to the cattle truck and took off again at speed.

In the quiet after the flurry, his mother turned to me and asked, 'Has he really won lotto, dear?' I felt a burning shame throughout my body; I felt inadequate as a wife and daughter-in-law. I was unable to give an honest answer, because I really did not know. Surely a real wife would have known.

'He said he has, but I don't really know,' I confessed.

'My dear,' Molly said softly, looking me in the eyes, 'he's told so many lies all through his life, we don't know when he's telling us the truth either.'

Cattle prices were at an all-time low in the south-west, and in February 2006 we struck a much better deal with the Murray Bridge meatworks in South Australia. Two double-decker road trains set off for Murray Bridge loaded with Wildwood steers, and I flew over with Terry to be there when they arrived.

We had come to scrutinise the Murray Bridge way of killing and butchering cattle and to check that the cattle were stress-free after their journey. If the butchered animals were free of bruising and there were no dark cutters (when the meat of a freshly slaughtered beast is darker than normal), we could conclude that the transport had been a success, since stress is believed to contribute to these conditions.

The manager of the meatworks was to guide us through the process as the cattle moved from the knocking box, where they are instantly killed by a bolt to the head, to the cardboard box. To visit a meatworks and watch my own cattle being killed wasn't new to me. I had followed many road trains to the Broome meatworks during the years I was managing cattle stations in the Kimberley. Each beast was no more than a number to me.

I was watching the yard hands pushing the cattle along to the knocking box when the bombshell hit me — and it hit hard. I recognised these big beautiful steers. I had been talking to them most evenings over my back fence at Wildwood. On the other side of the knocking box I fought a wave of nausea and had to look away from the animals' big dewy eyes, which were now vacant. I moved through the rest of the process in a daze, wanting only to get out of the meatworks as quickly as possible.

Terrible as it was for me, the whole process was a credit to all concerned. But I left with a heavy heart; I had grown too close to the cattle on the farm and recognised each one. I had not expected that. On the large acreages of the north, with such large numbers of beasts, the cattle are just that, a number. I love having cattle around me on the farm, but now I hate sending them to slaughter. I am getting soft in my old age.

Back in Perth, I drove Terry to the airport for his return flight to Broome and then headed back to the farm, very tired and beginning to feel empty inside. I was anxious, too, because Robby and Tara and a young friend Rachael were travelling south in a twelve-year-old Ford Laser that had seen better days. They had far more faith in this old car than I did, and no amount of reasoning would persuade them to buy a newer vehicle for the two and a half thousand kilometre trip. They had a fat gold Buddha perched high on the dashboard which they said would get them safely home, and I simply had to suffer sleepless nights in silence until they arrived safely.

Their journey was not to be without incident, however, and I was right to feel apprehensive for their safety, though not for reasons of the Laser's age. They had arrived at a roadhouse on the evening of their first night of travel feeling tired and dusty and looking for a room they could all share. Rachael was prepared to bunk down anywhere as long as Robby and Tara were close by, but she wouldn't take a room alone. She knew that all types of desperadoes frequent outback roadhouses. However, the last double room had just been taken. Realising they were out of luck, they returned to their little car.

Just as they were about to set off into the night, a man approached the Laser saying he had two rooms. He was a big unkempt-looking fellow and they felt a little uneasy about the situation, but they were tired and desperate for a shower and figured that three of them together were safe, so they followed the bloke to check the rooms out. To their horror, the rooms were occupied by other men, who looked like they could be members of some bikie gang. The three of them were worried and insisted that they all wanted to bunk down in the one room, whereupon the fellow who had approached them spun some line about that being 'against health regulations'. He was clearly trying to get the girls into a room away from Robby.

They managed to extricate themselves and run to their car. Shaking from anger, they didn't calm down until they were well away from that godforsaken place.

I was nineteen when I learned for myself the danger of outback desperadoes. It was the late sixties and I was a partner in an outback contracting team, sinking dams, clearing fence lines, dozing and erecting miles of new fences through the untamed Kimberley. I had a low-slung silvery Falcon 351 and almost never drove anywhere without my companion, a bull terrier cross boxer named Butch. On one particular trip, however, I left Butch behind at home.

I had left Halls Creek behind me and was travelling steadily towards Fitzroy Crossing, dodging stray cattle on the road and feeling that my day was going very well. It was late in the afternoon and I had seen only one other vehicle, a road train that rattled slowly over the corrugations, heading in the opposite direction. Then about fifty kilometres north of Fitzroy the Falcon began to chug and choke. It was losing power. I frantically pumped the accelerator, fuel burst through the lines and the car seemed to get a new lease on life. Maybe there'd just been a blockage. I knew there'd be no help in Fitzroy Crossing and that Derby was my only option; I prayed the car would get me there.

Then to my horror, south of Plum Plain, the car died. It just stopped dead. The sun had long gone by now and the night was pitch-black. Fitzroy Crossing was about two kilometres away as the crow flies, but it wasn't exactly the best place to trudge around on a 'pension night'. I could hear the racket going on from my car — cries, dogs barking, camp people yelling, and what sounded like a bloody good stick fight.

I had little choice but to wait for a passing motorist to give me a lift to the Fitzroy service station so I could ring someone. I walked around my car in the dark, stretching my legs while praying for a gentle breeze to cool the evening down and keep the mosquitoes at bay. Then I lay the passenger seat back as far as it would go, placed the biggest wrench I was carrying by my side and, after much tossing and turning, fell into a restless sleep.

It was still dark when I was woken by a road train pulling in beside my vehicle. Alarmed, I was unable to identify the truck as one I knew from the area, when a man's face pushed against my window. I screamed out, and then recognised the man as a cattle station owner from north of Broome. He had his own road-train business on the side. I knew of his reputation as a serious sleaze artist with women, but his son was a real gentleman. He smiled and tapped on the car window and I opened it an inch.

He offered me a cup of coffee; I thanked him, but refused it. He tried to get me to wind the window down further. I said, 'I'm not going anywhere tonight,' and he replied, strangely, 'You need me,' and walked back to his truck. He remained parked up beside my car. I slept restlessly after that, and at one point I woke busting to go to the toilet. While quietly opening the car door, my interior light came on, and in seconds so did his. He had clearly been watching for movement from my vehicle all night. I closed the door and sat tight, feeling as though I was involved in a cat and mouse game.

As the early morning light bounced across the plains the station owner came to my window with two steaming mugs of tea. I felt safer in the light of the day and wound down the window. No sooner had I taken the mug than he had the door open. He grabbed the mug and put it on the ground and in a moment had pinned me down in the passenger seat. Horrified, trying to shield my face from his, I found I didn't have the strength to push his body off mine. My left hand was frantically searching for the wrench. He stopped molesting me for a moment and said, 'What do you think you are going to be able to do with that?'

Realising I was probably unable to do anything at all, I remained still, with closed eyes, hoping and praying he would come to his senses. After what seemed like an eternity, he moved to untangle himself from the gear stick and steering wheel. 'Get off me,' I screamed, frantically kicking out at him with my legs and clawing with my nails, and somehow managing to get out of the passenger door.

I watched him go back to his truck and return with a small pearl-handled pistol. Unbelievably, he was telling me I should carry one of these for protection.

'Well,' he said, 'what are you going to do now?'

Somehow I felt he didn't have the guts to use the gun. Feeling quite brave from the opposite side of my car, I said, 'You have the choice to tow me to Derby without trying to molest me again, or I run to the Fitzroy police station.' Of course he could simply shoot me if he wanted to; I was as good as a sitting duck, but I was increasingly sure he wouldn't.

He was enjoying playing with me though, pointing the pistol and pretending to shoot at each side of my body. My heart beat rapidly against my ribs as I waited for this terrible man to make a decision.

'I'll back up and tow you,' he said. Relieved but still wary, I kept my distance while he hooked my car on behind his road train. Not another vehicle or truck had passed by in the last twelve hours, and that wasn't unusual in this part of the Kimberley.

I let go of the handbrake and he towed me flat out down the corrugated road, my car fishtailing from side to side with the swing of his trailers. In and out of creek beds and rivers, there was no stopping as rocks flew up from under the trailer wheels. The car was the least of my worries, though; all I wanted was to arrive in Derby in one piece.

Some four hours later we were coming into Derby, but the truck didn't appear to be slowing down for the service station. Frantic, I literally stood on my brake pedal, not caring for the consequences. Smoke billowed from my car as the tyres were dragged along the bitumen road and eventually the truck braked too, till it came to a standstill just beyond the service station. With a pounding heart I leaped from my car and ran for the security of the office.

'Don't let him near me,' I said to the man behind the counter. 'Can you please call me a taxi for Broome.' I explained what was happening and told him I would collect the Falcon later. He asked if I wanted the police and I said no. I went to the door and looked out to see if the station owner had unhooked my car. I waited for him to go, but incredibly he just stood there, leaning against his truck watching me, looking completely relaxed. He had a colossal nerve.

I stayed glued to the service station counter until my taxi arrived; the man behind the counter was looking at me as though I was some hysterical woman.

Why didn't I call the police? Because the man had a lovely son who was soon to marry a friend of mine and I didn't want to bring shame on his family. I was a cot case for weeks after this; I told my parents what had happened, but I wouldn't let them make any kind of official complaint, although I'm certain my father followed it up. I heard later that other truck drivers had sorted the bastard out, and I always wondered if the word had got through from Dad.

Robby and Tara stayed at the Shiralee for the duration of Broome's off-season. I was glad to have them there keeping an eye on things for me. I hoped they would stay and encouraged them to settle in, but as the new season came around in Broome they packed and returned to their old jobs.

By that time Kristy had moved south again and begun work at a top thoroughbred stud. She moved in with me at Wildwood and it was comforting to have another person sharing the large house. There was plenty of room for both of us. Kristy worked long hours and I was happy to do the cooking and washing to take the pressure off her.

When Brock spent weekends with me he would take over as the little man of the house, often helping me in the garden or cleaning out sheds. One day both boys were helping me pick figs to make jam. I was working my way backwards down the wonky ladder, balancing a full bucket of figs, when I slipped and landed like a sack of potatoes on the wet ground below. I was sprawled out among the squashed figs, rueful to discover I wasn't as nimble as in my bull running days — although I can vouch for squashed fig tasting far better than a mouthful of Kimberley bulldust. I wiggled all my limbs to check I wasn't hurt, then looked around to see an expression of absolute horror on young Cohen's face. Muddy tears were already making tracks down his face. Meanwhile Brock was frantically trying to help me to my feet. 'Shall I call 000?' he asked. 'I know how to, Nan.'

I got to my feet, dusted myself off and reassured them that I was fine. And I thought how lucky we were that if a real emergency occurred we could dial 000 and get the help of professionals in no time. In the outback we had the flying doctor, but help could be hundreds if not thousands of kilometres away, and sometimes it took time. And that could be the fine line between life and death. My son Kelly died as the pilot of the rescue aircraft walked through the homestead door. I still wonder whether, had we lived closer to civilisation, Kelly would have survived.

The fig jam ended up a bit on the runny side, and when Leisha arrived to collect the children after their weekend with Nan, she wasn't too interested in it. With her marriage over, she had plunged into studying psychology with a vengeance. She'd studied by correspondence all her life and she was very self-disciplined, squeezing in odd hours every moment she could. 'Keep at it, love,' I joked, 'I'll probably need a shrink in the family one day.'

They say what doesn't kill you makes you stronger, and for years I have sustained myself with that. I had been through a lot, losing my firstborn son, then McCorry's tragic deterioration as he sank into depression. His frightening black moods as he battled to kill his pain with alcohol. He was a strong man, that one, and I tried to remain strong for him and for the children too.

I worked long, hard hours on first Kimberley Downs then Napier, Kilto and Fairfield; my children pulled their weight too. I'd wanted to remain on Fairfield for the rest of my life and leave it as a legacy for my children, and it was another heartbreak when I had to sell it. I survived all of those cruel losses, but not one of them brought me as low as the madness of living with Terry. And yet maybe they also gave me the strength to come back to life, despite the psychological beatings I'd taken and all the mind games and confusion of living with a man who insisted black was white and night was day.

The writing played a big part in coming back to myself — all the hours I spent going over the past, remembering who I had been. This was the beginning of getting my strength and confidence back, though sometimes I feared I would never again be the woman I once was. Those were scary times, when I just had to give myself a shake and say, 'Sheryl, you got yourself into this, you can get yourself out again.' In my old life in the Kimberley I was such a can-do sort of person, I had to be. Out there, you had to be able to handle things on your own. It went with the territory. And that is one reason why I found it so hard to accept that I couldn't pick myself up without help.

More than once a doctor had suggested I see a counsellor. Now and then I did think I ought to bite the bullet and find the courage to do so. But I never did. To admit I needed that kind of help was like admitting I was a basket case. There wasn't much that was worse than that, I thought. Or maybe I was afraid that it wouldn't help. And if I tried and it didn't work — well, then I would be beyond help.

CHAPTER 16

Someone Wants my Story

*I*t was with a heavy heart I called up a real estate agent in Mount Barker to put my precious Shiralee on the market. Well, to begin the process of putting it on the market. When the call was over I sat for a moment as what I had just done hit home. I had worked hard for that farm, I loved it dearly, but it wasn't making a decent income. I wanted to get myself financially secure, and for that I needed more land and more cattle — and to be on hand to run it myself.

I was having a real tussle with myself. Because if I was living on the property and running it myself, then the Shiralee could probably run at a profit. After all, it had kept me going for the first few years, while McCorry was still alive. So maybe it could again — if I lived on the property full-time. But that was one fence I still wasn't completely ready to jump. I had hoped that Robby and Tara would stay and farm it for me, but they had returned to the caravan park.

Leisha and Kristy didn't care if I sold the Shiralee. Neither of them had a bond with it as I had. Leisha said, 'Don't hang on to it for us, Mum. You worked hard for it, it's your right to do what you want with it.' Robby was more concerned about where home would be if the farm was gone, but that didn't stop him wanting to go back to Broome. Terry didn't pay brilliant money, but at least it was wages, and on the Shiralee it would be lean times for a while until things were running smoothly.

In August I made a visit to my parents in Northampton. Living in this quiet little town was their way of remaining in the bush, away from the hustle and bustle of cities. We sat together on their back verandah, reminiscing and letting the winter sun give warmth to our bodies. I loved these quiet times with each other.

We laughed as we reminisced about the old days. There is one story of Dad's that I'm particularly fond of. Back in 1967, the Shell Company of Australia part-funded a documentary film about the exchange of culture and lifestyle between black and white. Whites were teaching Aboriginal men basic mechanics, and Aboriginal women were teaching the whites how to live and survive in the bush.

My dad, known by the Aboriginal people of Yirrkala as Mr Snow because of his white-blond hair, was hired as a guide for the project. It was his responsibility to make sure nobody in the film party became a main meal for a crocodile or got gored by a rampaging buffalo.

One morning's filming began at a beautiful billabong selected by the Aboriginal women. It was snuggled behind low sandhills and trickled into a stream that flowed slowly out to the ocean. The dark water of the billabong was covered with a blanket of blue waterlilies. Old paperbark trees dotted the surrounding area and provided shade, but also made it difficult to note any kind of movement in the waterhole.

Dad was aware that crocodiles frequented this otherwise enchanting billabong and wasn't happy that this particular site had been chosen for the filming. He had been taking readings from sand movement gauges on the beaches as part of his work at the time, and often found reptile tracks heading into the spring which led into the billabong.

A number of women were waist deep in the billabong, the water droplets on their breasts like jewellery in the sun. Floating coolamons — shallow dishes made from the paper-bark trees — carried the waterlily bulbs they were collecting for bush tucker. My father stretched himself out on an over-hanging paperbark branch, his gun at the ready.

It's a rule of filmmaking that the film always runs out in the middle of the best shot. The gofer for the second camera unit was sent back to the Landrover, a half-mile walk through the scrub, to collect more film. On his way back, he decided to take a short cut and in a thicket of tangled vines and pandanus trees met a sleepy old bull buffalo head on. 'AAAAH, HELLPP, HELLPP!' came his anguished cry, a mixture of pommy accent, city slicker and sick terror echoing out of the thicket.

Suddenly both man and beast burst into the open with a hell of a racket, the gofer screaming and the buffalo bull snorting as he charged straight for the film crew. Then the Aboriginal women joined in the chorus, screaming in panic; this somehow had the effect of diverting the buffalo, which changed direction and galloped obligingly in front of the first cameraman. The buffalo stopped suddenly, sending dirt and debris flying high into the air with his hooves. He was angry. An aggressive shake of those huge horns, a tremendous snort, and he charged again, lunging towards the terrified crew.

'Him proper angry one,' yelled Mary.

'You gonna shoot him, Mr Snow?' said another of the women.

Dad had no plans to shoot the 'old fella' buffalo — it was probably too tough to eat. He figured it would run out of steam and simply drift away shortly.

In all the panic, the first cameraman somehow kept shooting, right up to the moment he was thrown aside by the agitated beast as it made its final pass before heading off into the scrub again. Camera and man, tangled in metres of cords and unravelled film that had spilled out of the camera, went arse up on the ground, and yells and cries of fear and laughter filled the air as everyone converged to untangle the mess left behind by the buffalo.

Luckily other cameras were recording the exciting events, so all was not lost. The shoot in the billabong went on for another three days, during which time Mr Snow's crocodile count happily did not increase and the women harvested all their waterlily bulbs safely.

Back at Wildwood I sank myself back into writing. I felt an urgency to complete the story of my Kimberley life, to give the children a picture of their mother when she was firing on all cylinders! When I reached the point of old McCorry's dying, I knew I'd done what I wanted to do. I hadn't even realised it till then, but the memoir that was to become *Diamonds and Dust* was also a testament to my old cattleman, my children's father.

There were plenty of stories about McCorry that didn't make it into the first book. We had a lot of years together, and I couldn't put all of them in. There was a funny story — well, I didn't think it was so funny at the time! — when we were mustering out the back of the Robinson River on Oobagooma station in the late sixties. Competition in mustering the boundaries of your station before your neighbour did was ferocious. People would listen in on the party line to find out when neighbours were planning a boundary muster. The properties had no fences and the cattle wandered where they wanted in search of fresh green grass, from one property to the next. In my twenty-year-old eyes, the better cattleman was the one who knew and understood both the cattle and the untamed country — the one who mustered more cleanskins than their neighbour did. The Wild West had nothing on outback Kimberley!

I was out on a cattle muster with old McCorry, way out back on the boundary, years before we married. The stockmen rose each day at 4.30 am; we all had a pannikin of black tea made in Dingo Flour drums and warm damper smothered with treacle for breakfast. After breakfast I collected, checked and oiled the bull straps for the day's work. There was no point chasing feral bulls if I couldn't secure them safely once the bull buggy had them on the ground for me to strap. This was my morning ritual before I left the camp each day.

One morning McCorry walked over with an old .303 rifle in his hand, leaned it up against a gum tree, then turned to face me. Looking straight at me, his eyes black beneath the brim of his hat, he gave me orders that shocked me.

'I want you to spend the day on that hill over there,' he said, and he seemed deadly serious, although I couldn't always tell when he was joking, 'Keep your eyes out for any horsemen, and if the manager rides into camp, gut-shoot him.' He was always talking about gut-shooting someone, though to my knowledge, he had never shot anyone.

I looked at him, amazed. He pointed to the .303. 'There's the rifle, he'll be well over his boundaries if he gets this far. And don't worry about his stockmen, they'll only be following orders,' he added.

'What do you mean? You don't want me to shoot *them*,

only the manager?' I said, incredulous. Not that I was going to shoot anyone, in any part of their body, not even for McCorry. 'That's right,' he said and, not giving me time to question him further, turned and walked away, and in a moment was up in the saddle, off on another day's muster.

Bloody hell, I thought, looking from the gun to McCorry's disappearing back as he and the stockmen vanished against the thick scrub. *I don't believe this.*

Thinking about it, however, I remembered that the day before I had overheard the stockmen and McCorry discussing their find of three sets of shod horse tracks 'well inside our Oobagooma country'. From the tone of their voices I guessed that they were stirred up by this information.

When McCorry and the stockmen were out of sight, I walked across the flat to climb the rocky outcrop to the highest point. This was a long haul, lugging the heavy firearm; by the time I reached a point where I could look about the vast countryside to spot any intruders, I wasn't very happy. In fact I was very angry with old McCorry and wished I could tell him so.

I moved about the rocky plateau surveying the country below. There was no one to be seen, so I made myself comfortable, leaning my back against an old stump, the firearm beside me. *This is ludicrous, the whole idea*, I thought as I watched and waited. *How the hell can I tell whether it's the manager or his bloody stockmen from up here?* The heat of the midday sun was fierce, and the little black native bees were giving me hell, getting into my hair, ears, eyes, searching for salty moisture.

I got up off the ground and paced around the rocky outcrop. I decided maybe I would put two or three rounds into the air if I saw intruders, but hell, from this height, how was I to know who they were? Still, if they were intruders and this didn't make them turn their horses around and head back into their own country, the noise of the .303 echoing through the hills should be enough to bring McCorry galloping back to camp. Then again, he could be having me on. I just didn't know.

That was it, I'd had enough. I couldn't second-guess McCorry, never could. I stomped back down to where I'd begun and waited for them to return. And did I get a straight answer from the old bastard when he got back? No I did not. But I'm sure he was setting me up; they were probably all having a good laugh at my expense.

Now I had to work out what to do with my finished memoir. I made some enquiries and found an editor who would help tidy it up, correct the grammar — I had no illusions whatsoever that I could write — and present it in a printable fashion so I could run off a few copies for the family. When it was finished, it suddenly looked so professional, all properly paragraphed and set out on the page, that I decided, 'What the hell, let's see if anyone wants to publish it.' Over the years in the Kimberley, I had been the subject of a few newspaper and magazine stories, some of them syndicated around the country, and a lot of people had responded positively to the stories. It made good headlines — 'QUEEN OF THE WILD CATTLE RANGES' and 'ON KIMBERLEY DOWNS THE BOSS WEARS DIAMONDS', though Bob wasn't keen on that one, or 'NO BULL, SHE'S BOSS'.

I asked the editor how he thought I should go about finding a publisher, and was quite taken aback when he said, 'I doubt you'll ever get this published.' He went on, 'You'd certainly battle to get an east coast agent to take you on, and no east coast publisher would even look at it.'

Well bugger you, mate, I thought to myself. *I'll show you.* This was the nudge I needed to push me along. There's that cussed side to me, that if you tell me I can't do something, it only makes me the more determined.

As I said to Leisha, 'I've got nothing to lose, I've already achieved what I wanted to do, anything else is a bonus.' I felt so confident. I hadn't felt so much like my old self for a long time. All those days and nights writing, my strength had slowly seeped back through my veins.

I decided the local Western Australian presses were too small; I wanted to try for a major commercial publisher on the east coast first. If that failed, then I could always try the local press. And if nobody was interested, I would forget the publishing game and keep my story for my children as it was originally intended. So I printed out half the memoir and mailed it with photos to several large publishing companies. I didn't really care whether I heard back or not — in fact it never occurred to me that I would — I packed my bag and took a plane to Broome for a short break.

Less than two weeks later, while I was still in Broome, I got my first phone call of real interest, from Pan Macmillan in Sydney. The non-fiction publisher thought it was a great Australian story. I couldn't believe it, I was over the moon.

Of course, my situation with Terry had to turn this moment of triumph into burlesque. While I was taking the phone call on my mobile, my husband kept walking into the bedroom telling me loudly to, 'Hurry up, hurry up.' He wanted to go to the post office and for some reason needed me to go with him. Trying in vain to brush him away, I ended up turning my back on him in order to concentrate on the conversation. I couldn't believe it, the very phone call every writer wants to receive and Terry decided at that very moment he needed my undivided attention!

Once my manuscript was in the hands of the publishers, I had some moments of panic as I thought of how many people would get to read about my life. 'Don't be silly, Mum,' said

Leisha. 'You've done some amazing things, you should be proud of yourself. We're proud of you.'

Well, I thought, it was all in the lap of the gods. I'd just have to get on with my life now. So I took the Shiralee off the market. I had never really wanted to sell it; I'd just battled with not being able to care for it properly. Having a book deal gave me a more positive sense of a future and a new confidence that I could live on my farm and manage it as I once had.

I was coming back to life again, my heart and body waking up after a long sleep. Now the absence of love and sex in my life was making itself felt again. Sex with Terry had come to an end only eighteen months into our marriage.

It was an interesting pattern, I had to admit, to suffer a sex drought in two marriages. I once had a healthy sex drive, but now I worried I would become a dried-up old woman. Some nights I would lie curled up in my large bed, haunted by feelings of loneliness. Would I ever feel love from a partner again? I certainly wouldn't if I continued living in this sham of a marriage. Was it already too late? I longed to feel the intensity of desire, intimacy; the fire and heat of passionate lovemaking, but I feared that part of my life was over.

'Well, you made your bed and you have to lie in it,' I told myself, but I was beginning to doubt the wisdom of this 'hang in there at all costs' attitude of mine. Still, when a friend suggested I have an affair, I realised I couldn't do that; I didn't have the courage to break with the 'right' thing to do. I was more old-fashioned than a lot of people far older than me. My daughters called me strait-laced. Maybe that's why they decided a vibrator would be an excellent Christmas present.

'Everyone has them, Mum,' Leisha laughed. 'You can get them with lights and revolving pearls,' added Kristy. 'I can just see the headlines,' I said. 'AUTHOR ELECTROCUTED BY REVOLVING VIBRATOR!' This had Leisha rolling around in laughter on the floor. When the laughter had subsided, she said, 'So you will let us give you one then, Mum?' No, I would not! 'Not bloody likely,' I said. 'You can forget all about that bright idea.'

In November Terry was on one of his visits to the Wildwood farm when my doctor rang, asking me to come in to discuss the results of some blood tests. I organised to do this in a couple of days, for Terry wanted to visit his two grandsons. Leisha had recently moved off the farm to rent a place of her own in the Serpentine area, south of Perth. She had stopped studying for the time being. The coursework was too demanding with two small children, and she deferred it until she could give it her undivided attention.

Jumping at the opportunity to see Leisha and the boys, I thought how wonderful it was that Terry would drive me to see them.

Before leaving we stopped at the store to collect the mail and the daily paper. I sorted through the farm's mail, taking out only the personal letters for Terry. Jean always handled the business mail for the farms. Passing his personal letters to my husband, I was met with a very brusque, 'Is there any more?'

'Only the usual business mail for Jean,' I answered, and then he erupted. Yelling and abusing and slamming on the steering wheel, his jaw set in that terrifying way, his eyes dark and distant. Was there some letter he'd been hoping for? This was the behaviour of a thwarted child. I tried to ignore his angry outburst. Putting my head down, I pretended to read the newspaper, but he worked himself up even more, shaking his fists in my face as he threatened me.

I lifted my face from the newspaper and said very softly, 'Terry, the way you're carrying on is really stupid, this is not necessary.'

His face looked as though it was about to explode. He slammed the steering wheel again and spat, 'I'd rather be stupid than a coon!'

That took my breath away. 'Did I hear right, did you just call me a coon?'

For an answer, he forced an unnatural laugh and chanted, 'I may be a hoon, but at least I'm no coon.'

He obviously liked that, because he sat there repeating it in a singsong voice while I thought of Fanny Wannery and her daughter Dina. I was proud to have them in my heritage. In fact, it was a great day for me when I discovered that my great-gran Dina was of Aboriginal descent.

It was long after she had died. I was at my mother's, looking through photographs when I came across one of Dina in her youth — her skin was much darker than I remembered it in old age, and she was unmistakeably of Aboriginal heritage. I remembered visiting her in the Geraldton hospital; I sat by her chair and stroked her hand. Her skin felt like the softest silk — despite the fact that for much of her life she had chopped wood and done all manner of outside jobs around the place after her husband died of cancer.

Until this day I knew nothing of my mother's family history. Now my mother told me about my great-great-grandmother Fanny Wannery, born in 1852, the daughter of an Aboriginal woman and an English stockman from a sheep station in Western Australia's south-west. Fanny's mother was working in the station cookhouse when she fell pregnant to the stockman. Fanny's mother left her under a low scrubby saltbush next to the homestead, to be found by the English couple running the station. The couple brought Fanny up as their own, and she grew up as an English girl, well spoken and educated, and treated as one of the family.

Her daughter Dina rode horses, handled a horse-drawn buggy and was a good shot with a gun. She was a midwife, at the hub of a big extended family. When I learned all this it suddenly made sense of my ease and comfort being in the bush and my deep connection with Aboriginal people — it seemed we were family, no matter how white I was on the outside.

This made me laugh as I thought of an incident on Napier Downs station, long before this day with my mother. Back then the only way to help indigenous children achieve an education was to deliver them to St Joseph's Hostel in Derby at the beginning of each term and collect them at the end.

The school holidays had come to an end and the women on Napier Downs had a huge wash day: clean clothes were flying in the breeze from every fence line around camp. The stockmen were allowing the children a last ride on their stockhorses before Yardie the horse tailor (the stockman who keeps all the horses together during a muster) returned the animals to the paddock. The camp was alive with the sounds of happy chatter and squeals of laughter. The Aboriginal children were sprinting about, teasing mongrel dogs that attacked the camp chooks; a spray of white chook feathers would fly high into the air, accompanied by the poor hen letting out an affronted squawk. A mother's angry voice, another's laughter as a billy can landed in the middle of the flat, missing the dog altogether. The children all seemed fit and healthy; it was a shame they had to go off to school in Derby, but it was the only way they would learn to read and write.

The next morning, with a backdrop of bright blue sky, the heavy clouds sitting comfortably on the distant horizon, I called the women to have their children ready for school. The red cattle truck and crate was washed and shiny, and parents and grandparents were helping to load the children with their swags and bags. Using the cattle crate was the safest way to secure the children. Some of the older camp women were coming along as minders for the long trip into town.

In the midst of preparations, an argument started between two of the camp kids over who was going to ride in the front of the truck with me.

Lynette, whose skin was very dark, said to Mandy, 'You're mad.' 'No,' Mandy replied, 'you're mad.' Lynette answered with, 'You're mad, you're white.' Mandy's heritage was a mixture of black and white, and her skin was quite light.

'Hey, that's enough of that. Come here, you two girls,' I said. I hated to see this sort of thing. It was bad enough white folk discriminating on the basis of colour, but it really disturbed me to see the children attacking each other over who was more black or white.

The other kids had heard, and soon the whole group was standing around. 'Now, each of us put one arm side by side here,' I said, and all the children thrust an arm into the circle. 'What's the difference?' I said quietly.

One girl replied, 'All different colours, missus.'

'Yes, all different colours on the outside, but you mob remember, we are all the same on the inside, all right?'

'Yes, yes missus,' the girls replied happily, and the cheap shots of the earlier argument were forgotten.

And that was what Terry had been doing, taking a cheap shot at me. Too bad for him it missed the target.

When we eventually reached Leisha's — after a predictable detour to check on two of Terry's horses — I was emotionally drained and in need of a cup of tea.

'Mum, it's him, isn't it?' my daughter asked when she saw

my face. She put her arms around me while I tried to pull myself together.

Terry was pacing the verandah and his true reason for the trip emerged. Not giving me time to drink my tea, he insisted on leaving to visit a thoroughbred stud at Serpentine.

Leisha, wary of his unpredictable temper, said, 'Hang on, the kids and I are coming too,' and gathered her nappy bag and a bottle for young Cohen. We all piled into the Landcruiser, and when we arrived at the stud we left him to it.

'Mum, you've got to do something about this, he's turning you into a nervous wreck, can't you see that?' said my girl.

'Right now I simply don't have the strength, but I'm sure once the book is completed I'll be stronger,' I replied. It was the best I could do.

Terry returned, his face dark as thunder, and we sped off down the dusty road, not a word spoken between us, my head bowed, hoping for peace.

'The lights are flashing!' yelled Leisha suddenly. Lifting my head, I saw we were approaching a railway crossing. I screamed, 'For god's sake, stop, Terry,' but he only sped up.

'Can't you see the lights? A train is coming! Stop the bloody car, think of the children!' I screamed at my husband, and at last he did, slamming his foot hard on the brake and sending us flying forward against seatbelts with a terrible jolt.

Terry's blind aggression had taken me by surprise. It had been a while since I had felt its full force. I didn't know what triggered it, I hardly ever knew, but I was starting to wonder just how sick he must be. For a moment I even felt sorry for him. He carried so much tension and anger, and I don't know if he had anyone he could talk to, anyone who could help him. I don't think he had any real friends, he turned on everyone who tried to get close. I don't suppose he was ever one of a bunch of twigs.

As my children grew up and other children joined our family — some abandoned, others wayward, all from different walks of life — I introduced them to the story of the bunch of twigs.

Not long after sixteen-year-old Bert turned up, courtesy of the welfare department, we sat under the massive canopy of a ghost gum on the banks of a billabong. It was peaceful except for some bickering between Bert and another of the children staying with us. I got up from where I was sitting and collected a handful of twigs, returned to my little group and sat down cross-legged in front of them.

'Look here,' I said, holding out my bunch of twigs to Leisha. 'Can you break them?' I asked her, and then suggested she pass them around the group to see if anyone could break all the twigs in the bunch. When they came back to me, some twigs were bruised and a little damaged, but no one was able to break the bunch as a whole. I explained to the children that the bunch of twigs was like us as a group.

'See how strong we are,' I said as I applied strength in vain to the task of breaking the bunch. Then I took one twig from the bunch and broke it. 'This is one person — it is easier to break one person than break a group of people who look out for each other through life.'

This, I explained to the two squabbling teenagers, was how my family worked, and I welcomed them to be part of it. Today we still get visits from Bert and the others, 'Just checking to see you're okay,' they say.

Two days after my visit to Leisha's I went to my doctor's for the results of the blood tests. It wasn't what I wanted to hear — not that it was life-threatening, it wasn't that. I had aggressive rheumatoid arthritis. It explained all my joint aches and pains, which was good, but the prognosis wasn't great. Some days the aches and pains became so unbearable that I would retreat to my bed four times in one day. Constant joint aches and pains contributed to such an overwhelming tiredness so that all I wanted to do was sleep it away. This would be my life; I couldn't expect it to go away.

Terry stayed at Wildwood for six weeks. At the end of November I woke to a beautiful day. As I lay basking in the sunshine that filtered through my bedroom windows, I could hear movement in the house. I got up in time to catch Terry leaving the house with his suitcase.

'Are you just going to Perth or back to Broome?' I asked. He hadn't given me any indication he'd be leaving.

He turned around and yelled back at me, 'You attacked me!'

'I what?' For days on end I'd had no idea what Terry was doing or where he was. 'That isn't remotely true and you know it,' I said. 'It isn't even funny.'

He didn't answer, just threw his case into his old Holden Statesman and left the farmhouse with wheels spinning, sending a cloud of dust drifting through the open door. The next morning he rang and spoke to me as if nothing had happened. I should have been used to his erratic behaviour, but I was left feeling ragged and confused again. It was clear to me that no matter how strong I became, he still had the power to knock me sideways.

CHAPTER 17

Like Mother like Daughter

*I*n March 2007 I travelled to Northampton to pick up my mother and take her back to Wildwood for a holiday. My father was happy to stay at home and potter around. After the green of the southern country, the farm paddocks around Northampton were shockingly barren, not a blade of grass to be seen. The country looked like a desert, and I wondered just how many of the sheep and wheat farmers would survive this terrible dry spell. The men were taking jobs far and wide — in mines, on road gangs and driving trucks — while the women remained on the farms trying to keep some stability in the lives of their children. We really felt for them.

After a few days at Wildwood we drove through the forests to the Shiralee, reminiscing about life in Arnhem Land where we scavenged on beaches for shells and pieces of coral. My mother was always a collector of beautiful or interesting things.

As we drove I got her talking about her childhood. I wanted to know more about Dina, her grandmother. Mum had been very close to her gran, who had lived with her family for many years before the Second World War. This time she told me a story Dina had told her, about a white dingo.

There were two brothers in the family, and they had travelled by horse and buggy across country on their way home and found a gold nugget lying in a creek bed they were camping in. After they arrived home, they decided to go back with packhorses and try to find the place where they'd found the gold nugget. Three days after they were due to return, people were starting to worry. Dina was sitting outside when she saw a white dingo coming towards her. She remembered hearing a story from her mother, Fanny, about how seeing a white dingo meant someone was in trouble, so she packed food and water and a swag, and went out following the dingo. In the end she found the brothers, nearly perished: they'd run out of water.

Eventually, as Mum and I drove, the distinctive outline of the Porongurups came into view way in the distance, amethyst daubed with a palette of earthy colours. The sleeping princess looked so peaceful in the late evening, and warmth flooded my heart as it did every time I got this close to home. Mum loved the Shiralee as much as I did; it had such a serenity about it. I took her around the farm, checking on the fences, although that wasn't really necessary as Richard was still keeping an eye on things for me. Mainly we just had a relaxing time there. It was restful and rejuvenating, waking each morning to the tap-tap-tapping of the little blue wrens on my bedroom windowsill.

From the Shiralee we made a trip to Ravensthorpe, the town where my mother and grandmother were born. We visited the graves of my great-great-grandparents in the pioneer cemetery, and I saw the little old house Mum was born in, with her own grandmother as midwife. Dina was often called on to deliver babies as the local doctor was frequently unable to attend — due to being plastered, apparently. From Ravensthorpe to Hopetoun to Mason Bay (named after my great-great-grandfather John Mason, Dina's brother), it was a journey of going back to beginnings, and it was wonderful to do this with my mother. We travelled well together; we were soft with each other, it was a revelation that two people could get along so well.

My mother came from a musical family. Most of them could sing well or play a musical instrument by ear without ever having studied music. Johnny Mason was a horse breaker who handled horses for Australian soldiers shipping out to Gallipoli. He wanted to go to war himself, but they wouldn't let him because he was needed to break in horses. However, at the age of thirty-three he accompanied a shipment of horses to Perth and managed to sign on with the 10th Light Horse Regiment. He served in Palestine and was one of the lucky ones as he survived the war, despite being wounded twice. Apparently Johnny Mason was famous in his unit for bursting into song on the battlefield, as I learned from the family memoir written by my aunty Ethel Coleman, who was Johnny's niece.

There was a news article in the old Western Mail. *It said that a halt was called after a day of hell, fighting in the desert. Everyone was weary and dispirited, the men just threw down their gear and lay down to rest in the still, silent desert night, when gradually the wonderful voice of Trooper Johnny Mason rose on the evening air.*

On our trip Mother and I sang and listened to music all along the way. I felt connected to my mother in a new way, and connected through her to a long line of strong, determined, hard-working individuals. It reminded me that I had inherited some of their strength and uniqueness and that I should not lose sight of that.

The day I received the advance copies of the book was unbelievable. Over the past months I had been fine-tuning my book with different editors and they had made me dig deeper, until I was expressing more than I had ever intended to. I was excited about the end result, but a little uncertain too. The kids all wanted the first copies out of the box, but I posted these to Mum and Dad. My tough old dad later said he cried most of the way through. Nobody had read the manuscript, and for all my family it was a revelation as to how deeply I had been affected by things.

It was a revelation to me too. I read my copy from start to finish in one go. It was like reading about someone else's life. I couldn't put it down. It felt surreal, as though I was a stranger in my own life. That was the power of seeing the whole story, all in one piece, polished up and complete for the first time. I couldn't really believe my own life — it gave me a big boost to see myself in that way.

Finally, in October 2007, *Diamonds and Dust* was officially released, and then the interviews began. Flooded with invitations for speaking engagements and back-to-back phone interviews, fright and fear of facing the public and the many questions almost overcame me. But I surprised myself and found after my first interviews that I enjoyed talking about my life in the outback. And the enthusiastic response from the many readers who sat down and wrote to me was wonderful. People related deeply to what I had written, and that was more gratifying than I could have imagined.

The time came for me to head to the east coast for a *Diamonds and Dust* publicity tour. I was very nervous. I had never flown alone to Sydney before. I forewarned Pan Macmillan's publicist that I had never been to Sydney and was afraid I'd become lost — and I very nearly did so, before I had even left the airport! I wondered would I ever find my luggage and get out of the building, and regretted all my remarks about city slickers. I took a bearing on another passenger from my flight, hoping that would lead me to the carousel to retrieve my suitcase — and it did.

A taxi took me to my hotel in the heart of Sydney. I was surprised that my driver wasn't taking corners and bends on two wheels, as I had been warned before leaving the west. Maybe Robby had been pulling my leg!

By the time I reached my suite I was looking forward to a bath and a cup of tea. I opened the door onto what initially looked like an entire wall of lights but turned out to be a huge picture window looking onto Sydney's city lights. It was a beautiful view and could have passed as a fairyland, until I suddenly registered how far up off the ground I was — and quickly pulled the blinds.

For the next week I moved around in what seemed to me another world. With so many media interviews, and only time to take a cab from one studio to another, there was never time for fear to set in. I was whisked in and out of hair and make-up to be interviewed live on Channel 7 by Kylie Gillies and Larry Emdur. This was my first television interview and I was absolutely terrified. But Kylie and Larry made me feel so at ease and as I stepped down from the cameras after the interview several cameramen wrapped their arms around me and said I had done very well. One said he had filmed hundreds of these and mine was one of the best. This gave me tremendous confidence to go out and face the world, although I'm sure he was only saying it to help me out.

In Melbourne for a live Channel Ten interview with David and Kim, I grasped for the first time how deeply *Diamonds and Dust* had affected readers who were complete strangers to me. As I talked I noticed Kim's eyes fill with tears. When we went to an advertisement break, the make-up artist raced in and fixed her face. I glanced up, only to notice a cameraman wiping tears away too. After the interview I got up to walk away, only to have people wrap their arms around me in big hugs. I was so surprised, and happy; I needed that. But I never wanted to make people cry.

After that hectic week I returned to the west carrying with me new visions and broader horizons, though at the same time it all seemed unreal. Back at Wildwood I had many more phone interviews lined up for me from all over Australia.

Some weeks later Terry asked me to spend a fortnight with him in Broome. I decided to say yes. I had book signings to go to, and radio and newspaper interviews there anyway. People at the park were buying the book and wanting it signed. I was stopped everywhere, by friends and friends of friends who wanted to congratulate me on it. Suddenly Terry got caught up in all the excitement too. When people stopped me to ask about my life in the outback he came and stood tall by my side, beaming and happy for me. He seemed proud of me at last. A bit late, I couldn't help thinking.

We hired a car and travelled to the Aboriginal community of Yiyili, halfway between Fitzroy Crossing and Halls Creek on Louisa Downs, the cattle station I once managed. I wanted to visit Katie and the many other old friends who kept in contact. Katie still called me regularly and once we started talking it was as if I had never left the station. I wanted to hand Katie my book personally. There were hugs and laughter, tears and joy as the women crowded around me, then Katie showed me the new art studio built on Yiyili land.

'You got more photos, missus?' Katie asked me, having turned straight to the photo sections and exclaimed over the people she knew. She and the other women on the community who had been on Louisa and Bohemia Downs were keen to look back over the pictures of our years together. I promised that I would make multiple copies of any photos I had and deliver them at the first opportunity.

Arriving back in Perth I caught up with the news that *Diamonds and Dust* was on its fourth reprint, and that one was selling out fast. I was delighted, though it didn't feel quite real to me. As Leisha and I drove home to the Shiralee I realised I couldn't have been happier. Life looked so full of possibilities and promise. I decided it was more than time for me to take a darn good look at my marriage.

Being treated with so much respect and admiration for the book made it impossible for me to take Terry's insults and put-downs any longer. I was finding my confidence, courage and determination coming back to me in waves. To hear my book described in such positive terms gave me an amazing boost. It was a very strange experience, suddenly to be a public person, but with every passing day I was becoming less of a stranger to myself.

CHAPTER 18

The Nightmare is Over

*I*t was Christmas 2007 and Robby and Tara had come down from Broome to be at the Shiralee. Leisha had moved back to Wildwood to be with me, and Kristy was away working with horses, further to the south-west of the state.

Terry came to Wildwood, and I used the opportunity to tell him that I could no longer see any future for us as a married couple. In response, he told me he had threatened to do away with the solicitor of his last wife if she didn't agree to his divorce terms. He boasted that he had kicked in the front door of his last matrimonial home.

Other than that, he never responded directly to my saying I no longer saw a future with him. Perhaps to him that would have meant taking me seriously, and I think he never felt I was worth that. The pride he seemed to feel for me in Broome, when people were making a fuss about the book, had vanished.

It was good to have Leisha and the children around. I didn't know whether it had a physical or emotional cause, but suddenly I felt extremely low again. My bones ached and I had a fever. I felt miserable because I had thought all this was over; I had not thought Terry could still reduce me to such a state.

Then one evening, while standing under the shower, I was in for an even ruder shock.

'Leisha, Leisha!' I called out in a panic.

She came running, and I cried, 'Come here, love, look,' pointing to the plughole which was full of my blonde hair. I ran my fingers through my hair and looked down in horror to find my hands full of my own hair. What was happening to me? Not even my cancer treatment had taken this much hair from my head.

A few days later I drove with Terry to Perth so he could fly back to Broome. Again he reminded me of threatening to do away with his ex-wife's solicitor if they didn't agree to what he wanted.

I suggested that maybe he needed some help at the park. 'Why?' he demanded, and I answered, 'Because you're always so angry and stressed.' He tensed up even more, so I tried again. 'What's really wrong, what's worrying you, Terry?' I should have known better, he had never given me a straight answer before. His face stiffened, his jaw twisted and he slammed the steering wheel. Leaning over towards me while driving with one hand, he shook a fist in my face, angrily jerking the steering wheel from side to side. We were on the highway and the traffic was heavy. I was terrified he might kill other motorists, let alone us.

'Keep this up, Terry,' I said, 'and I'll go to the solicitor myself with all your threats and aggression.' This stopped him; he went quiet and remained calm until we got to the airport. As he got out of the vehicle he fumbled while taking out his suitcase and I saw him standing on the curb, looking suddenly lost and lonely. He could switch moods in a split second. I felt so sorry for him, but still I drove away as fast as I could.

The next week I went to see my doctor about my hair loss. He ruled out physical causes, and at his first kind words suggesting I must be in a pretty bad way for my hair to be falling out like this, I burst into tears, apologised profusely, then told him I needed help, I needed to talk. All of a sudden the penny had dropped and I realised I *couldn't* sort this out by myself. I had always felt that I *had* to be able to, but if I couldn't do it now with all my renewed confidence, I knew I never would be able to.

Something about Terry kept hooking me back. He knew just how to play me, and every time I fell for it. I don't think he once felt guilty for the way he treated me, and yet I couldn't help seeing that picture of him, lost and alone as I drove away from the airport. I felt guilty, as though turning away from him, despite how difficult he was, was turning my back on the chance to add a little more love to the world, instead of misery and confusion.

My doctor let me talk it all out, and by the time I'd finished I felt so much better. He thought I'd do very well with a short course of counselling, but he didn't push it. I walked out of his room feeling much lighter. I would go and see someone, soon, but for the moment all the talking had let the pressure out, and I didn't need it straightaway.

Yes, I was still putting it off. In the cold light of day, needing that kind of help still felt like telling the world I couldn't cope. And maybe deep down I was still afraid of talking about what was going on. I didn't know why I was afraid, though; it didn't make sense to me. But it also didn't make sense that I could be a successful author one minute and a nervous wreck the next.

*

Diamonds and Dust had taken on a life of its own. By January 2008 it had already gone into its fifth reprint and was still in the top ten in some bookstores. Letters and cards poured in at the farm from people who had enjoyed my book. Many people wrote because they had similar stories to mine. Some were struck by my staying with McCorry through his depression, not abandoning him. 'Your book is a revelation for all the women who married older men, had a good life earlier on, and are now shadowed by the older men with chronic depression,' wrote one.

Another, who had also lost a child, wrote, 'But I have not written to you to talk about grief, but to say I admire your courage in writing your story. I rejoiced in your frankness as I live in a small town and I know that what people don't know, they make up.' One woman finished her letter with: 'On bad days I tell myself, if Sheryl McCorry can do it with two million acres, what do I have to complain about with two hundred! Your book has been not only inspiring but also very healing.'

Speaking invitations were rolling in, as were film offers on *Diamonds and Dust*. Leisha visited one day and told me she was taking Cohen to the doctor regarding his hips. He was only two years old and suddenly it had become clear to her he had a sway in his walk like a tired old stockman. The doctor ordered X-rays and in a week we were all heading to Perth to see a specialist. The news was terrible. Cohen needed major surgery on both hips, and soon. Our darling boy had not complained of the pain he must have been suffering from his serious hip displacement. And it wasn't only his hips; his back was curved like the letter 'C'. The specialist was amazed that Cohen could walk, run and ride a bike.

My girl broke down in tears and I knew just how she felt. Kelly had to have an operation in Perth at ten months old — that floored me and it was only a minor procedure.

Cohen had his operation in June 2008, followed by three more over the next ten months. For each operation he was a couple of weeks in hospital. Leisha never left his side, and I moved into her house to take care of Brock until they came home. Between operations, Cohen wore a full cast from his waist to his toes. In a year's time the specialist will remove the two little metal rods inserted in his hips, but Cohen will have to live with metal plates bolted to his femur for the rest of his life. For now he is home and mobile again, healthy and happy, and we have learned to celebrate the victories and be thankful.

So much was happening in such a short time. Change was in the air whether I liked it or not. We were in the throes of worry about Cohen when Terry came south to Wildwood again, supposedly to work on the farm, though he spent most of his time at the races in Bunbury. He had a win and a second place with two of his horses, so he should have been happy, but he was full of anger and tension.

This may partly have been because he wanted to accompany me, smiling at my side, for book signing events and interviews, and I wouldn't let him. I didn't want him there, pretending we were happy, when he had no more interest in me or my life than he'd had for all the years of our marriage. Nor did I want to give him the opportunity to upset me or embarrass me in public again. A friend had told me of a recent conversation he'd had with Terry. My friend had read the book and said to Terry he thought I'd had a great life, and that he was fascinated by the stories. Terry apparently replied, 'Sheryl's left me now she's famous. I haven't read the fucking book!'

One afternoon, after two weeks of unpredictable and volatile behaviour, Terry came running through the farmhouse covered in dust and cow shit and said, 'I'm leaving. I've got to get back to Broome.'

He kept running towards the shower while I looked at the lamb casserole I was about to put in the oven for dinner. One of his favourite dishes. He hadn't given me any inkling that he'd be leaving, and I knew then, finally, that this was the end of our marriage. I turned the oven off, boiled the kettle and made myself a cup of tea, silently willing myself not to shed another tear. It wasn't worth it.

I sat alone on the verandah drinking my tea, listening to drawers and wardrobe doors opening and slamming as he collected his belongings from the bedroom. After several hurried trips between the bedroom and car, he came to the verandah where I was sitting gazing across the dry paddocks and said, 'I'll have a cup of tea before I go.'

There must be something he wanted to say to me, I thought as I got up and went to the kitchen to make his tea. But when it was made I found him in the lounge room, his gaze fixed on the racing repeats blaring from the television. I put his cup on the little wooden coffee table beside his chair. There was no 'thank you', he simply ignored me; it was as if he was mesmerised by the repeats playing over and over.

I returned to the verandah to finish my tea in silence, and a few minutes later I watched my husband leave the house in a cloud of dust and flying gravel. There were no goodbyes, just a spectacular display of his leaving. I sat there and I thought, *Well, another one bites the dust.*

And that was the last time I saw my husband. Perhaps I had been waiting for him to leave all along, since I was never able to cut the knot myself.

In March 2009 I applied for a divorce. I expect it to be as nasty and dirty as his treatment of me over the nine years of our marriage. But I'm no longer scared of his threats. Now that the marriage is over, there is no more fear.

Over the next few months, while I was biding my time at Wildwood, I took up several speaking invitations.

Being interviewed was one thing. I simply sat there and answered questions, and the interviewer was usually doing their best to make it easy for me. It was a walk in the park. But to stand up and deliver an address to a room full of strangers — the whole thing terrified me. I'd get out there and be shaking like a leaf. But I soon came to realise that what people really wanted to hear was stories of the outback. And I had plenty of these. Real stories about ordinary people doing things that were very different from what your average city slicker was used to. Or stories about city slickers out of their depth in the bush. That could be very amusing, and not always in a kind way.

I liked telling the story of the govy from hell.

I would employ a governess through an agency in Broome to oversee the children's correspondence schooling. Some were trained teachers, but that wasn't a necessary part of the job. Govies came and went, some staying longer than others.

In 1987, when I was managing Kimberley Downs, we had the govy from hell. Most days after their school lessons Leisha and Kristy, who were about ten and eight, rode or swam their horses in Cammera Creek. After a rough week with their latest govy, who had come to the station directly from Melbourne, my girls invited the woman to go with them down to the creek. The govy had not been 'sparing the rod', although I did not know this — I do not believe in physical punishment, and never countenanced its use against my children — and Leisha and Kristy had decided it was payback time.

Leisha was riding her performance horse, Lady; Kristy was on Beauty, and the govy, who didn't ride, was on foot. As the three rambled in and out of Homestead Creek, which flowed into Cammera Creek, the govy soon had blood-sucking leeches hanging from her legs. In no time she was in hysterics and her screams were frightening the horses.

'Don't panic,' chorused the girls, 'they don't hurt you.' That didn't calm her at all, and when they said, 'We'll take you home and burn them off,' this only brought forth more hysterics. The girls were a little shocked at how effective their payback scheme was proving. They walked her to the cook house where they saturated the blood-fattened leeches with salt so that they quickly dropped off.

I knew my girls were not always angels, and they weren't getting away with this. I scolded them for taking the govy for a walk where they knew there would be leeches, and in her defence Leisha said, 'We didn't mean to freak her out that much, but it's not as bad as what she does to us.' And they both held out their hands, showing me the welts on their wrists. The govy had been sinking her sharp fingernails into the girls' wrists whenever she wanted to drive a point home.

Now I thought about it, I could see a dark moodiness to her. She could have been a heavy drinker whose hide was cracking. It wouldn't have been the first time — a lot of people who are in some kind of trouble, who aren't dealing with life and its problems, come out to the bush thinking the experience will cure them. She was out of her depth, and she was taking it out on the children.

Well, that was it, I thought to myself. She'd be off Kimberley Downs by the end of the week. In fact she left earlier than that.

I woke two nights later from a deep sleep to the smell of burning. In a flash I was out of my bed and flying to the children's rooms, terrified of losing them in a house fire. Finding the children safe, I realised the fire wasn't in the house. I ran to the front verandah and immediately saw the flames licking out from the window of the govy's flat and lighting up the night sky.

'Fire! Fire!' I yelled as I ran into the building. Govy was out cold on her bed. I thought at first it was smoke inhalation, but as I came closer the sour reek of alcohol overpowered the smell of smoke. I shook her shoulder. 'For god's sake, help yourself!' I screamed. She opened her eyes, looked at me blankly and closed them again. 'Move,' I yelled as I tried to pull her out of danger. Thankfully I could hear the stockmen's voices as they arrived with garden hoses. One of them grabbed the govy from me and dragged her clear, and I got out of the building and stood back to let them fight the fire. The blaze was soon out, though the bedroom was a write-off.

Govy left the next day, without any prompting from me, hitching a lift with a bull runner passing through from a neighbouring property. She admitted to nothing, but I feel pretty sure she'd been smoking in bed after some dedicated drinking and had fallen into an alcoholic stupor. She certainly looked like a wardrobe drinker.

One thing about living and working in the outback — you can't ignore the climate. Sometimes it really can be the difference between life and death. In 1986 the west Kimberley had a dry year, probably not a drought as such, because eventually the wet season did come in, but it didn't bring the usual abundance of rain.

Clear blue skies, humidity high, it was hot as hell. The natural waterholes were drying up, as were many of the silt-filled dams. These were difficult times for us, as Australian

Land and Cattle had gone into receivership. There was no money to spend on improvements for the stations; even repairs to windmills and waterholes were done with patched-up gear. We could have rolled up our swags and left the stations but I loved a challenge. I stayed as manager and helped pull Kimberley and Napier Downs through those tough times.

Twice a day I drove the bore run on Kimberley Downs, checking that windmills were pumping and looking for cattle bogged in the hungry mud that now filled Telegraph Dam. The air was filled with the stench of decomposing flesh, and eagles constantly circled the dam. Yesterday's casualty, an old cracker cow (who had missed being mustered and was too old to breed from), didn't have the strength to stand after I dragged her out of the dam with a rope hooked to the bullbar of my Toyota. There was no hope for her, she was suffering and barely alive. The eagles and scavengers hadn't waited for her to die, but had begun to feast on her alive, attacking her large eyes. Something had been gnawing on her nose and tongue, dingoes probably, and the maggots had moved in. She was a sad, terrible sight.

It was one of the rare times I didn't have my .308 rifle with me in the Toyota, and I had no choice but to cut the beast's throat. I hated doing that. It's a lot easier to stand back and fire a gun. But I knew I had to put the cow out of her misery.

Alone, exhausted and covered in stinking grey mud, I sat for a while afterwards, resting my back against an ancient boab tree, and cried my heart out. It was tough times like this that I wondered what the hell I was doing in such a godforsaken place. Then the rains would come, and the rugged outback would flourish and come to life again, and nowhere was more beautiful.

*

And then there are stories that have everything in them: ordinary people doing extraordinary things, wild country, wild weather, wild adventures — and the quiet wisdom of a people who lived in this land long before we arrived.

A lot of the city people who came and listened to me talk had very little experience of Aborigines or their country. Very few of them had even talked to an Aboriginal person. Their opinions were formed by things they had seen on television or read in newspapers. Yet I have learned so much from the Aboriginal men and women I've worked with throughout my station life.

Up in the Kimberley, the rains would come, and sometimes they wouldn't stop. Out of my six years at Louisa Downs, two years had record-breaking rainfall. The spinifex-covered desert country usually had an average fourteen inches a year, and then out of the blue we received twenty-six inches in 1983 and thirty-three inches the next year.

We had more than an inch the day I organised a light aircraft to evacuate two people from the top end of the Louisa Downs airstrip. One was an old Aboriginal woman called Judy and the other was a truck driver with a bad case of food poisoning. Old Judy was well into her eighties. She was thin and always wore a long dress and a jumper, no matter how hot the day. She had a temperature and a rattling cough in her chest.

The evacuation was accomplished in the rain with no dramas, although we were just in time — it looked as if the airstrip would soon be too wet and soft for a landing.

Late the following evening, after even more rain, I found we had another sick person in the camp. The old man was an elder who usually lived in Halls Creek, and was the grandfather of several of the station's stockmen. I was feeling a bit frustrated; if I'd known the night before, we could have flown him out with the others. Now the airstrip was definitely too wet. It seemed I was forever having to make emergency runs to one or another of the region's hospitals. McCorry was no help — he was away mustering on Roebuck Plains. But my feeling frustrated wasn't helping anyone. I had one of the largest Aboriginal groups in the area camped by the Louisa homestead; out in the middle of nowhere, I was literally their lifeline in emergencies.

I went up to the camp and talked to the old man and his family, who told me he had prostate cancer and was unable to pass urine. I took him back to the homestead and made radio contact with the Halls Creek hospital. The doctor on duty asked me questions and I relayed back to him the answers the old man gave me. It turned out the old man hadn't passed urine for several days. *My god*, I thought, *he must be busting*. He had my sympathy — I was pregnant with Robby at the time and knew what it was like to have pressure on my bladder.

It was more serious than that, of course. Sitting by the radio with the medical kit at hand, I paid close attention as the doctor told me what I was to do. I had to measure two finger widths up from the top of the pelvic bone, get the syringe and put the needle in there to withdraw the urine.

I hadn't done anything like this before, and I soon realised I didn't have the confidence to tackle it properly. I looked at the old man. His face didn't seem to be showing too much pain, so I said to the doctor, 'I'll do this procedure if I must, to save his life, but I don't think he's at that point yet.' At least I hoped to god he wasn't. 'At this stage I think I'd rather just get him to you as quickly as I can.'

It was a hundred and fifty kilometre drive into Halls Creek. I got off the radio and called for the latest weather reports. Everywhere was pretty well flooded, but most of the terrain should be passable for a while yet. I got back to the doctor and said, 'There's only one river we might have trouble with between Louisa and Halls Creek, and at last report that was the Laura.' There was no saying if it would be crossable when we got there. In such heavy rain, river rising was unpredictable. I suggested that the hospital vehicle travel as far as they could to meet us, and I would take the medical kit and radio. We would meet, God willing, even if on opposite sides of a flooded creek. If the old man took a turn for the worse before that, I would make radio contact and do my best to follow the doctor's instructions.

We would have to take two vehicles. We couldn't all fit in my brother Michael's 4WD tray-back, yet we needed that vehicle to make the tracks for me to follow in the Ford. I made the old man as comfortable as I could on the mattress in the back of my Ford F100, his son Leslie sitting beside him. Leisha sat in the front with me. Then I set off, slowly following in the tracks of the tray-back. With a firm grip on the wheel I manoeuvred the vehicle as steadily as I could along the boggy and slippery highway — which was still a gravel road then. Even so, I was sliding from one side of the road to the other and tense with the effort of trying to keep from going over the steep banks.

There were several creek crossings between the station and Laura River. Prior to entering any swift-flowing creek, we would stop and cover the front of our radiators with a piece of tarp or a mail bag. We also attached one end of the long wire rope we carried for such emergencies to each vehicle. Michael would enter the water first and, once he was through the rushing torrent, I would follow down into the murky creek, keeping the vehicle moving slowly forward even as the water reached halfway up the cab door. I burned with fear when the floodwaters entered the cab and swirled around my feet; I felt the lift of the vehicle then the feeling of floating as we were moved by the current. Then a bump and the massive relief as the wheels gripped the muddy bank on the opposite side.

We went along in this fashion as far as the Laura River, but here the murky floodwaters were too powerful to even think of crossing. The old man was holding his own when I radioed the doctor for his location, which was some thirty kilometres away. Not far. Although maybe a case of 'so near yet so far' — in the vehicle's headlights we could see the debris being churned up by the rapidly moving floodwaters. No way was I going in there. Standing by Michael, ankle deep in mud, I wondered how we would cross this one. Then one of the stockmen called, 'Lights missus,' and a sudden relief came over me as I looked towards the moving headlights in the distance.

Checking on my patient, I said, 'Old man, doctor is nearly here.' He acknowledged me with a movement of his eyes. He lay quiet and still, making no fuss at all, surrounded by the sounds of nature. The rushing floodwaters, the odd bullfrog calling for a mate, the high-pitched drone of the thousands of mosquitoes buzzing around, and somewhere out there in the darkness, the intermittent bellow of a lonely feral bull.

Soon the doctor's 4WD ambulance was facing us on the other bank. By now we had ascertained that the water level was slowly dropping, but it was another two hours before the Laura River dropped enough for us to consider crossing. Michael and I hooked up our vehicles as the current was still too strong to take the slightest risk. Visibility outside the beam of our headlights was nil and the darkness could be deceiving. We would each in turn be an anchor for the other.

I watched Michael go in first with the Toyota to test the water. My heart was in my mouth as I saw him get pulled slightly downstream, but soon he was out of the main current and had manoeuvred himself up the opposite bank. I unhooked the wire rope so I could back up the bank — I wanted to load the Ford with a few heavy rocks, hoping the extra weight would help keep me grounded. Back down at the water's edge I hooked back onto the wire rope. Entering the river slightly to the right of the crossing I could visualise approximately where the strongest current would hit me. With a firm grip on the wheel I steered the Ford gently down into the rushing floodwater and moved steadily across the river, listening to the gurgling sounds as the vehicle lifted gently in the current, water seeping into the floor of the cab. I felt the tension drain out of me as the tyres started to grip on the opposite bank. 'Not long now, old man, the doctor is just at the top of the bank,' I assured my passenger behind me. 'Yull,' was his answer, telling me he understood what was going on.

Once the elder was safely in the hands of the doctor and nurse, I heard him speak to his son. Leslie came over to me, unfolding a dillybag, and pulled out a boomerang. 'This is for you, missus, from that old man,' he said. 'He wants you to have this.'

'That's very good of him,' I said, 'but I don't need anything.'

Leslie pushed the boomerang into my hands and said, 'You must take this,' and I did. It was a true gesture of thanks from the old man. It had been a long and weary night, our patient was now in good hands, and Michael and I turned our vehicles around and started the slow trip home.

CHAPTER 19

Stars over Shiralee

Once Leisha had gained faith from the doctors that Cohen was going to come out the other side of his operations happy and healthy, she started to feel her old self again — in fact better than her old self: there was a new man in her life.

Midway through 2008 she became engaged to Nigel Millington, a man she had known since the previous winter when she was living in the second farmhouse at Wildwood. One of Nigel's friends was a farmhand at Wildwood, and through this connection Nigel had come to the farm to do a bit of casual work. One day I noticed him chopping a great stack of firewood for Leisha, and I said to her, 'I see he's cutting firewood for you — funny that he hasn't cut any for me!' We had a laugh about that, but I was pleased to see a bit of a spark between them.

In Nigel I believe she has met her match. She needs a good strong man by her side and Nigel stood by her and Brock while Cohen was undergoing his operations. Nigel has a large farm-style house in Boyanup, a small country town south of Bunbury, and Leisha and the boys have moved in with him. It is a real home, and a good safe place for the children to live and play.

Their dreams included having a child together — it would be Nigel's first — and my phone rang one day in August 2008 and it was Leisha, bubbling with happiness, announcing that she was pregnant. 'Leisha, my girl, this is the best news,' I said, excited as well. 'I can't wait to be a nan again.' But for the first two months of her pregnancy she suffered the most shocking morning sickness; she was unable to leave her bed for days. I practically moved in with them to help out, she was so ill. I visited doctor after doctor with her, but no one was able to identify the problem. Nigel was pulling his hair out with worry, and I was too — I had never seen my girl so ill.

Then one day while she was lying on her bed and I was sitting there holding her hand, she cried, 'Mum, I can't see the baby's face any more. I can't see a baby in my arms.' Each time she has been pregnant she has been able to see her baby's face and name them before they were born. She worried there was something wrong with this pregnancy because she couldn't see this baby's face in her mind. 'Leisha,' I whispered, 'you're going to be okay. You're strong, darling.' But four weeks later she woke in pain in the middle of the night, losing blood. Nigel drove her into the hospital, where they learned that their unborn child's heart had stopped beating at about eight weeks — the time she had told me she could no longer see her baby's face. She had been carrying the dead foetus all that time. She was so maternal, her body had been holding onto it, wouldn't let it go.

She and Nigel both suffered terribly, and I shared their pain. When she recovered, I drove Leisha and the children through the Nannup forest to the Shiralee and picked up her two quarter horses to take home to Boyanup. This brightened her up. She needs her horses around; they are good medicine for her soul.

Robby and Tara had the Shiralee looking good. They had left Broome at the end of the 2008 season and were planning on staying this time. They were painting the posts and rails around the farmhouse, cleaning out sheds and keeping a watchful eye on the cattle.

I'd done a lot of emergency runs for other people. Now I needed to do one for myself. It was time to go home.

On that day at Wildwood when Terry left without a goodbye I felt the tie between us break. As though something had snapped. I didn't decide it was over. It simply was. Over the months since that time, my strength had returned; the real me had come to life again and I was no longer afraid. I had been moving my things one trailer load at a time and finally I had almost all of my possessions back at the Shiralee.

On the day I closed the door of the Wildwood farmhouse behind me for good, I didn't have much left to pack. All of my boxes of personal belongings, which had never been unpacked in the nine years I'd been married to Terry, had already gone. Every inch of Molly's house — all the cupboards, wardrobes, even under the beds — was packed tight with family possessions; there was never any space for mine. Molly had told me to dispose of her things, but I couldn't bring myself to do that after feeling the wrath of Terry's temper when he couldn't find the hay record book in a kitchen cupboard one year.

Maybe that was cowardly, but having faced his fury so many times, I desperately tried to avoid triggering it. I thought I could do that by steering clear of the things that set him off — and yet I also knew from experience that anything could set him off, at any time. There were no guarantees of safety. So maybe it was cowardly. But that is not what my counsellor thinks.

Yes, I finally began to see a counsellor — and before long realised that, aside from the writing, it was by far the best thing I had done for myself in years. It was as confronting as I'd feared, but it was also comforting in ways I'd never anticipated. I felt supported and encouraged by my counsellor, who never pushed me further than I wanted to go.

Funnily enough, the reason I overcame my fears and consented to see someone had nothing to do with Terry's behaviour. It came about during the month before we realised Leisha had miscarried, when she was in a lot of pain. It was such a terrible time. Cohen was in plaster then; my health wasn't the best, and Nigel was frantic with worry. One day I was with Leisha visiting yet another doctor, and feeling frustrated that they weren't able to identify her problem, when I just broke down and cried. I couldn't stop crying. The more I cried, the worse I felt. It seemed they already thought Leisha was crazy with her wild talk about not being able to see her baby's face. Now they must think her mother was an absolute lunatic too.

I had never felt more hopeless. I couldn't hold everything up a minute longer. I could barely hold my back up straight; I just wanted to curl up in a little ball. When I finally managed to stop the tears I told Leisha's doctor I wanted to see a counsellor.

It turned out there was a counsellor operating from the medical centre, and they made me an appointment for the following week. She is a lovely young woman, and she has given me so much perspective on my relationship with Terry. The question that puzzled all the doctors, and which puzzles me too — why didn't I, why couldn't I, leave him? — is a subject we keep coming back to in our talks together.

It seems Terry's behaviour indicates a man who must control his partner, and keep her in a state of disempowerment and disorientation through constant criticism, blaming, manipulating, verbal abuse, physical abuse, threats, affairs, mind games and humiliation. So disoriented, the woman is unable to see the mess her own life is in; so disempowered that even if she *were* able to see the mess, she'd feel it was impossible to do anything about it. I think I must have been a textbook case.

I don't know whether Terry acted consciously in all this, but whether or not he purposefully tried to destroy me, the fact is that he *did* hurt me, and he was never sorry, and for a long time he got exactly what he wanted out of me. There are no excuses for any of that.

Unspeakable things go on behind many closed doors, and abusive people get away with terrible behaviour because their victims don't speak out. Thanks to my counselling I am no longer ashamed to show my weak side; in fact, I want to say to any women, or men, who are the victims of abusive relationships that it can happen to *anyone*, no matter how strong or celebrated you are. It is not your fault if you find yourself paralysed into inaction — that is what the abusive behaviour does, it makes you unable to act in your own best interests. And also I want to say, you *can* escape it, though most likely you will need help for that, as I did. Indeed, that may be the biggest step, admitting that you can't do it alone, that you need expert help. There is no shame in that.

I was singing as I loaded my trailer to cart the last of my things back to the Shiralee. I could have hired a removalist, but it felt wonderful to be taking charge of things myself. I had been unable to act for so many years, I was relishing the idea of moving on. It was another ending, and I felt truly happy.

To unpack my things at the Shiralee, to share the farmhouse with Robby and Tara with their youthful energy — it was absolute bliss. I felt alive for the first time in years. The sky looked bluer, the air was crisp and pure. I was fifty-nine years old, and every day I felt younger and healthier. There was even less pain from the arthritis.

I got stuck into the general maintenance that needed doing on the Shiralee; it's never-ending, as on any farm. Robby and Tara worked hard by my side and were very good company. When we couldn't work out between us how to do something, I would call my father in Northampton for advice. Then call him again when the job was completed, because I was proud of myself for doing it.

One day I phoned for advice on filling cracks in the lounge-room ceiling. 'Hang on, love, Mum and I'll jump in the car and come down and do it for you,' Dad offered, worried that I might fall off the ladder or glue myself to the very high ceiling. Dad was eighty-four and Mum wasn't far behind. 'Dad, it's okay, I can do it,' I told him. 'Anyway, I always wanted a chandelier' — though I would have made a far from elegant light fitting.

Late one evening, after I had finished painting the external walls of the farmhouse, I was feeling tired but contented, satisfied because the job was completed. There was a chill in the night air. I took a moment to gaze up at the sky — there was a glittering canopy of a hundred thousand twinkling stars.

I had never seen so many, not even in the Kimberley. The night was magnificent.

Finally, I thought to myself, *the stars are shining again over the Shiralee*.

CHAPTER 20

Good Things Come to Those Who Wait

Diamonds and Dust brought me many unexpected blessings, but none more unexpected than Michael. It was August 2008 and I was attending a book club meeting at a Kojonup farmhouse. By chance, Michael was there too. He wasn't a regular member of the book club, but a friend of the people who were hosting it. Those friends introduced us at the end of the evening and Michael told me he had enjoyed my book immensely. In a few minutes I learned that he lived alone and was a big reader in the evenings after a hard day's work on his cattle farm.

A few months later I was considering restocking the Shiralee — I had run no cattle on it for two years — and had heard from a stock firm that a cattle farmer south of Kojonup had good quality Angus cows for sale. Apparently he wanted to take advantage of predicted high canola prices, and needed to free up a couple of paddocks to plant canola in the coming season.

It turned out that the farmer was Michael. We discovered this over the course of a couple of phone calls discussing the cattle. I decided the cattle sounded worth looking at, and we arranged a time to meet to look them over together. In fact, I think I might still have lined up a meeting even if the cattle hadn't sounded so interesting. I remembered Michael very well from our initial meeting — he was over six foot tall, tanned and with the muscular physique of a hard-working man. I was struck by his massive hands, which he moved with great sensitivity. His brown wavy hair had a sprinkling of grey in it, and I thought he had a very kind face, though I hadn't registered the colour of his eyes.

I found myself suffering butterflies for days before our appointment, but on the day itself I was soon at ease. It is very relaxing to be around cattle, great gentle beasts that they are. We both knew what we were talking about when it came to Angus cows, and we could see there was no bullshit in each other. I was more than impressed with the cattle — and with this lonely farmer as well. His eyes, I noted, were large and velvety brown, and as warm and compassionate as any I had ever seen.

I went home feeling very pleased with myself, and not just because Michael and I had shaken hands on a sale of seventy head of cows to start the herd again on the Shiralee. There seemed to be all sorts of possibilities opening up in the attraction between the two of us, and I felt ready to grip them with both hands. Gone was the depression and darkness that had shadowed my world through those nine long years with Terry.

The next morning I awoke and I knew my body had really let go of the past. 'I'm free, free, free!' I cried out to no one but myself as I ran through the back paddock, dancing and twirling in the brilliant spring sunshine, the crisp cool air fresh against my cheeks. I felt the enormous weight of sorrow had lifted from my shoulders. I was truly ready to start living again.

*

It was getting known around the district that I was living back on the Shiralee, and neighbouring farmers dropped by to offer a helping hand. Some would stop for a cuppa and leave homemade cakes and biscuits. It is wonderful to be surrounded by such good kind neighbours, both men and women.

In just a few months back at the Shiralee I felt more at home than I had in all the time since old McCorry died. I was beginning to think I was acclimatising to life in the south — so much tamer than it was in the Kimberley — when we had a ripper of a storm.

News flashed across the local radio and TV channel early one evening that violent weather was expected in the south-west, with winds up to a hundred and thirty kilometres an hour. We put the tractors and trailers in the large shed by the farmhouse, and all smaller items into the lock-up shed, then retired to bed to see what the night would bring. About 10 pm gusting southerly winds buffeted the farmhouse windows, rattling the glass and whistling in through the cracks. The power failed and plunged us into darkness. I heard the crashing of a eucalyptus gum tree hitting the ground, then another crash, which I hoped wasn't my bird-attracting flowering gum by the house fence. By torchlight, however, I discovered it was.

'Mum,' said Robby, 'I reckon the wind is that strong it could blow a dog off its chain.'

I wondered what would be destroyed next. Inside, I checked the ceilings for leaks and found water running down the walls of the spare bedroom. We brought towels, rags and buckets to stem the flow, then I thought, bugger this, the work wasn't going to go away. 'Let's go to bed and face the mess in the morning,' I said to Robby and Tara and it wasn't long before I was snuggled down in my warm comfy bed, the covers pulled over my head. Whatever the storm was doing out there, I slept like a baby.

Next morning while surveying the extent of the damage, I received a phone call from my new friend Michael. 'How did you weather the storm, any damage?' he asked in his deep voice.

'Not too good,' I said, 'trees over everywhere.'

'Do you want a hand? I've got two chainsaws, I could bring them down and help out,' he offered.

I hesitated. It was a lovely offer, and I did want to see him again, but something made me hold back from saying yes. I needed to stand on my own two feet for a while. I had only just found my own belief in myself and I wasn't going to give that away again, ever.

Weeks later, however, there was another wild storm. By morning, this one had brought down a large tree, blocking access to the cattle-loading ramp and putting several trees over the boundary fences as well. Michael was due to arrive that day with the herd of Angus cattle I had bought from him. Not only was access blocked, but the fences needed repair or the cattle would easily be over them — and would beat Michael's truck back to his Kojonup farm if they were so inclined.

My own chainsaw went on the blink after the first few cuts, and with the cattle arriving that afternoon I called Michael. 'If you want to unload these cattle you'll have to bring your chainsaw,' I said.

'What are you going to do, cut the cattle yard up for firewood?' he said and laughed. Well, he would laugh, not having seen my new steel yards. I wasn't feeling so happy about the storm's trail of destruction — he'd see the Shiralee when it looked a mess. But he said, 'I've done nothing but fix up fallen-down farms all my life, so this won't be a problem.' I thought, *Holy hell, you sound like my sort of guy.*

'Do you have a tractor?' he asked. 'I'll bring both chainsaws and the fencing gear.'

By sundown, with Michael's help, we were in a position to release the cattle into the now secure paddocks. A week later he returned to the Shiralee and helped me repair the electric fencing. As we worked side by side, laughing and joking through the long day, we found we enjoyed each other's company. He was a very playful man. We were out near the dam when he suddenly dropped his fencing tools, grabbed me and threw me over his shoulders as if I were light as a feather, then ran towards the dam with me screaming my head off. He stopped just two steps from the muddy edge, his strong arms holding me firmly as he lowered me slowly down in front of him. For all his size and strength he was a very gentle person. I shivered; I could feel the warmth of his body, but I could not lift my face to his yet. I was still a little wary of men, only slowly beginning to admit the possibility that there might really be decent men to be found.

Michael understood how I was feeling, because he had been in a disastrous relationship too. He had battled in a marriage to a woman who already had four children from as many different men, who loved the plonk more than the man, and who had no qualms about shoving the barrel of a loaded rifle into his stomach or holding a butcher's knife to his throat in view of their little daughter. Luckily for everyone he was strong enough to report these incidents, and man enough not to have retaliated.

I felt as if I had known Michael forever, he was so easy to talk to and get along with. There was not a trace of the mockery and ridicule I had grown to expect in my relationship with Terry.

He was an impressive farmer too, and that counted for a lot with me. He worked the whole outfit alone, managing eight hundred head of fine Angus breeder cows and their offspring, as well as an Angus stud, and putting anything from three thousand to three and a half thousand head of mixed young cattle for fattening through his feedlot in any one season.

'I don't know how you do it, this is a three-man show,' I said, amazed, when he showed me around Forrest Downs. 'It's a tough job.'

As our friendship grew, so did our respect for one another. He would help me on the Shiralee, and in return Robby, Tara and I would go up to his farm each week and help him process two to four hundred head of young cattle through his yards. Working with Michael was more like fun than work, and we all enjoyed it immensely. If something went wrong he dealt with it with good humour.

Leisha took an instant liking to him. 'He's fair dinkum, Mum. I know he'd never let anything bad happen to you,' she told me calmly. 'He's not selfish, it's not all about him — and I have never seen you so happy.' I didn't say anything to that.

'I bet your mojo's come back,' she said with a mischievous smile.

'Leisha Marie, I don't know what you're talking about,' I said, trying to keep a straight face.

'Mum, all we want is to see you happy, especially after everything you've been through.'

'I am happy, darling,' I said. 'But I have to go carefully, you must understand that.'

'Let the past go, Mum,' said my wise girl. 'There's a liveliness and enthusiasm about you now. It's wonderful to see you let your spirit fly.'

How true it was, I thought, that God's greatest gift to us is the people who love us.

*

One evening Michael was driving me home when he said, 'I'll wait for you as long as I have to — so long as I'm not wasting my time.'

Holy hell, I thought, *that's laying it on the line*, and I suddenly burst out laughing, probably because I was nervous.

Michael started to stutter and stumble with his words, trying to explain himself more clearly, and I realised in that moment that he was sincere, that his intentions were warm and honourable. I realised too that since I had known him I had been waiting for things to turn ugly. Part of me just expected that they would. But they hadn't because he was a truly decent man.

'I like you a lot,' he finally managed. 'I don't want to frighten you away.'

I let myself sink into a deep feeling of contentment. I liked this man too, very much. I could no longer deny to myself that I was falling for this rugged bushy. I loved his steady good humour and playfulness.

I had begun to refer to him as my 'gentle giant' when talking with my family. My parents were very happy for me. They came down to the Shiralee after my glowing reports, anxious to meet him, and found Michael to be a kind and happy person. Best of all, he had put the twinkle back in their daughter's eyes.

Best of all for me was the difference in Robby. With Tara he had grown into himself; gone was the anguish that had burdened him while I remained with Terry. Laughter filled his eyes now and he had an enormous zest for living. Robby and Tara both had a wonderful connection with Michael. Happiness embraced my entire family, and as a mother I could not ask for more.

Throughout my life I have observed that my intuition has nearly always been right — if only I'd had the courage to believe in it, I might have saved myself and my children a lot of heartache. Now it's telling me I have met my gentle giant, a man who isn't out to impress anyone; an honest, hard-working gentle man; a genuine and compassionate human being.

As the weeks turned into months, our friendship developed into a deep love for one another. Sitting together one evening on the back verandah at the Shiralee, feeling the electricity between us grow, so that a brush of his arm as he reached for his cup made me shiver, my only worry was whether I would be able to give myself to Michael completely, having been celibate the past seven years. But I need not have been concerned.

As the sun set to the west of the Shiralee, and the evening star rose high in the night sky, our desire to be together only grew. Our eyes met and my gentle giant lifted me in his strong arms and carried me across the threshold and into my bedroom. My yearning to be held in my loving man's arms was finally satisfied and our feelings for each other were released in alternating waves of slow tenderness and uncontrolled passion the whole star-studded night long.

As I lay in Michael's arms contemplating a happy future together, I realised the emptiness had left my soul, replaced by deep love and a new enthusiasm for life.

As morning came I tapped him on the chin. His eyes flew open and his face lit up in a beautiful smile.

'Do you realise, you bushy old bastard,' I said, 'you've got one hell of a grip on my heart.'

Acknowledgements

A big thank you to Alex Craig of Pan Macmillan for believing I had another book in me. Thank you also to my editor Janet Blagg for convincing me to let my feelings flow, and making the process so easy — it was truly enjoyable to work with you. Thank you Tara for typing the whole manuscript for me.

Special love to all my family, you know who you are, and to you Michael.

Sheryl McCorry
Diamonds and Dust

Sheryl McCorry grew up in Arnhem Land carrying crocodiles to school for show and tell. When she was 18, Broome beckoned, and it was there that – only hours after being railroaded into marriage by a fast-talking Yank – she locked eyes with Bob McCorry, a drover and buffalo shooter. When her marriage ended after only a few months, they began a romance that would last a lifetime and take them to the Kimberley's harshest frontiers.

As the only woman in a team of stockmen, Sheryl soon learned how to run rogue bulls and to outsmart the neighbours in the toughest game of all – mustering cattle. The playing field was a million acres of unfenced, unmarked boundaries, But Sheryl soon saw that to survive in the outback a woman needed goals. Hers was to become the first woman in the Kimberley to run two million-acre cattle stations. But it was to come at an unimaginable cost.

Inspiring and unforgettable, *Diamonds and Dust* is a classic story of a woman finding her destiny in the further reaches of the outback.

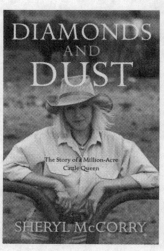

Fiona Higgins
Love in the Age of Drought

When Fiona meets Stuart at a conference in Melbourne she isn't
looking for a relationship, let alone the upheaval of falling for a
cotton farmer from South-East Queensland. But then life never
quite goes according to plan . . .

When Stuart sends Fiona a pair of crusty old boots and a
declaration of his feelings sixteen days into their relationship,
it's the start of a love story that endures – in spite of distance,
the strain of Stuart's farm entering its fourth year of drought, and
Fiona's issues with commitment.

Something's got to give, and eventually Fiona puts everything
on the line – her career, her Sydney life, her future – and moves
to Stuart's farm. Nearest township? Jandowae, population 750.

Here, Fiona encounters an Australia she's never really known,
replete with snakes on the doorstep, frogs in the toilet and the
perils of the bush telegraph. Gradually, she begins to fall in love
with rural life, but as Stuart struggles to balance environmental
and commercial realities she realises that farming isn't quite
as simple as she'd imagined. Ultimately, Fiona has to learn to
cope with the devastating impact of the drought that grips the
countryside, and what it means for Stuart, the farm and their
future together.

Love in the Age of Drought is a delightful fish-out-of-water story
about the city–country culture clash overcome by the course
of true love. Written with heart and humour, it's also a moving
portrait of country Australia's capacity for survival and renewal
amid a drought that won't be broken.

Tammie Matson
Elephant Dance

It's the middle of the night in the Namibian desert when Tammie Matson wakes to find two bull elephants standing just inches from her head. Totally vulnerable in her tiny tent, she promises the night: 'If you just let me survive tonight I will give up Africa. I'll give it all up. Just don't let them stand on me.'

It's not a promise she will easily keep. At 29, Tammie has spent half her life in Africa working as a conservationist. Africa – with its big skies and extraordinary wildlife – is her first love, and Tammie has just landed her dream gig researching human-elephant conflict.

But as her thirties approach, Tammie is conscious that Africa has left little room for pursuit of dreams that are becoming increasingly important: a partner, kids, a house . . . With her visa running out and close to broke, it seems like Africa may just force Tammie to give it up after all.

On returning to Australia, Tammie unexpectedly lands a job at the World Wide Fund for Nature in Sydney. There she meets Andy, a charismatic Brit, and Africa suddenly has a rival. But she's not ready to give up on the elephants yet . . .

From the magic of Bushmanland in Namibia to the civil strife of Assam, India, *Elephant Dance* takes us to the heart of a quest for elephants to live peacefully in a world with too many people and too little space.

Passionate, funny, and wise, *Elephant Dance* is also a young woman's story of self-discovery, love and the courage it takes to follow a calling, especially when life has other plans.

Jane Stork
Breaking the Spell

Growing up in post-war Western Australia, and embarking on the familiar path of marriage and raising children, Jane Stork's semblance of a normal life began to unravel as she entered her thirties.

She sought answers at a meditation centre, and quickly became devoted to the Indian guru Bhagwan Shree Rajneesh, changing her name, adopting the orange robes of a 'sannyasin', and uprooting her family to live first in an ashram in India and then in the Bhagwan-created city of Rajneeshpuram in Oregon, USA.

It was here that Bhagwan's behaviour became increasingly bizarre. He began promoting a siege mentality among his followers, ordering them to amass firearms. He encouraged his secretary Sheela to use drastic methods to take over local governments and punish the local communities who objected to their 'utopian' city.

For Jane, what started out as a journey seeking spiritual enlightenment descended into darkness as she sacrificed her marriage and children, and eventually – through a monstrous act of attempted murder – her freedom.

After serving time in the US, Jane started a new life in Germany, but soon realised she could never truly be free until she had faced up to the past . . .

With an international arrest warrant hanging over her head, and a son who is gravely ill, Jane finally does so with devastating clarity.

Utterly compelling and deeply moving, Jane's incredible true story is a profound meditation on the nature of self-determination and the human spirit's capacity for redemption.